Quest for Equilibrium

By the same author from The Johns Hopkins University Press

BEYOND KISSINGER: *Ways of Conservative Statecraft*

STATES IN EVOLUTION: *Changing Societies and Traditional Systems in World Politics*

ALLIANCES AND THE THIRD WORLD

WAR AND ORDER: *Reflections on Vietnam and History*

IMPERIAL AMERICA: *The International Politics of Primacy*

NATIONS IN ALLIANCE: *The Limits of Interdependence*

EUROPE ASCENDANT: *The International Politics of Unification*

Quest for Equilibrium

AMERICA AND THE BALANCE

OF POWER ON LAND

AND SEA • *George Liska*

The Washington Center of Foreign Policy Research,
School of Advanced International Studies, The Johns
Hopkins University

THE JOHNS HOPKINS UNIVERSITY PRESS
Baltimore and London

The Johns Hopkins University Press, Baltimore, Maryland 21218
The Johns Hopkins Press Ltd., London
Library of Congress Catalog Card Number 77–4780
ISBN 0–8018–1968–7

Library of Congress Cataloging in Publication data will be found on the last printed page of this book.

For Yendo

CONTENTS

FOREWORD

Twenty years after the appearance of *International Equilibrium*, I am returning in this volume more than casually to the theme of equipoise. Whereas the early effort dealt with international organization of collective security and stressed the smaller powers, the present one emphasizes great states involved in the balances of land- and sea-based power in the raw. If the motivating personal experiences are different, however, the intellectual concern to bring together past and present, doctrine and diplomacy, into a potentially instructive relationship remains unchanged.

More immediately important than any sentimentally rewarding anniversary or association is the much closer connection between the present study of equilibrium and its forthcoming companion volume on empire. The latter study, relating the American to the Roman and British imperial experiences, addresses the problems of expansion and control, just as the present study deals with conflict and accommodation within the European and the global systems. Thus the two studies complement one another in focus as well as, consequently, in the kinds of data they select and enlarge upon from the different, indigenous and foreign, backgrounds of contemporary American foreign policy, all too often treated as unique in type and rootless in tradition. Both discourses are set in long-term temporal perspectives; and they apply a corresponding method which, for lack of a simpler term, might be styled "analogico-historical." At least in intention, finally, the two volumes, while individually self-contained, add up to a particularly slanted restatement of enduringly salient issues of international politics and foreign policy in the conventional or classic manner on one level and, on another level, to a not wholly orthodox reevaluation of the international strategic, domestic, and economic environments and determinants of America's lifepath in world affairs, with implications for the fundamental choices facing the United States in the future.

This study was completed under the auspices of the Washington Center of Foreign Policy Research of the Johns Hopkins University and is published as a special volume in the series Studies in International Affairs.

INTRODUCTION. *Historical Recurrences and Contemporary Responsibilities*

As American foreign-policy statecraft entered its third century, it continued to be bounded by a fact and haunted by an ambition. The fact was one of cyclical recurrences, while the ambition was to transcend history in a radically new direction. From before the inception of the Republic, three phases or policy emphases tended to recur. They reflect the inability or unwillingness to adopt and pursue with adequate means or steady motivation either one of two basic strategies, for politico-militarily sustained empire or likewise promoted equilibrium. And they bear testimony to a consequent vain pursuit of a third way, in the guise of economic policies and emphases in more or less complete separation from contemporaneously pertinent strategic frameworks and commitments.

At the outset, the idea of empire dominated the period preceding and attending American independence, as an object of opposition in the form of British mercantilistic constraints, and the target of aspiration for the Americans themselves, in the form of independence (*imperium in regno suo*) within an elastic territorial habitat. The succeeding equilibrium or balance-of-power phase had likewise two sides. One consisted of the balance between or among geographic sections (increasingly focused on the issue of slavery), which regulated continental expansion; the other side was the Anglo-American balance of power. If the stage for the latter contention was initially confined to the North American continent, the British factor controlled also the actual or potential impact of the larger European balance of power on the Americas at large. Once the American Civil War had resolved the issue of both the internal and the external power balances in favor of Northern supremacy in the United States and of American supremacy on the North American continent to begin with, the United States was released from the most pressing politico-strategic quandaries for an undistracted preoccupation with economic growth culminating in the depression of the early 1890s.

The inadequacy of both capitalism and continentalism in isolation from world currents and in the absence of a global strategy, which the depression seemed to demonstrate, refueled the cyclical process. Reproduced was, first, the empire phase in the guise of the brief spell of imitative overseas imperialism of 1898. A subsequent equilibrium phase reflected the meanwhile enlarged setting as it assumed the form of Theodore Roosevelt's great-power diplomacy extending an active American role as mediator to the Asian, and as moderator to the European, equilibrium systems. The "large policy" soon enough gave way to politico-strategically unsupported "dollar diplomacy," covering the period from William Howard Taft to Herbert Hoover and interrupted only by the short-lived and essentially sterile interlude of American participation in World War I. It took the renewed bankruptcy of inherently nonstrategic economism in the Great Depression and in the worldwide crisis leading up to World War II to relaunch the United States on a sustained strategic course, first toward empire in conjunction with the Cold War and, along with its subsidence, toward classic balance-of-power politics on the great-power plane. It was no meaningless accident, therefore, that Theodore Roosevelt was one of Richard Nixon's heroes, since both prepresidential archimperialists veered toward balance-of-power diplomacy when acceding to the White House in the wake of an empire phase. Nor was it wholly accidental that one more rejection of both empire and equilibrium in their classic forms was to generate in the later era pressures for one more phase of a strategically vague and timid emphasis on economics. The third way was henceforth propounded under the aegis of economic interdependence, just as it had been previously trodden in behalf of economic independence (after the Civil War) and economic expansion (in recoil from the Spanish and the first German wars).

The contemners or both empire and the balance of power equated the first with a war in Asia and the second with the diplomacy attending and following the war's termination, while failing to discriminate between valid principles and questionable performances. But the rejection of both classic formats of order seemed nonetheless to clear the conceptual terrain for the affirmation of the third formula. Variously labeled, it focused on a specifically undefined "world order" while postulating a near-spontaneous compatibility of the material utilities that nations had presumably come to pursue as the primary and, indeed, sole major objective in transnational or interdependent relations. Correspondingly deemphasized was both control (empire) and conflict (equilibrium), along with their twin roles as distributive mechanisms in conditions of finite supply, or scarcity, and as legitimizing mechanisms for the graduated status among nations which reflects their unequal sharing of, and access to, both material and immaterial values.

Torn between fact and fancy, American statecraft continued thus to be prey to a paradox fathering a perversity. The paradox was that the statecraft unfolded repeatedly in three phases or emphases in a conceptual setting that did not actually comprise, in any lastingly practicable manner, the third strategy formula toward which that statecraft sought repeatedly to escape from the demands of, and the tension between, empire and equilibrium. Since the coveted third formula, however styled and applied, did not exist, the three-phase cycle had to be repeated sooner or later. A perverse urge to innovate covered up for the situational compulsion to revert to the empire and equilibrium modes of action, previously rejected because either mismanaged or misunderstood; and, eventually, the striving would recommence to realize the third mode only to see it prove itself wholly sterile because radically unreal for a nation of America's massive size and embattled vitality. *E pluribus unum*, projected abroad in one diffuse way or another, obscured again and again the stern injunction of *tertium non datur*.

Taking its clue from the just-cited dictum, the following study of America-and-equilibrium has only one companion volume, on America-and-empire. The presiding idea of both studies is a simple one. Just as the unification of Europe requires the reexamination of past national differences, so the unity of the West and, indeed, accommodation with the people and the state too long alienated from both, demands the deemphasis of American differentness. If this entails the explosion of patriotic myths, just as the other task required the prior erosion of nationalistic mystiques, the primeval contents of either has little meaning in the contemporary setting. That setting, far from superseding the state-system form, was, instead, one in which an authentic system of states on a global scale was crystallizing conjointly with polarized and polarizing conflict of two ideological (as before, at the analogous European stage, hereditary dynastic) enemies giving way to incipient flexibility in constellations among great and between greater and smaller powers. As the European continent had first been self-sufficient in balance-of-power terms, and only gradually came to depend on extraneous, British, reserve power; and as the European system including Britain retraced the two phases, ending up dependent on American reserve power, so the global system of today is at its early and vital stage because self-sufficient, maintaining itself and assuming discernible shape through subtle changes in alignments. It has relieved thus for the time being the problem that the absence of significant reserve power (outside the nuclear one, anywhere or, specifically, at the back of the American Atlas) had posed in the bipolar beginnings or, better, antecedents of the post-European world system.

Finally, if the United States loomed large as the full-fledged founding and participant member of the emergent global equilibrium, it did not come to that role from the latest spell of empire either as a complete novice or as completely simon pure in relation to the earlier European one. Nursed to independence and nurtured in growth by intra-European imbroglios, America came subsequently to bear her share of responsibility for the older system's decline and disruption, first by virtue of her very nature, then of her mere existence, and finally of her basic disposition. In that sequence, the Anglo-Saxon ethnic makeup of the original American ruling class precluded an escalating Anglo-American contention over continental and subsequently maritime empire which, in cold geopolitical logic, was inscribed in global topography and would have relieved intra-European conflicts by allowing some to attach themselves to, and others to exact absorbable compensations for the dividend from, an effective British resistance to the rising American empire in and off the Western Hemisphere. The mere existence of the United States encouraged Britain thereafter in the hope of avoiding, at a cost no greater than Anglo-American sharing, the price of accommodation with Imperial Germany from a position of progressing weakness. And finally, perpetuating the innate instability of America's immature statecraft as to passing designs concealing from self even more than from others the steady persistence of ultimate pretension, the intervention by the United States in World War I helped bring about an outcome displaying a greater, and more dangerous, disparity between real power and ostensible role or formal status in Europe between victor and vanquished than would have caused a finite triumph of the Central Powers emerging from a negotiated settlement. And America's prompt withdrawal from sustaining the discrepancy by opposing hers to Germany's latent organic strength created all the greater need for the deserted European "associates" to sustain the artificial constraints on the dynamic balance of vital forces. In the twilight of traditional Europe, climaxing confusions and misjudgments of at least half a century, the explosive reaction of the constrained to injunctions of self-restraint, setting off the second global conflict, could, in the perspective of the natural history of states and the natural instincts of statecraft, be justified by leveling the charge of hypocrisy against the weakening states' professions of a new, transcendant political morality in the relations among rising and declining powers.

If history repeated itself for American statecraft, the critical question in the era of American world power was whether it had to repeat itself for the international system as well. Supposing that the contemporary American retreat from empire made room for the strategy of the balance of power, the hinge of that balance was the American-Soviet relationship. The continuing priority of that relationship was firmly rooted in the implications of a degenerated conflict over either power's supremacy. Moreover, the relationship ramified into all the other issues, also in view of the potentially moderating effect on these of a progressing accommodation for mutually acceptable parity between the two superpowers. The priority status implied questions of substance. What was, at the critical point of transition from empire to equilibrium, the guiding American vision of the Soviet Union, of the United States itself, and of the current and likely future American-Soviet relationship of forces and vital energies? And what was to be the basic long-term American design or strategy following from the prior assessments?

Under any descriptive label one might choose, the Soviet Union, despite weaknesses at home and setbacks abroad, has evolved into an ascending as well as an assertive power. A more controversial question was how to interpret the assertiveness. Were the Soviets perpetuating the Marxist-Leninist commitment to carry the Soviet state to supremacy and Communism to triumph by exploiting class struggles in the world's industrial centers and other disorders in the developing peripheries? Or was the Soviet foreign policy more usefully understood, for purposes of both analysis and response, as but the latest example of an upthrusting and outreaching continental state that seeks a place in the sun, perhaps above but certainly by the side of, the so-far dominant and more favorably situated insular or near-insular maritime world power? In the latter interpretation, the contemporary Soviet globalism and navalism did not so much represent an assault on the contradictions of bourgeois society, as they enacted continuity with the earlier European challenges to the British command of the high seas and control of widespread colonies. The ideological factor has doubtless a role of sorts to play, mainly for internal exegesis of policy and for its obfuscation externally. But it is the geopolitical framework that can be identified historically, analyzed concretely, and managed practically. Reinjecting the holy writ of Marxist-Leninist "socialism" into the post-Cold War debate about Soviet foreign policy has been no more illuminating than was the use of U.S.-style "capitalism" as the all-sufficient cause of American globalism at its pre-Vietnam peak.

More important still than to identify the well-springs of Soviet policy was to assess the state of health of the American body politic and its perception by the makers of official policy. If the Soviet Union was not an irresistible giant, had the United States shrunk to the size of a dwarf bested first by Hanoi (in Asia) and then by Havana (in Africa)? If the intramural perception of the United States was one of absolutely declining power, it was hardly right to enter upon a major accommodation process with the Soviet Union on the mere assumption that an inattentive adversary could be parleyed into moderation by even the most subtle diplomacy. If, conversely, the intimate official perception was confident of the continuing superiority of the United States to the Soviet Union, there was no readily apparent reason for irresolute response and alarmist rhetoric in connection with relatively minor efforts and slight or transient gains of the Soviet Union in remote world areas.

Without probing into the conflicting symptoms of internal American decay and resilience, it ought not to be far wrong to hold that the United States and the Soviet Union have come to be locked in the classic contention between what seemed to be a relatively receding world power and the commensurately advancing continental state. Whereas America has continued to be wedded to the comfortable pretensions bred by the geography of a near-insular position and resisted their exposure to the exactions of an authentically global sway, sovietized Russia has remained burdened with the residues of her tormented, virtually landlocked past and was anxious to transcend parochial limits at considerable cost or even risk. Although modified by technological and other factors, the resulting dilemmas have been far from original with the two superpowers. While the current environment injected additional risks as well as restraints, it was also propitious to reducing the danger of cataclysmic conflict so long as the two countries could continue to perceive the future as an open-ended one. That is to say, so long as they, unlike their earlier European analogues, could see the future unbounded by both the pressures and the temptations arising out of predictably uneven rates of ascendancy on the part of rival continental adversaries of the preeminent offshore insular power, itself vacillating between grants of major concessions and fears of even small ones. So long as such a situation was not present, the United States could engage with some confidence in assorting concessions with denials to the Soviet Union over the kind of stakes that continued to constitute a genuine measure of national power. Evolving a dual concession-denial policy for avoiding such a situation had precedence over combining traditional military counterforce with questionably innovating economic entanglement in any search for constraints on external action and stimulation of internal transformations. After all, even domestic liberalism can be expansionist, and will be so with a vengeance in cases when it has broken out only recently from the chrysalis of autocracy and seeks to legitimate itself by reaching out for the historic goals of the body politic.

A rising power will be more likely to accept limits on the rate and scope of enlargements if it has been accorded qualitative symmetry at an early stage, and has thus the assured prospect of eventual equality. Conceding symmetry to the Soviet Union has meant entangling the progressively navalized and globalized Soviet empire in all of the intricacies and frustrations of overseas reach, presence, and influence. Such an experience was more promising than was any hope for, say, enhanced internal bureaucratic complexities to carry the Soviet political class over into the neglect, benign or other, of opportunities for expansion. And the hostages that both stable and unstable overseas Soviet gains were apt to offer to an effective American policy were more readily exploitable than could be any imaginable leverages ensuing from economic exchanges and uneven interdependences. They are tangible; and action upon them is not paralyzed by the immaterial impediments that the internal sovereignty and international status of a self-conscious great power will oppose to the application of economic strings.

Modulating opposition to geopolitical gains by the Soviets should make it easier for American policy to implement its own priorities, while lessening the inevitable ingredient of conflict in any kind of relations with a globally expanding Soviet Union. Other things being equal, it would be easier for the United States to pursue its priority goals in the Middle East, for instance, if it were simultaneously tolerant of Soviet political access elsewhere. The Soviet Union might or might not overextend itself by piling up involvements in several areas, while disposing still of only limited material resources. More significant was the likelihood that the Soviets would be less liable to overcompensate in the Middle East for effective denials of influence everywhere else by seeking a maximum return on investment in an overseas area most readily accessible to the still limited reach of Soviet military and naval power. If properly synchronized, a policy committed to systematic efforts to devolve regional role and responsibility to lesser regional powers was apt to reduce the sum of American assets to concede to the Soviet Union as gains before consummating the ''terminal'' geopolitical parity, whereas the rivalries among the local powers and their consequent rebounds from one to another of the major states were apt to reduce the sum-total of political gains that either of the latter could one-sidedly acquire and assets it could reliably retain in the meantime. Nor was it impossible for effective globalization to relax Soviet regional controls in Eastern Europe, as central attention was diffused and overseas tasks were delegated to the European clients. Globalization was more promising in this respect than was any foreseeable liberalization in its absence, just as a merely platonic détente confined to the abstractions of the nuclear arms race and the ambiguities of interbloc exchanges could not but reactively tighten regional Soviet controls as a matter of ideological compensation for functional contacts with, and nominal concessions to, the West.

Allowing a certain latitude for unopposed Soviet gains overseas was likely, moreover, to brighten whatever outlook there has been for a common stand by the superpowers as either global-maritime, trading-or-fishing, or mature-industrial states against merely irksome or altogether intolerable impositions by third-world countries. No common stands were likely to amount soon to anything like an American-Soviet "northern" solidarity. But their occasional occurrence would lessen American dilemmas relative to medium-sized (or middle-income) third-world countries, which are potential devolutionary surrogates for geostrategic purposes regionally, while being also and simultaneously effective challengers or disturbers of the U.S.-sponsored world economy in regard to both terrestrial and oceanic surfaces and depths. Joint superpower constraints on the third-world bias to hard-to-assimilate aspirations or hard-to-contain anarchy could be no more than marginal occurrences until the Soviets had acquired the standing and the needs of a fully developed industrial economy. Even that was preferable, however, to the Soviets' unrelentingly exploiting the South-North cleavage or to the Cold War conflict over the South reviving in full. The more benign state of things would reduce the need for economic concessions by the United States for the purpose of holding onto the political allegiance or neutrality of third-world middle and small powers. A reduction of such material costs could be charged against the political costs of earning Soviet neutrality or better in the confrontational interludes of the Northwest's negotiation with the South over a new world economic order.

Defining the tacitly understood tolerable rate and scope of Soviet acquisitions at any one time will be eased when their effective bearing is actually seen as contained and curtailed by concurrent reconfigurations of power and policy involving a range of other states; and when the costs to the United States of enlarged Soviet access on one "chessboard" of action are reduced, and are seen as being offset, by benefits on another. To manage effectively the rise of an upcoming power is possible only if the bestowal of latitude goes with limitation while firmness is closely at the back of forbearance. The United States was not yet sufficiently weakened, nor did it have ready at hand a preferred recipient of yet more sweeping concessions (such as declining Great Britain had had in the United States), to reenact with respect to the Soviet Union the British mismanagement of the rise of Germany from the late nineteenth century on; nor was the United States still so inexperienced and only fitfully engaged in world politics to be doomed to repeat its own mishandling of Imperial Japan's integration into the state system. Besides, the emerging contemporary global international system disposed of more space and dimensions for accommodating the play of compensations and cancellations of gains and losses than had been true for the not only economically but also psychologically mercantilistic state system with a decaying center in Europe. Alternations between seemingly or transiently conceding much and denying near-everything had ended by finally decimating all of the parties most directly involved in the earlier transactions. The exception had been the United States, as the not wholly unintended or unwilling beneficiary. The possibility of repetition in favor of a third party other than the United States remains. A partner in blocking the expansion of one power may still erect his supremacy on the ruins of the policy of denial. But his involvement in merely regulating such expansion can be more fruitfully a source of larger stability.

Failing to properly assimilate a rising power via equalization along with containment used to be outwardly manifested in catastrophic wars. Such a dénouement cannot be ruled out for the future. If helplessly drifting declining powers are apt to be frustrated, so are hopelessly denied rising powers; and the frustration of either can be released most readily by a resort to a major, including nuclear, act of violence. But mismanagement can engender something even worse than a major war, which may at least clear the slate for a new beginning by clarifying the distribution of power and endowing survivors with a sharpened purpose for a period of time. Protracted anarchy in the interstices of an aimless great-power competition is not inherently preferable to war-wrought catharsis; nor is so preferable the lapse into appeasement, if to conciliate means surrender to small-state anarchy or to an enforced transfer of ordering influence to a successor in empire whose assimilation to an order of equilibrium was missed or mishandled in the process of relinquishing one's own hegemony.

In the relations with the Soviet Union and the related ones with China and Europe (and Japan), the United States stands at a point in evolution that recalls in basic structures the decades preceding World War I, while the current symptoms resemble the final play-out of the earlier misjudgments in the years preceding the second global conflict. To a large extent, Soviet Russia is the Imperial Germany of the earlier era, just as the United States is the British Empire, while Western Europe is erstwhile France, and China replicates Tsarist Russia. Despite the climactic fury of the second world conflict, the reassertion of Nazi Germany in conjunction with militaristic Japan was only the near-ineluctable postscript to the earlier plot's unfolding between still relatively vital and still relatively moderate participants within an expanding system. The seeds of the futility of the interwar Briand-Kellogg Pact (among other utopias) were in the sterility of the much prior Anglo-German attempts to agree on the meaning of parity comprising naval-colonial-continental assets as a basis for common course or even alliance in Eurasia and beyond; and the Stimson Doctrine of nonrecognition of the fruits of agression was just one more impotent attempt to deal with the explosive consequences of denying Japan equality with the West in Asia and reciprocity outside it. Inverting the sequence, an incipient American doctrine of nonrecognition of Soviet (right to) global expansion has been building on one particular interpretation of the Nixon-Brezhnev ''Pact'' (of

1972). It bade fair to initiate and rationalize the mismanagement of the Soviet ascent to parity.

The post-Vietnam United States has been setting out to reshape a new economic order out of disarray; a new balance of military power by means of arms-limitation; and a new internal Executive-Legislative balance of control over foreign policy. The corresponding efforts in the period between the two world wars were to cope with economic depression; control the rearmament of Germany; and subject American involvement in the world to Congressional legislation. It has become essential to see to it that the surrounding and sustaining conditions of such combined efforts be radically different in the next phase, and promise, therefore, a different outcome. As different American foreign-policy elites bade for succession to the Nixon-Kissinger-Ford interregnum, proponents of so-called planetary humanism (encompassing the Third World) and industrial trilateralism (comprising the United States, Western Europe, and Japan) vied with advocates of reactivated polarization (of the United States with the Soviet Union). The first viewpoint played down the need for appropriate configurations of politico-military power to support any larger values or purposes, including those of welfare and interdependence; the second one would not clearly tie a resimplified power equation to any larger systemic analysis and longer-range evolutionary insight or purpose. The first set of ideas would seem to reflect the belief in the ready solubility of political problems by economic devices and in the easy satiability of third-world claimants to a larger share of wealth, sidestepping as a result the issue of force; the other set has viewed the hypothesis of Soviet insatiability as a sufficient warrant for the adequacy of more American military power and more forceful policy alone. While appeasing the third-world claimants would be self-defeating, however, describing any policy of concession-mongering as appeasement is apt to be self-fulfilling if the nation proves unready to revert to strenuous conflict on the strength of insufficient evidence as to its necessity.

The American world empire that grew out of the Cold War justified itself by secreting the half-made elements of a functioning international system. This was its unique claim to posthumous fame. It was also a repayment of the debt that an earlier America had incurred to the Europe-centered international system while ascending to national independence and regional empire. The task of American *après-impérialisme* has become to take a lead in constellating the previously spawned elements into a stable equilibrium susceptible of reconciling the contrary principles of a competition-dependent international *system* and a conflict-controlling-or-confining international *order*.

The initial major step in an orderly retreat from empire to equilibrium is to identify firmly the main kinds of equilibrium from which to choose; the next, to consider ways in which to apply flexibility when moving steadfastly in the direction of the preferred one. Is the principal equilibrium to be one of overall parity with the Soviet Union, evolved progressively and eventually achieved in an environment so changed as to devalue the bearing of the intervening American concessions or even convert them into a joint asset against new principal forces of disruption? Or is the equilibrium to be the steadily manipulated one of a multipolar balance-of-power system, involving several major and, on the lower or regional tiers, also lesser powers? And is such a multipolar equilibrium politics to be a lastingly preferred condition, circumscribing a new economic world order and a new oceanic order politically? Or is it to be mainly a mechanism of transition to the terminal goal of a U.S.-Soviet understanding, stimulated eventually and ultimately justified as the necessary barrier to radical disorder in the economic and oceanic arenas? Before the main roads out of empire would bifurcate in sharply diverging directions, they were apt to be parallel and the movements along them tactically complementary for long enough to spare the makers of American foreign policy the ordeal of a premature and irreversible choice. But keeping the strategic alternatives constantly in mind was a necessary part of implementing the strands of military counterpoise to the Soviet Union and of an economico-political entanglement of the Soviets along with others. It had no lesser a part in orchestrating concessions and denials vis-à-vis the growing number and variety of claimants, currently no more than including the Soviet Union.

The following chapters explore a number of questions that continue to affect world politics along the just-sketched lines. The explorations take place in the setting of the European international system with emphasis on the period preceding more or less closely the First World War (chapters I to V), before returning to the more recent and the wholly contemporary scene (chapters VI to X and Conclusion). The theoretical purpose of the earlier chapters is to expound certain ideas of continuing relevance within an already completed historical record; the practical objective is to lay a basis for discussing more recent developments. The principal themes are two. One inheres in the interpretation of intra-European international politics along lines that, while not original in fundamental bias, are not the most generally accepted ones in the English-speaking world. There may be some utility in continuing to reexamine the European diplomatic past with a view to its psychological if no other bearing on Europe's present and future, as well as an analogical one on the contemporary global system. The other theme is implicit in the relationship of the United States toward the European or Eurocentric international system. It constitutes a background for assessing the American contribution, already made and yet to make, to the emergence and consolidation of the modern global system in the light of

America's role in the system of states from whose ruins the modern one has fitfully grown so far in function of the American-Soviet contest and its byproduct, the American world empire.

The conceptual centerpiece of the study is equilibrium in different manifestations, including balance-of-power and interallied politics and the parity-evolving process between adversaries. Since the postempire future of American foreign policy is yet an unknown, hypothetical speculation about alternatives will not be avoided. It differs from the speculative hypotheses about the completed past that dominate in analyzing the European state system in this study, just as they inform the dissection of the so-far completed American imperial past in the other study.[1] Taken together, the two blends of hypothesis and speculation are as inseparably complementary for the so-called classic or conventional approach to international relations as the two perspectives, from equilibrium and empire, are mutually reinforcing for the conceptually aided grasp of the America foreign policy experience in its historical roots and both recent and continuing dynamics.

---

1. Tentatively entitled *Career of Empire* (forthcoming).

Part One

BRITAIN AND EUROPE

I

LAND VS. SEA POWER. *Alliances and Balance*

International system and empire coexist at all times as either fact or norm. Ideally, empire is to the interstate system as deference within a hierarchy is to the dissension of equals, and as stately permanence is to incessant turmoil. Actually, empire and system share the trials of both contention and change, in ways that are comparable in kind although not in frameworks, levels, and protagonists. In both, evolution is inseparable from conflict; and catastrophe threatens to be the delayed product of cleavages deeper than mere contentions. Similarities strain the symbiosis rather than easing it when empire and system function or founder side by side; and strains among the actors become schism when clashing anxieties and ambitions are compounded by disparity in the natural and structural environments that define group experience and expectations.

The interstate, or international, system depends for continuity on prolonged spells of reequilibration from upheavals or innovations, and it depends for energy on conflicts ranging from minor to hegemonic. The system works and evolves best when two kinds of basic processes activate one another, even while they contain each other's potential for disruption. The processes are, one, the operation of mechanical checks and balances in the short run, identified with the conventional balance of power; and two, longer-range transformations of a partially organic kind. The international system undergoes such transformations as individual states and powers rise and decline, relative to one another and to the norm that the leading or most viable state sets at any one time; and as the system itself expands or contracts in ways that fit more or less well the rise and decline of key states. The system can expand or shrink either in terms of the space that is actually taken up by transactions that are genuinely systemic because they revolve around some form of balancing among partially autonomous actors attending to their interests and roles; or it can be more or less capacious in terms of the variety of stakes and of methods for coping with actor interests.

The expansion or contraction of the international system can be historically associated with basic cleavages or schisms in interstate relations that are fundamentally different from routine rivalries or antagonisms. The differences giving rise to schisms will be qualitative rather than quantitative and give rise to incompatibility of assessments and aspirations at any moment of time without being subject to erosion over any practically significant length of time. Schisms will typically attend the emergence of new issues or resource potentials favoring expansion of both actors and system, even while tending to restrict either the range of significant players or the application of previously available techniques for adjusting conflicts. They will, finally, tend to pit against one another states or other actors bent upon controlling and exploiting values and media other than mere territory and having as a result strictly undefinable or universal characteristics and implications. The precipitant and object of a schism can thus be religion or ideology and imperial succession or alternative international orders. Last but not least, it can be the sea with its significance for naval power and maritime commerce.

The schism between powers situated in a continental and a maritime setting, between states enclosed by territorial rivals and states enclosed by protective moats, is a recurrent focus of interstate relations and was a critical one for the European system. The qualitative disparity between principally land-based and sea-oriented states proved commonly incapable of assimilation by competitive or other interactions. It deranged and finally disrupted as a result the evolution of the European system depending, as will any interstate system, on the capacity of the balance-of-power mechanism to encompass, and thus both mute for ultimate stability and mobilize for evolutionary momentum, the organic rise and fall of qualitatively as well as quantitatively different states. The schism was conspicuously manifest whenever a strong land power staged, and the dominant maritime power resisted to the point of vetoing, a drive for seaborne outreach that would expand the scope of the balance of power and adapt its functioning to overseas extensions of the system's continental core. The resistance of the maritime state implied an artificial restriction of the system while responding to a natural tendency inherent in the sea element. The tendency will urge the insular or near-insular maritime state to seek a monopoly of qualifying assets conveyed by the command of the sea and the control of the overseas realms that make such command technologically possible at any particular time and both materially and immaterially fruitful.

The phenomena identified so far are the mechanical balance of power, the organic divergence of rising and declining states, and the radical, schismatic heterogeneity of land-based vs. sea-based power. They entail a different role for alliances among states. In a descending order of efficacy, the role is regulative in regard to the balancing; at best moderating in regard to the fluctuation; and only variably interactive with the schism.

The regulatory function of alliances in the balance of power is a partial remedy to the many problems of the balancing mechanism itself. Some of the problems are due to a misplaced desire for precision in a concept that is at once the dominant myth and the fundamental law of interstate relations, and as such with some reason highly elastic. There is, however, one genuine difficulty. It lies in establishing the connection in both theory and practice between individual act and systemic result. The difficulty is not entirely removed by even a high degree of confidence that the unintended consequences of even wholly self-regarding individual actions will tend toward balance in a world where several states of comparable power have diverse conflicts which, in this respect at least, are complementary. To that tendency rooted in structure can be added, within a full-blown "balance-of-power system," the analytically easier and actually rarer cases of a deliberate effort to restore the equilibrium against what is somewhat undiscriminatingly called "hegemony." When he exists, the quasi-oligopolistic leader-in-equilibrium or the pseudoaltruistic balancer will mediate between dynamic and deliberation with results mainly profitable to himself or also propitious to the larger system.

The climactic event of a hegemonial drive will tend to take care of the conceptual problem with equilibrium by converting it into a critical predicament. In its absence, the oft-criticized proclivity of states to seek more than "balance" in their favor, if it is practiced by at least some of the more important states at the same time and in contrary directions, is apt to cancel out into a rough equilibrium on a somewhat higher level of realized capability than would be the case otherwise. This tendency and this likely, if unintended, outcome goes far to weaken the practical bearing of the impossibility to precisely measure "power." If states do indeed seek as much power as they can bring forth, and all who are able do this in critical situations, there is no practical need for them to quantify "power" in order to determine the point of equilibrium. The existence and location of that point in the judgment of states can be mostly inferred from their conduct. As a matter of fact, the ability to measure power might even undermine balance-of-power politics. A major initial advantage of an aspirant to hegemony, which could be precisely assessed, would tend to discourage the initiation of what might then appear to be hopeless efforts to first narrow and then overcome his headstart by initially weaker defenders.

What is true of individual states applies also to alliances. They too will seek to generate as much collective power as is economically possible. And the quest of allies for a "balance" favorable to them will be thwarted not only by analogous efforts of the rival alliance for more than a match in hard-to-specify power, but also and much more reliably by the specificity of particular conflicts among actual or potential allies themselves. In a universally competitive context, the role of alliances in regulating the balance of power will reflect and implement a tendency. The tendency is for the marginal utility of any additional ally or alliance effort (including commitment) to start declining at some point so that liabilities come eventually to exceed the gains to be derived from ostensible increases.[1] Within this framework, alliances regulate the balancing process insofar as each actual or prospective alliance-member strives, as a minimum, for parity with fellow-allies in the advantages to follow from his individual contribution to, and value for, the collective effort. In practice this ambition will translate into regulation by way of the value that the adversary power or alliance attaches to having a party deny or cease his contribution to the other side.

Like any other process, the regulatory process has its starting point, its course, and its conclusion or outcome. How unequal competing alliances are initially will depend on the outcome of the early bargaining and transactions. These are conditioned by the nature of the issue at conflict that is responsible for the alliance-making; and they will reflect the importance of the originating issue relative to other conflicts, some of which may be so intense as to rule out adequate compensations for even temporary association between the rivals. While a conflict unfolds, alliances will be subject to more or less complementary equilibrating tendencies. One such tendency is for strains to grow among members of a defensive alliance that appears to be engaged on a winning course. When a defense coalition is initially losing, without being hopelessly outnumbered, its members are disposed to tighten their bonds and suspend interallied conflict for the time being. When such a coalition begins to win, however, internal strains will tend to increase, reduce individual military efforts, and transfer the energy so withheld to attempts to secure the greatest possible political advantage from the past material efforts, if need be by way of a strategy for separate peace. The

1. See also the author's *Nations in Alliance* (Baltimore: The Johns Hopkins University Press, (1962), pp. 26-27. The idea has been expressed more elaborately in terms of the "minimum winning coalition" by William H. Riker, *The Theory of Political Coalitions* (New Haven: Yale University Press, 1962).

corresponding tendency is for an aspirant to hegemony who has been stalemated in his drive to intimate his readiness to concessions, and to offer concessions sufficient to convert into secessions the strains that have been evolving within the winning defensive alliance. An offensive alliance of relatively equal parties is a less frequent historical occurrence than is challenge by one major state with the aid of lesser clients. When a predatory alliance is in being, however, and is being fought to a stalemate, its failure to achieve the anticipated gains with a sufficient speed and in a sufficient volume to permit frictionless distribution among the predators will activate yet another tendency. The rarely-great strategic coordination of the offensive alliance will be further diminished, as even the most reckless expansionists give priority to their divergent defensive needs over the joint or parallel pursuit of offensive ambitions.

Yet another situation obtains when two different but complementary conflicts have precipitated two rival alliances and conditioned their composition, without clearly identifying either association as offensive or defensive. The case arose, for instance, in the mid-eighteenth century's conflicts over the German and the overseas balances. It is then unlikely that any one ally would aid and support any other ally to the point of helping the beneficiary to a "total" victory in the contest that concerns him in particular. To do so would be to make the benefiting partner independent of further aid by the improvidently altruistic one and, therefore, reluctant to run risks while aiding the latter to achieve *his* objectives within what was originally, and should have remained, an opportunistic alliance of convenience.

The probable outcome of these and subsidiary tendencies will be to equilibrate power. The nearly automatic tendencies will also reduce the need to be self-consciously concerned with the balance of power as a standard of conduct, and will confine the need to instances when the structure of conflicts is exceptionally lopsided or when there is an exceptional incentive to rationalize alliance-making and behavior by reference to an unimpeachable norm. Whereas precombat internal strains and conflicts tend to limit the initial size of an alliance, the course of the conflict will tend to limit the size of victory as it engenders new variations in interallied strains that will be sufficient to cause individual diminutions of effort, defections, or realignments. A minimal *winning* coalition, in numbers that are considered necessary and sufficient for insuring joint success, will be thus converted into a minimal-*victory* coalition, just sufficient to satisfy the irreducible objectives of members and deny even those to some of them if a separate peace has been the vehicle or precipitant of the final settlement. The incidental consequence will be to avoid eliminating the major loser or losers from the balance-of-power universe. His or their survival is rightly represented as being the key requirement of a continuing equilibrium system. Abstention from decimating the losers is not, however, the dependable product of statesmanlike foresight implementing an acknowledged rule and recognizing in the defeated enemy an essential future player. It is as much or more the beneficial side effect of the gut instinct of allies to keep one another either manageable or allied. Selfish instinct will be more dependable than systemic insight in a setting of constantly changing ratios of power among adversaries and inherently questionable parities of advantage among allies, the first to be shielded and the second to be derived from continued, reduced, or redirected effort within the existing alliance or in a revised alignment.

This balancing mechanism worked better for the European system than it had for the Mediterranean one prior to the rise of the Roman empire. And it worked more reliably for the European and the Eurocentric global systems in the seventeenth and eighteenth centuries than either in the sixteenth century or the nineteenth and twentieth centuries. That is, it operated more efficiently in the wars of Louis XIV and Louis XV than in those of Imperial Spain, of the Napoleonic empire, and of the two German empires. When the key tendencies failed to assert themselves fully or at all, it was because either local discords or domestic disarrays inhibited the formation of defensive coalitions (against Spain), and the expansionist power was checked not so much jointly as by individual opponents successively; or conversely, because strains within defensive coalitions (against Napoleonic France and Germany) did not produce individual secessions, so that joint counterbalancing lasted too long after starting too late. When it works at all, the regulatory mechanism works best in alliances that aim primarily or only to aggregate power, that is, to add up weights without also instituting controls among unevenly stable allies or a quasi-constitutional union among unevenly evolving ones. The so-called rigidities that impede the regulatory role of aggregative alliances range from hard-to-reverse mass sentiment to the hard-to-disrupt technological and logistical integration. Nor will regulation through alliances be increased when deficient identification of only crystallizing interests in an incipient system gives way to a growing number of relatively declining states within a late or overmature international system, to be at once upheld and controlled by alliance ties.

The proliferation of declining states moves the center of crisis away from the inequalities of power to be balanced in the short run, and toward divergences in the organic rise and descent of states to be contained or absorbed in the longer run. States rise and decline in response to determinative factors such as differences in material resources and immaterial attributes and their management. To the extent that the vertical fluctuations can be at all contained extraneously, they are subject directly to the working of the balance of power system itself. Alliances will be only the secondary, institutional device for flattening out farther any too abrupt oscillations in conditions, status, and practically available policy goals, and for easing thus the immediate effects of individual transitions from one power position or status ranking to another.

As for the balancing process itself, it can affect the issue of rise and decline only as an incident to other concerns or as a matter of deliberate management. Ascent is fostered incidentally when material assets or status advantages go to a not yet manacing junior member of the system as part of attempts by senior powers to upset or to restore the balance. France and Britain promoted the rise of Brandenburg-Prussia and her expansion into Germany at different stages in both ways, and against one another; so was, to a degree, Japan's rise aided by Britain against Russia. Conversely, when a dynamic balancing process activates outlying or depressed regions, it helps incidentally to cushion the decline of the mature states, which turn to the lower-pressure areas to compensate for their diminishing adequacy in the central balance; or, when the system is stalemated, declining states will have a better chance to redefine the scope and stakes of international relations in ways that could prolong or partially restore their preeminence in a new framework. France and (less conspicuously) Britain sought the first kind of boost in the colonial realm, beginning with the nineteenth century. More recently, in the twentieth, they looked to a "new" international politics, first in a League of Nations and secondly in a European Community that emerged from wartime dislocations.

When balancing is applied more deliberately to the rise-decline issue, it can also work both ways. Opposing power will normally be mobilized to contain the rise of a state or an alliance beyond a level that would exceed the capacity of individual members to reverse, and the capacity of the system to assimilate, the resulting displacement in the center of gravity either at all or by tolerable means. Balancing can also uphold a failing member of the system and retard his decline by infusions of strength from the outside. Whereas failure to resist rise in time might make it necessary to include hitherto peripheral members in an expanded system at cost to its charter members, uncompensated failure to uphold decline would constrict the operative system and bracket out hitherto essential players or materials for compensation at likely cost to equilibrium. At different times, Milan in the Italian state system as well as France and Germany in the larger system were both held down and upheld. In contrast, Britain eluded the first operation without forfeiting the benefits of the second. Attempts to antici-pate future trends will be precarious and may be perilous. They will be both when one power acts preventively to undo or match the early tokens of growth in a neighbor, thus Germany vis-à-vis Russia in 1914; or when joint action is taken, thus in partitioning Poland, to neutralize the hypothetical future effect of a state's continuing decline on the great-power balance. It is no less unsettling, however, when perceptions of relative strengths lag behind events and delay or distort balancing responses. Thus Britain did not always rightly resolve the question whether to ally with Spain or France in the early days of Elizabeth and Cromwell and with France or Prussia-Germany during the Victorian climax.

Be they right or wrong, the decisions regarding with whom to ally against whom in the face of actually or presumptively rising and declining power will tend to be inspired by calculations of long-term trends with relevance for adversary balance-of-power politics. Thus, choices will *not* derive primarily from transactions within and between alliances by means of which both waxing and waning actors pursue an immediate equal opportunity to realize an appropriate gain from comparable units of concrete effort. Alignments responding to "organic" rise and decline are keyed to too-long time spans and are subject to too-large margins for error in assessing divergencies among states to be particularly effective in regulating the short-term "mechanics" or "dynamics" of the balance of power. If their general function is not to regulate interactions, however, it still can be to moderate or attenuate fluctuations; and if their specific function can still be to aggregate power, it will be more characteristically to control the use of power or to conceal power deficiency. A quasi-constitutional alliance, approximating a union, will typically ease the decline of one party and facilitate the transfer of primacy to its past rival. England and the United Provinces implemented the transition in the Protestant Alliance, France and Spain in the Family Pact, and Germany and Austria in the Dual Alliance. On a larger basis, a Grand Alliance will constitute a genuine concert of powers if it sublimates disparities in standing among great powers so as to insure the declining ones against too-abrupt loss of status or independence. Pragmatic balancing of power is then supplemented with the ideology of "just equilibrium" and "legitimacy"; and it is correspondingly modified within an institution that replaces military with diplomatic containment (e.g., the European Pentarchy) or mutilated within one that sets out to supersede both military and diplomatic balancing with normative constraints (e.g., organs of international organizations centered on great powers).

Such arrangements include an element of cover-up that deceives no one for long. But fiction does facilitate accommodation to fact, and recourse to institutions may soften the adverse verdict of reality outside them. Alliances alone will be about equally effectual when they are employed by one ally to control another's immoderate reactions to either a sudden decline or to a sudden increase of strength. Decline and increase are alike in that they can produce a superficially similar effort to extend one's position in the balance of power: in the case of compulsive reactions to sharp decline, beyond what is possible for the individual power; and beyond what the system can encompass and absorb in the case of an exuberant attempt to capitalize on surging strength. France's alliance with Sweden and Britain's with Japan illustrated the limitations of attempting control over an ascending state at widely separated critical points in time and space. And essays at control over a declining one in Germany's alliance with Austria-Hungary and Britain's several alliances or ententes with France produced similarly mixed results, as they either terminated or briefly departed from customary relations of conflict between the parties.

Mechanical balancing and organic divergence may be complemented by radical heterogeneity in the makeup of states, and are then further complicated by such heterogeneity. The schism between land and sea powers is a case in point. For a schism to appear in full bloom, there must be overlap as well as diversity, a ground or object in common as well as differences of emphases and approaches. For a land-sea power relationship to be schismatic, therefore, the maritime power must not be just a seafaring trading nation like one-time Portugal or Holland, readily vulnerable on land. It must be a state like Venice in regard to Italy, Great Britain in regard to Europe, and Japan in regard to Asia, disposing at the critical juncture of sufficient immunity and resource to affect seriously the field of forces on the adjoining mainland in both offense and defense. It is likely that such a state will be actually or virtually an insular one. Its obverse is an essentially continental power like France, Germany, and Russia, off and on under different regimes, both capable and willing to extend its territorially focused concerns and resources to the maritime theater. Both kinds of power are thus amphibious, but with sufficiently different ratios of the solid and the liquid elements to make their posture schismatic and their contact explosive. In consequence, the structural differentiation of land- and sea-based power has a very definite impact on the balancing of power as a mechanism. But the schism does not by itself invest alliances as an institution with any distinctive or definite new function. It merely injects additional asperity or rigidity into the regulatory and moderating roles, and deranges in one way or another their rapport with the balancing process.

The radically different situations of predominantly land- and sea-focused powers will dominate their divergent perceptions of reality, including the conditions of security, status, sufficient capability, and the balance of power itself. This will inhibit the emergence of consensus about basic procedures and norms. Such a consensus facilitates normally the operation of the balance of power among otherwise heterogeneous states, and it is even more importantly the key byproduct of a routinized operation of the balance of power over time. The peculiar heterogeneity in continental and insular make-ups and mentalities, moreover, not only intensifies but also frustrates the search for an elusive parity in overall capability and standing. In a situation when neither side can decisively subdue the other, the misperception of each other's strengths and weaknesses makes for reciprocal stimulation of goals. It also makes for attribution of objectives to one another that are still more exorbitant than are those actually entertained. Thus, on the least provocation, the land power will be taxed with the pursuit of continental hegemony as a preliminary to invading or dispossessing the insular sea power; and the maritime state will be indicted with driving for overseas monopoly as a basis for isolating the land power from the peripherally located means to existence.

Until the advent of airborne instrumentalities of destruction, conditions favored sea powers like Venice and Great Britain beyond their intrinsic strength. They had the situational advantage of immunity to a direct assault and possessed a wide range of options with regard to the land powers, which tended to neutralize one another. A related advantage was the tendency for the balance of power to operate somewhat one-sidedly in favor of the insular sea powers. Great Britain was the tendency's especial beneficiary. In this respect, the issue is no longer one of consensus-creation having to do with perception, but is one of actual equipoise-formation in practice.

The balance of power worked commonly to favor the insular sea power in terms of both national capability and alliances. In the course of a protracted and generalized conflict, the disposable resources of land powers like France or Germany tended to decline in relative terms and moved the continental states from preponderance to stalemate and worse. By contrast, the naval superiority of Great Britain and its maritime allies tended to grow in such a conflict to the point of virtual monopoly at the expense of both the military and the merchant navies of adversaries. The advantage was not effaced even by the advent of submarine warfare. Internal strains and counterbalancing responses will tend to decrease the marginal utility of additional national and, yet more, allied power at a relatively early point for ascendant land-based powers. Conversely, the marginal utility of each added national, allied, or impressed naval resource has the obverse tendency to increase as a sea power attains superiority. Moreover, because the less extensive seaborne control mechanisms engender less frictions and consequent costs than do overland ones in most situations, a preeminent maritime state will be less vulnerable to erosion from sheer overextension. Such erosion will beset most conquering land powers when they fail to integrate dependent elites within an empire framework, and will do the job of counterbalancing response over a not-too-long run.

As an insular sea power, Britain had in addition a superior capacity to readily win allies and keep or drop them with almost equal ease. Her ability to dispense subsidies, from profits of overseas trade and related homegrown industries, substantiated her geographic advantage and attractiveness in Europe whenever she was ready to meet an actual or purported hegemonial threat from the major continental power. In order to keep essential allies well-disposed in the short and sufficiently strong over the longer run, Britain had only to abstain from direct acquisitions on the continent and, when called for, limit voluntarily her wartime gains overseas. For example, Britain returned Indonesia to the Netherlands in the peace settlement of 1815. The magnanimity had not been matched in the seventeenth century, however, when the issue between Dutch and English seapower had not yet been decided to the near-monopolistic advantage of the latter. The ready supply of allies with whom to start a campaign permitted Britain to practice a cavalier neglect of allies toward the end of a war or as a means of avoiding one. Discretionary disinvolvement by way of a separate peace was the reverse side of engagement in grand coalitions, so long as Britain's role as "balancer" was an element in the broader regulatory role of alliances as such. Only once, in the War of American Independence, did the prior practice seriously reduce Britain's alliance-worthiness. The European chanceries heeded then briefly the frustrated protest of the French Minister, the duke de Choiseul, to be resumed more than a century later in Wilhelminian Germany, against Britain's destroying a defenseless balance at sea while claiming to protect a much safer balance on land.[2]

As a rule, the sea power could plausibly invoke the adversity that would befall the balance of power if superior land-based capabilities were combined with matching sea-based capability. This hypothesis compromised the position of each of the successive preeminent continental states, which, regardless of any momentary superiority, were actually exposed to an adverse balance-of-power equation. Faced by an impregnable but interfering insular power, no major land power could ignore the continent, nor was it in fact able to organize continental rivals against the dominant sea power on the basis of either consent or coercion; and it could in no other way escape dilemmas born of an inherent disparity in resources and options, favorable to the insular sea power. This thwarted any attempt, however sincere or sincerely counseled, to avoid dissipation of resources by con-

---

2. Brief treatments of related issues are Gerald S. Graham, *The Politics of Naval Supremacy* (London: Cambridge University Press, 1965); Roger Soltau, *The Duc de Choiseul* (Oxford: B. H. Blackwell, 1908); and Ludwig Dehio, *Germany and World Politics in the Twentieth Century* (New York: A. Knopf, 1959). Germany is more thoroughly discussed by Fritz Fischer, *Krieg der Illusionen* (Dusseldorf: Droste, 1969).

tinental involvements and concentrate on the unbounded oceanic horizons and bottomless treasures of the Indies.

Neither France nor later Germany was able to win independence from the continental balance of power by dint of either determined disinterest in its affairs or stabilized defensive predominance relative to any conceivable continental coalition. The course of disinterest would isolate the premier continental state from even the most indispensable ally and set his ship of state adrift toward a British haven.[3] The fact that fickle Austria was the vital ally for both France and Germany at critical periods did not ease the predicament. The other course, of defensive predominance, was impossible to achieve without arousing continental apprehensions and triggering British involvement against even a potentially stable, moderate imbalance. For a preeminent land power to gain a reprieve from the one-sided balance of power, Britain had to either consent to stay neutral or be neutralized. British neutrality on continental issues was sought often and occurred but rarely—as in the war of the Polish Succession in favor of France and in the wars of German unification in favor of Prussia, each time muffling Britain's voice in the peace settlement. Neutralizing Britain by matching seapower was tried without success by both France and Germany. Naval build-ups with national means were no more effective than alliance with Britain's declining maritime rivals. French diplomatic approaches to the declining Dutch Republic had had no more success in the seventeenth century than had the later idea of a "risk-fleet," which would enhance Germany's value as ally (against Britain) for a colonially ambitious and diminished France among others. Being, but for the dykes, also a continental state, the seventeenth-century Dutch feared the elimination of their British protector against France on land more than they resented Britain's abuses on the seas. This left France with conquest as the only alternative to alliance. The German problem with the French was similar in kind, if larger in magnitude.

Only when Britain's troubles within her empire coincided with a compromised diplomatic position in Europe could Britain be even temporarily neutralized. This happened at the time of the independence wars in North America and South Africa. The continental power had then to limit itself to sentimental and prestige gains barely compensating for previous material injury (France) or denial of concrete ambitions (Germany). But it could at least get near organizing the continent against Britain in a way that would give the slightest political expression, in the form of "armed neutrality" or antiwar propaganda, to the normally suppressed resentment of Britain's use of her special position on the allegedly free seas. In no circumstances could

3. Thus France could practice a separate-peace approach only when she was clearly losing or when her land-power ally was exceptionally magnanimous or dependent (Austria and Spain, respectively, at different points of the Seven Year's War, for instance).

either France or Germany be strong enough, however, to give plausible leadership in global strategy without being so strong as to represent a more immediate threat in Europe. This fact of power supplemented widespread economic-commercial dependence on Britain, which militated against participation in any overt challenge to the British Peace. As a result, to win and hold a major land-power ally in a conflict involving Britain, both France (in 1756) and the Second German Empire (in 1914) had to go to war ostensibly in defense of the interests of an at once decaying and ambitious state, Austria. To adopt this remedy meant bypassing more congenial *casus belli* that would avoid the costs of a major war on land as well as on sea.

The apparently more positive way out of the dilemma was to redefine the balance of power expansively, to comprise also the balance of commerce and naval power next to land power. In actuality, neither France nor Germany, while ascendant on the continent, were able to achieve more than tolerated coexistence as an inferior sea power entitled to only minor territorial compensations for a larger prior loss (Corsica for Canada in the French case) or for the denial of a larger prize (Southwest Africa for *Mittelafrika* in the German one). Anything more would risk, in Britain's calculations, weighting the superior land mass too perilously into disequilibrium. As seen by the continentals, however, Britain's criteria for overall parity spelled a discriminatory denial of anything approaching equal maritime capability and overseas access for them. In theory at least, to mitigate the conflict in perceptions and assessments, it would have been necessary to expand the scope of the relevant land-sea balance of power to comprise new areas and actors, other materials of compensation for both parties, or new competitors to be shared by them. The eighteenth century had not yet witnessed the growth of a new world sufficient to help redress the balance of the old. Consequently, France and Great Britain could only temporarily dissolve rivalry in alliance against the new (Bourbon) Spain and the old (Habsburg) Austria, in the aftermath of Europe's first global war (over succession to Habsburg Spain). If the balance of power was expanded at all, it was only to encompass common interests in the Baltic region and in the similar dynastic succession issues of the provisional partners.

Even a temporary consummation was not realized in Anglo-German relations before World War I, although it may have become materially possible by then to evolve a genuinely global balance of land- and sea-based power. No Anglo-American alliance including Germany or counterbalancing her with the aid of a rising Russia came into being to make a peaceful German expansion tolerable for the Euroglobal equilibrium, any more than did a "United States of Europe." In one of the premature visions of the German Emperor, such a union would "Europeanize" Great Britain within a politico-economic bloc capable of effectively competing with the United States and

Japan (or China) under Anglo-German direction. Instead, the "classic" balance of power continued to operate to the immediate advantage of the insular balancer. The result was to postpone the expansion of the scope and the redefinition of the stakes of world politics by a few decades, in the course of which two world wars were necessary to secure whatever gain has been implicit in altering the shape of Germany's economic predominance, and of the Russo-German balance of military power, in Europe.

Alliances accentuated the one-sided operation of the balance of power in the guise of the maritime state's privileged access to allies and alignments. Beyond that, alliances can have also a more direct effect on the land-sea power heterogeneity when they narrow down and then aggravate the schism as part of variable interactions. Alliances can superficially obscure the land-sea power heterogeneity by way of occasional cross-alignments between preeminent sea and land powers in bilateral or, more frequently, multilateral alliances against assertive but second-ranking land powers. The latter will be more typically the subordinate allies of the dominant sea power, however, from which they derive supplies and subsidies even while they surrender oceanic ambitions in exchange for a seemingly gratuitous protection by the ostensibly invulnerable island state. Secondary differences of colonial or commercial interests, such as those between Great Britain and still-allied Austria over the commercial exploitation of the Scheldt River outlet in northwestern Europe, were dwarfed by the common concern for European liberties and decided in British favor. Conversely, an alliance of the sea power with the dominant continental state as either established fact or an elusive potentiality will aggravate the schism in depth. In order for the alliance to be acceptable to the dominant sea power, it will have to be an unequal alliance between materially equal or even inversely unequal parties. Before the land power can accept the status of junior ally even temporarily, it will have to be chastened by a just-endured coalition war or by otherwise induced frustration of larger ambitions. But it must not be so greatly weakened as to lose its eligibility for intimacy with the maritime empire to the next-in-line aspirant to continental supremacy. Beginning with the Peace of Utrecht, France remained England's intermittent junior partner. She continued in that position past her zenith because Germany never fulfilled the basic condition for such an alliance for sufficiently long or to the full in the decades from 1870 to 1940.

The Anglo-French alliance following upon the wars of Louis XIV is a prototype. It suggests that even a temporary accommodation of parties to the schism will require outright alliance, and one that subjects a tentative condominial thrust to the more solid fact of control by the sea power. The land power is required to reduce its goals in regard to world commerce and overseas conquests; and it is expected to play an active secondary role in the promotion of continental peace, even at the expense of its own longer-range interests (thus France's in the Scandinavian North and vis-à-vis Bourbon Spain). In return, the land power will partially achieve that which it was unable to accomplish in militant confrontation with the sea power within the one-sided balance of power. While it can, and indeed must, remain a pre-eminent continental power, it can also enjoy conditional immunity from the sea power's anticipatory restraining responses to even minor continental gains. These are the very restraints that, in the absence of alliance, tend to precipitate the hegemonial drive they ostensibly serve to avert. If such was on different occasions France's position from the early eighteenth century on, Bismarckian Germany was too strong and Weimar Germany too unstable to substantiate the surface appearances of similarity. In addition to improving his continental balance-of-power situation, the junior ally will be also admitted to coexistence in the global, overseas arena on terms compatible with the unquestionable supremacy of the sea power. This need not surprise, since an irreducible measure of maritime superiority was a condition of British alliance, even when an exceptionally weak government (of Charles II) was in dependent association with Louis XIV in the most prestigious early phase of his reign.

Neat in concept, the arrangement injected the frictions of unequal alliance into the dilemmas of heterogeneity. In the wake of the first (post-Utrecht) *entente cordiale*, the pent-up French resentments sank ever deeper into traditional Anglo-French antagonisms. Fueled by subsequent spells of alliance, the asperity was intense enough to survive the briefer period of more violent French hostility toward the continental German enemy.

If alliances exacerbate the land-sea cleavage on balance, the cleavage itself makes for alliances exceptionally close in the political domain and subject to extraordinary strains in the economic area. It may not be altogether an accident that exceptionally close alliances appeared first in connection with maritime-continental contest. One example is the Family Pact of the two Bourbon powers against Britain, in virtue of which "France was Spain, and Spain was France." Another is the Austro-German Dual Alliance, which incarnated similar sentiments in words and in the post-Bismarckian period also in action. Both alliances represented an ultimately abortive effort to offset the one-sided operation of the balance of power by reducing the superior capacity of the off-shore maritime power to exploit political frictions on the mainland. To the extent that the close alliance would stabilize the continental side of the balance of power, to that same extent would it ease the land powers' problem of back-breaking costs of a war to be prepared or waged simultaneously on land and sea. The cost of "integration" was to reduce the regulatory capacity of alliances in the balance of power, by abridging the freedom of action of both the stronger and the weaker continental ally. The cost seemed to be an acceptable one so long as the tendency of the sea power to monopolize overseas assets diminished the interest in keeping one's alliances flexible on land.

Although continental states facing the dominant sea power had also economic differences as trading nations, they were more subject to political strains to be expressed in conflict or overcome in close alliance. By contrast, keen economic competition for a favorable balance of trade encouraged close alliance between mercantile sea powers with common political or security interests. The prototype of alliance constraining intense trade competition is the Anglo-Dutch connection. On more than one occasion it came close to evolving into a full-fledged union, initially in order to consummate painlessly the transfer of maritime primacy from the Dutch to the English and subsequently in order to facilitate a common front against France on the mainland. Anything resembling an equal alliance is even less likely between maritime states than between land and sea powers. Given the tendency of seapower to seek monopoly, "fish eats fish" is a more apt adage still than is its territorial counterpart, *homo homini lupus*. Once a narrowly based sea power loses its superiority, it rapidly subsides into cumulative inferiority. The Dutch had fallen relative to the English in maritime capability, trade, and colonies, no less rapidly and totally than the British lost out vis-à-vis the United States. The very dispersal of seaborne instruments that calls for unified control and command will also work in favor of both close and unequal alliance. So will the vulnerability of a weakened sea power and its coasts and harbors to preemptive attacks from the sea, which will make it less attractive to a competing land-based coalition and reduce its bargaining power within the sea-based alliance. In the early stages of their decline, the Dutch were compelled to exchange sacrifices in maritime trade to their British ally for gains in overland security against French enemy. When the direct French threat declined, the United Provinces became able to partially right the adverse bias. They could regulate Britain's foreign policy to an extent by playing on the British reluctance to go to war without having the Dutch in tow and having them share war-related risks for trade as a result.

The failure to absorb the land-sea power schism within a revised or expanded, but still Eurocentric, balance of power led in the end to the destruction and demotion of the European system itself. It was a system of states that had successfully weathered the strains imposed upon it by conflicting territorial expansion, rival religious and other ideologies, changes in both productive and destructive military technologies, disparities in growth and decline of key members, and even, initially, by the overextension of its materially yet ill-equipped members outside the Continent. Yet the same system failed to deal with the problem created by the emergence of an authentically amphibious actor, in the guise of Great Britain, uniquely endowed with both sea- and land-based power and unwilling to permit the only traditionally tested method of assimilating a novelty into the system, by its diffusion. This reluctance caused the situational disparity to persist and progressively aggravate the divergent perceptions of reciprocal security needs by two kinds of major states, only further alienated from one another by attempts at alliance. No way could be devised by which to reconcile the continental view of "parity," as comprising also maritime balance, with the British application of the balancing principle to the Continent alone.

If it was to continue evolving over time in fundamental stability, the Eurocentric, like any other international system, depended on a structurally uninhibited interplay between balance-of-power mechanism and the vertical fluctuations in national power within a scope expanding horizontally in terms of both space and stakes. Such an interplay ground to a halt some time in the eighteenth century, contributing to the end of the *ancien régime* before undoing its continuation updated by a series of revolutionary interludes. Checks and balances operated henceforth one-sidedly in terms of both access to allies for war and to separate-peace arrangements for ending war. The result was to restrict the actually operative politico-diplomatic system to the disadvantage of all continental powers, and especially the rising ones, at a time when expanding material forces and energies were pressing beyond the henceforth too narrow European framework.

The effort by the late prerevolutionary statecraft, acting for a France no longer threatening on land, to stabilize the continental balance of power for long enough to "right" the balance on the seas failed. The failure insured the thereafter irreversible continuance of two parallel systems, narrowly European and global, which both pressed and permitted Britain to oppose, and by opposing to exacerbate into hegemonic fury, attempts of the leading land power of the day to equip the Continent with a degree of unity required for the global age. Britain's mere existence as an exemplar of the real or imagined advantages of overseas empire, and her actions as a force for equilibrium on the Continent barring access to empire by others, imparted the scope, length, and ultimate destructiveness to what, on this interpretation, were Europe's only partially civil wars. The rhythm of waxing and waning power, assimilable previously, continued. It did so in conditions of an ever greater ease to mobilize resources, of an ever greater apparent urgency to provide against an unpredictable future economic order, and of a growing success of the satisfied nations in setting up psychological and normative barriers against forcible self-assertion by the unsatisfied. On the Continent, Louis XIV and XV were as a result about as inexorably followed by Napoleon as William II was by Hitler. And Britain, at once hero and villain, the Continent's safeguard against ambitions she helped create and wholly intensified, at long last subsided into the condition (in Lord Curzon's words) of a "second Holland" and was taken in tow by the United States, while Soviet Russia stepped forcefully on land and eventually also on the seas into the challenger role vacated first by France and then by Germany.

II

THE GREAT
SCHISMS: *Parity*
and Preeminence

Shifting alliances and protracted antagonisms evolve around the issue of parity. Alliances foster parity when they help adjust gains of individual parties to their actual contribution in a stable balance of power of fixed compass; or help adjust restraints and reinforcements to fit a prospective rise or decline of the participating states in material and other capabilities; or, which is least likely, help secure comparable access to military power, economic opportunity, and strategic dispersion for both land and sea powers within an expanding, dynamic balance of power. Likewise ideally, long-lasting rivalries can be stabilized short of warfare by agreements on parity. Actually, "parity" is no easy criterion to apply on either the conceptual or the practical plane.

In its meaning of equivalence or equivalent standing, parity differs from both "equality" and "balance." From equality it differs because "equivalence" between divergently rising and declining states, for instance, may well mean unequal restraints and reinforcements. It may also mean unequal distribution of material assets: less than equal amount for the ascending state, which may be compensated by anticipatory concession of status, and more than equal amount for the absolutely declining state, whose material advantage is apt to be offset by diminution of will. Moreover, equivalence differs from quantitative balance because it may entail complementary imbalances as well as disparities between any two parties. The particular imbalances and disparities, to be encompassed in overall "parity," can comprise a range of hererogeneous factors such as material capability in both land- and sea-related assets; role or function within the system; status or prestige; recognized prospects of future power or function; and, last but not least, power as means to wealth and wealth as a source of power. It is comprehensible that in such a situation "parity" will not connote accomplished "balance" or "equality" so much as the equal right or opportunity of access to the different sources or manifestations of power—a *Gleichberechtigung* rather than a *Gleichgewicht*.

The problem is thus not one of "measurement," which (we have noted) takes care of itself more or less automatically in the actual world of the balance of power. It is, instead, one of evaluation bearing on both tangible and intangible, present and future, actual and potential assets. As a result, parity as fact or guideline or goal will lend itself to misrepresentation as much as to misperception between both allies and adversaries, especially when they are radically heterogeneous. To offset this bias, criteria of evaluation broadly shared by the parties will have to preside over the pursuit and the acknowledgment of "parity" bearing on status or function as much as on material or geopolitical assets.

As if the conceptual problem were not sufficient, the parity issue comes to life typically in the dynamic framework of tension between parity and its counterpart, preeminence. As parity is to balance, so preeminence is to preponderance in that it connotes overall acknowledged standing rather than superiority in sheer weight alone. For the same reason, preeminence connotes even more strongly than does preponderance both a potentially vulnerable basis and a privileged possession of assets momentarily crucial for a role and inciting to matching efforts. Thus the spells of preeminence by the Papacy over secular rulers in medieval Europe were rooted in both its anterior origins and in the politically relevant exercise of the then critical, spiritual power. Similarly, Britain's preeminence over France and Germany was anchored in her prior possession of increasingly critical maritime and industrial capacities. And, most distinctively, the precarious diplomatic preeminence of a materially declining France under Napoleon III was based on wider options and greater or more reckless initiatives.

The twin concepts, of parity and preeminence, betoken the essential stakes between any two comparably strong and potentially equal powers. In the face of different kinds of intractability, however, the contention over parity and preeminence will undergo either expansion or constriction. The contest is expanded when a two-sided contest, including initially that between Popes and Emperors or more lastingly between Germanic Emperors and Kings of France, either abuts upon or activates other parties and is thus converted into a multipolar balance of power; and the contest is, moreover, intensified when the difficulty to define, consolidate, and accept a "mere" preeminence of one party produces a hegemonial conflict within an international system that is congenitally biased toward precautionary anticipation of threat and its exaggeration. Nothing is harder to attain or maintain in relations among states than the condition of a *primus inter pares*, combining primacy and parity in one notion. The instability was converted into empire by Rome in the Mediterranean basin and by Britain in the world's oceans. And while the notion of a "first" monarch was familiar to early Europe, hegemonial conflicts engulfed nonetheless the successive preeminence of Spain, France, and Germany on the Continent.

Whenever the parity-preeminence issue does not give rise to climactic encounters, the reason for this may be with a different kind of intractability. The obstacle is then a built-in or temporary inability of the contending parties to effectively engage or subdue one another because of the lack of appropriate means. Such ultimate limitations affected the contentions between the Carolingian and the Byzantine empires, between medieval Church and Empire, and between Catholic and Protestant during the Reformation, before being augmented by developing land- and sea-based military technologies. When this happens, the parity-preeminence issue will be constricted into formulating the stakes in terms of formal parity in crucial respects as almost an end in itself. The aim is then to evolve agreements on both substance and standards that would be sufficiently precise to avoid misperceiving actual stalemate as either the frightening superiority or the enticing inferiority of the other party. And the related effort is to confine competitive balancing of power to secondary issues or instruments, and to avoid converting the denial of parity or escalating its pursuit in key areas into the search for preeminence, which would unavoidably reopen the dread issue of hegemony.

Acknowledgments of parity that formalize a stalemate or consolidate coexistence are peculiar in nature. They differ from coexistence that is marked by intermittent warfare and a fluctuating relationship of forces, such as the centuries-long interplay between the Byzantine and the Moslem realms. They differ also from a merely factual promotion of a previously inferior power, thus of the Carolingian empire in the West relative to the eastern Byzantine empire in the period between Charlemagne's coronation and his recognition by Constantinople. And, finally, they differ from formalized sequelae (including schemes of union) to an effective prior transfer of primacy in struggles between rising and declining powers of the same category, such as those involving England and the Dutch and France and Spain in the seventeenth century and France and Germany beginning with the nineteenth.

Formal parity agreements will be sought when two basic requisites obtain. One, the parties feel unable to destroy one another in a context that may well include a schism comprising both diversity and overlaps in their attributes and goals. And two, the parties are also in some ways inter-dependent for assured survival or standing within an elementary order in relation to third parties or environmental factors. Among the just-mentioned conflicts, the Arab-Byzantine contention lacked compelling interdependence relative to third parties, while the hegemonial conflicts between maritime powers or between land powers lacked both the schismatic quality and reciprocal impregnability. Only the relation between the Carolingian and the Byzantine empires invited attempts to formalize parity. It did so on the question of status, bearing on continuity with the Roman Empire. In addition, the parity issue between the Holy Roman Empire and the Papacy concerned primarily function in contemporary order-maintenance, and that between the Catholic and Protestant confessions bore most explicitly on institutional representation and weight in the organs shared by the ide-ologically incompatible parties. The three subjects for parity adjustment—status, function, and institutional standing—were related to material capa-bilities and specific interests and tended to be involved and often to combine in subsequent contests.

The issue of equal status for the Carolingian or western empire, concerning imperial title and coinage equivalent to the Byzantian or eastern one, was entangled in conflicts of doctrine between the two related churches and their parallel expansion by way of the conversion of pagan peoples. The seapower-oriented eastern empire continued to enjoy material advantage. Its acknowledgment of the western emperor's formal equivalence (in 812) was precipitated by the older empire's need for assistance against the Arabs, a third party to whose different branches both of the Christian empires stood in a comparably ambivalent relationship of hostility and alliance. Such ambivalent relationships expose two principals to options and temptations that are more likely to inspire attempts to stabilize their relationship than does sharing an unrelieved hostility for the third party, which will compel opportunistic cooperation even in the absence of parity agreements.

The Byzantines disrecognized the Carolingian empire after it was divided into three artfully, if futilely, equilibrated parts. The issue of parity arose next within the West, between the Holy Roman Empire, as it had been enlarged by the military and missionary activities of the Saxon emperors, and a Papacy asserting itself against initial subordination. A parity agree-ment was embodied in the Concordat of Worms (1122), which formulated the equivalence between the secular and the spiritual authorities within their parallel spheres and hierarchies. The issue involved complementary rights for emperors and popes in selecting and materially endowing the higher clergy, which was itself a potential balancer between the two supreme authorities of which each was endowed with partially interdependent assets in the still more genealogical (familial-matrimonial) than geopolitical dynastic politics of the earlier Middle Ages. The papacy's quest for parity with the initially Church-dominating emperors was facilitated by parallel challenges from "third" forces, comprising disruptive localism within both Empire and Church and the rival universalism of Constantinople. The interdependence of the secular and the spiritual powers for maintaining a Christian order and for surviving at its summit individually encouraged the search for a compromise to be formulated in an abstractly doctrinal setting. The material stake was the allegiance of the clergy as the initially sole purveyor of key administrative services that exceeded the importance of feudal chivalry as the key resource. As a result, the interdependence of the two powers was matched by interpenetration of the two spheres. This in turn favored a competitive quest for the preeminence of one party within both of the spheres, to the temporary advantage of first the emperors and subsequently the popes.

The next major parity issue was between Catholic and Protestant confessional camps, within the organs of the Holy Roman Empire itself. It was in large part engendered by the failure of the earlier effort to stabilize relations between the popes and the emperors. The issue was provisionally compromised in the Peace of Augsburg (1555), which followed from inconclusive prior conflict and futile prior efforts to secure a de facto coexistence by renouncing force in doctrinal matters unilaterally. The compromise reflected, moreover, interdependence of the two camps for effective resistance to the outside Ottoman threat and to the extreme internal threats of either an authoritative centralization by the emperors or an unchecked anarchy wrought by lesser actors. Including provisions for reciprocal nonintervention, the religious peace instituted also parity representation for Catholic and Protestant rulers in major organs, ideological partition of biconfessional cities with assured protection to the minority creed and, last but not least, institutional inaction in the absence of agreement. When the parity arrangement broke down, warfare resumed and escalated into the Thirty Years' War.

Parity agreements were hard to evolve in view of disparities in the situations of parties. Their recurrent breakdowns showed that the agreements were even harder to perpetuate in view of uneven trends in relative capabilities. The unevenness turned against the agreement the very factors that had originally facilitated accord. One such factor consisted of ambiguities introduced into agreements to reflect the overlaps in either attributes or interests of the conflicting parties. An example of an ambiguity that fueled antagonism in the longer run is the reservation inserted in the Peace of Augsburg on the subject of a continuing revolution in regard to secularization of ecclesiastical properties. Another such factor consisted of the complementary imbalances favoring different parties in different areas or spheres and originally supporting the quest for parity. Their inherent impermanence required, as a supplement and eventually a partial substitute, a self-sustaining definition and institutionalization of parity. When these failed to crystallize lastingly or at all, the latent inseparability of the relevant spheres of authority or action—secular and spiritual, religio-doctrinal and territorial, institutional and politico-military—reasserted itself in the drive of the temporarily stronger party for preeminence or outright supremacy. Resumption of conflict was also promoted by some forms of convergence between parties. One antagonizing form would replace partial overlaps with integrally identical stakes, as when the secular-territorial interests of both popes and emperors converged on Italy. Another would replace or supplement a partial qualitative symmetry of original and relatively moderate parties with the converging thrust of diametrically opposed identities, as when Catholicism evolved in the Society of Jesus its own internal reform in extreme opposition to the simultaneously radicalized offshoots of the Protestant Reformation.

Whether or not interrupted by parity agreements, contests over supremacy fostered the rise of ever new third forces, which would eventually supersede the principals in the parity-preeminence drama. In the medieval context, the actors tending to universality such as church and empire and confessional movement were superseded in due course by more particularistically defined and oriented dynastic or ''national'' actors with pragmatic goals. Whereas the French monarchy abducted the previously triumphant papacy into ''Babylonian captivity,'' the German territorial princes utilized the confessional issue to dislocate the Empire to their advantage. The secularization of politics set simultaneously the stage for an integral maritimization of the dominant schism.[1]

The dichotomy between secular and spiritual power is most closely comparable with the schism between land- and sea-based power in regard to the issue of parity in role within a system and access to key values. The related issue of parity in status, such as that which engaged the senior (eastern and maritime) and the junior (western agricultural) successor-empires to Rome, will be likewise intrinsic to the enactment of conflict between major land and sea powers whenever the oceanic realm offers special advantages. Only in respect of ideological or doctrinal and the

---

1. For historical backgrounds see Robert S. Lopez, *The Birth of Europe* (New York: M. Evans, 1967); Alfred F. Havighurst, ed., *The Pirenne Thesis* (Boston: Heath, 1958); Robert Folz, *L'idée d'Empire en Occident du Ve au XIVe siècle* (Paris: Aubier, 1953); Walter Ullmann, *The Growth of Papal Government in the Middle Ages* (London: Methuen, 1955); Gerd Tellenbach, *Church, State and Christian Society at the Time of the Investiture Contest* (Oxford: B. Blackwell, 1959); and Hajo Holborn, *A History of Germany*, Vol. I (New York: A. Knopf, 1961).

derivative institutional ramifications of the parity quest is there a difference, since neither extension is automatically engendered by the contention between land- and sea-based powers except insofar as militant propaganda plays upon the elusive peculiarities of each in world-views and value systems deriving from their distinctive material conditions. But similarity reappears, in that both spiritual authority and seapower, as the more pervasive forces exerting the less tangible influence, will tend to win an at least temporary, if in the end hollow, victory over their more concretely bounded and tangibly focused secular and land-based adversaries. Such as it was, victory rewarded intervention of the ecclesiastical power in mundane affairs and of maritime power in "continental" affairs, departing from the initial impulse of one to escape from temporal dilemmas into spiritual contemplation and of the other from territorial struggles into seafaring enterprises.

When they were concretized in the ecclesiastical successors to Rome and in Rome's insular British imitators, to embrace the world meant to dominate it for the spiritual authority and the seafaring adventurers alike. Such domination could be direct or indirect, through control of the essential elements and from a posture of ostensibly impartial arbitrament, employing crusades against more or less authentic threats, be they those of unauthorized heresy or hegemony. In their ascent, both the militant church and imperial Britain shared the advantage of ultimately impregnable, either transcendent or natural, safeguards in relations with correspondingly handicapped rival powers of secular or continental character. They were, moreover, both strengthened and stimulated to intervention by possession or control of major assets in the rival territorial sphere (middle Italy by the papacy and different continental enclaves by Britain) and by natural alliances with the geographically caused "hereditary" or "historic" enemies of the rival power or powers. The advantage turned into a liability and assets became hostages only in periods of weakness. The weakening coincided with the liberation of the secular-or-continental powers from dependence on the spiritual-or-sea powers. And liberation could bear on either essential services or essential sanctions. Among the services were ecclesiastic administration and spiritual solace by one and mercantile-industrial supplies and material subsidies by the other; among the sanctions were excommunication and, more importantly, denial of matrimonial dispensations in dynastic politics on one side and maritime blockade and confiscation of vital colonies in global warfare on the other side.

The difficulty to evolve mutually satisfactory terms of a parity formula between dominant land and sea powers is matched only by the recurrent pressures for evolving one. They were due to the reciprocal impregnability of the two kinds of powers and their interdependence for a stabilized order against third parties. Just as dogs and sharks, major land and sea powers cannot destroy one another in their respective elements.[2] Thus no continental great power could invade Britain so long as it lacked prolonged naval domination of the treacherous Channel. Nor could any British-led military coalition reduce either France or Germany permanently to impotence from the eighteenth century on. Similarly, Britain could win climactic naval battles, and naval encounters could materially contribute to the outcome of decisive land battles in any one war. But the typically slow and relatively cheap strangulating effect of superior seapower was indecisive against the recuperative potential of the major continental states. Consequently, ultimately inconclusive contests or attempts to avoid them produced efforts to stabilize relations on a basis that would express in a formal or de facto parity agreement the disparately structured equivalence. Such efforts engaged Great Britain with France beginning with the early eighteenth century, as well as with Germany from the end of the nineteenth century on. The essays expressed the interdependence of the disparate powers for an order and welfare that would entail all kinds of reliefs: from the costs of a competitive dual (territorial and maritime) military capability for France or Germany, or the two-power plus naval standard for Britain; from the need for political alignments, with often even less cognate or compatible third powers, notably Russia in both the French and German contexts; and from the danger of reciprocal destruction profitable only to third parties.

The situational disparity (which engendered the need for somehow formulating parity while rendering the challenge intractable) meant different things for the two different powers. The major land powers faced a two-element environment (land and sea) and often a two-front strategic situation in its continental sector. Their internal political dynamic and foreign policy responses to the environment were complicated by a two-culture social and economic structure: feudal-agricultural and maritime-industrial. The resulting predicament commonly overtaxed both the available material resources and the existing creative capacities for reconciling contrasting priorities. For the insular sea power, the situation seemed to provide little middle ground between integral immunity and total insecurity in its absence. If immunity seemed to require an unqualified command of the sea, insecurity reflected a constitutionally augmented inherent demographic weakness in land-based military capabilities most of the time. The resulting calculations constricted the extent of naval capabilities, and of overseas geopolitical or economic assets, which, in a strictly bilateral

---

2. "The struggle resembled the contest of the dog and the shark; neither could get at the other." Horatio F. Brown, *Venice: An Historical Sketch of the Republic* (London: Rivington, Percival & Co., 1895), p. 272, with reference to the contest between Sigismund of Austria and the Venetians in 1412.

context, Britain would or could readily concede to the dominant land power of the day as part of an overall parity mix, allotting to each kind of power a comparable margin of intrinsic and situational assets over liabilities. The technical problems alone were formidable. To be taken into account in the naval domain were not only numbers but also the quality of ships in matters of design, mode of propulsion, and armaments; the size of presumably required British, and tolerable continental, navies relative to different, offensive or defensive, strategies; the uneven scope of overseas imperial responsibilities, and consequent dispersion; and the extent of required access to politically controlled overseas facilities that would be implicit in different kinds and ranges of naval capabilities allowed to the land power. The gravity of the stakes for Britain fostered speculative visions of maximum imaginable threat arising from even inferior or only locally superior navies. And anxieties were augmented by inexperience in periods of technological change. One such transition was to steam, innovated by the French in the 1840s; another was to superbattleships of the dreadnought type in connection with the German threat. An untested and, in the light of the subsequent wartime performance, exaggerated enemy capacity for surprise, speed, or striking power distorted calculations and bred naval scares and arms-races in peacetime.

Contrasting with such complexities was the real or apparent simplicity of two basic forms of a parity mix. The first would approximate equality and complete symmetry, in the guise of parallel equilibria including Europe-wide balance of land power and correspondingly distributed sea power at large. Britain would then be on a par with the major continental state or states in both elements. The second would express only equivalence by means of complementary imbalances, adding up to a largely if not wholly asymmetric overall equilibrium. A preeminent position of a land power on the Continent would match Britain's on the seas. The two imbalances would be supplemented, and kept in overall equilibrium, by a comparable capability of each in the complementary sphere: maritime for the continental state and continental for the insular. Although inferior, the supplemental capability would be sufficient to serve as a rallying point and core-potential for collective resistance against abuses of preeminence on land or sea.

If nothing else, Britain's constitutional aversion to a standing land army ruled out receptivity to the first, egalitarian version of parity. No less powerful habits of thought and fears impeded, however, also her whole-hearted acquiescence in the alternative form of equivalence. Historically, ascendant Britain insisted on highly unequal ratios of naval capability and maritime-mercantile potential in her favor with regard to both enemies and maritime and continental allies. Thus even the allied Dutch were consigned, at the early stage of the War of the Spanish Succession, to a ratio of five-eighths to three-eighths in naval contributions and to an inverse ratio in military contributions on land; and, thereafter, the Austrian empire was even more drastically inhibited from engaging in the maritime exploitation of the Catholic Netherlands (Belgium) transferred from Spain to augment joint security against France. The British requirements were anything but modest. An indisputable command of the Channel and of the Atlantic approaches to Gibraltar en route to the Mediterranean was seen as necessary to guarantee an unimpeded wartime passage through key maritime gateways and to eliminate enemy threat to either the Low Countries or Spanish-Portuguese coastlines. Immunity of the first was deemed vital for Britain's physical security, of the second for the security of her trade. Moreover, a superior central strategic reserve was considered mandatory to effectively relieve transient inferiority in remoter waters. So defined, the requirement readily evolved into a two-hemisphere naval supremacy following the Napoleonic wars, when Britain's fleet equaled the sum of all other fleets on the "free" seas. By then, and pending Britain's later surrender of her naval self-reliance, her "minimum" naval requirements had drastically reduced the scope for "tolerable" naval capabilities of the major continental states. And Britain's bias to preemptively seize and retain even immediately valueless peripheral real estate limited the access of the continentals to supporting overseas possessions as well.

Any effort by continental states to move the maritime balance to a point closer to an overall land-sea power parity disposed of two basic types of capabilities and strategies. One had but limited peacetime and diplomatic impact and was not decisive in war. It consisted, as the offensive supplement to ships for coastal defense, of privateering raiders (France in the eighteenth century) or long-range light cruisers and submarines (Germany), designed to disrupt British commerce and supplies. This option downgraded climactic naval engagements between high-sea fleets. The French saw such engagements as something that the enemy could avoid at will or that would not produce decision if he did not (before Nelson's tactical innovations); the Germans as a wager lost in advance (in conditions of clear British or Allied naval superiority). The other capability-strategy formula assumed that a combination of the naval capabilities of several continental states could both decisively and successfully engage Britain's main force or home fleet. This option presupposed that one land power could develop a sufficiently great tonnage in capital ships to tie down Britain's strategic naval forces, strain her finances, influence her military and diplomatic conduct, and, in consequence and crucially, constitute an adequate nucleus for a continental maritime alliance against an otherwise but impotently resented British management of the "freedom of the seas." After Napoleon retreated from the concept in the wake of Trafalgar, the viewpoint was represented by

Thiers in France in the 1840s and by Tirpitz in Germany in the 1900s. Both men postulated a 2:3 naval ratio in Britain's favor as both šufficient and intrinsically nonprovocative. The heightened status that would result was attractive especially for the self-conscious German statecraft. But British strategic thought had anticipated and implicitly rejected Tirpitz's risk-fleet theory as early as the mid-nineteenth century. It was then preoccupied with the capacity of a strong French navy to invade Britain and with the potential of even a temporary enemy success to trigger naval hostilities against Britain by a third power such as the United States.

An inferior but substantial naval capability could be dispersed or, more likely, gathered into local superiority in a sea that was critical for the continental power. This meant the Baltic and the eastern Mediterranean for Russia. For France, it meant the western segment or the entirety of the Mediterranean Sea, and for Germany the North Sea, abutting most directly on Britain's territorial security. Russia's maritime deployments in the eastern Mediterranean, beginning with the mid-eighteenth century, were alternately repugnant and acceptable to Britain up to 1914, depending on the momentary state of British relations first with France and then with Germany and her Italian and Austrian allies. France's naval ambitions in the Mediterranean were in large part compensatory for losses in the Atlantic and Indian oceans beginning with the 1760s. They were steadily opposed by Britain up to the early 1840s (coincidentally with the Mehmet Ali crisis over Egypt) and were only intermittently tolerated thereafter as a southward diversion for the French navies and a hostage for the British navies. They also served as a basis for an Anglo-French political alliance whenever it was desired. And, finally, after the spell of an inhibiting Franco-Russian cooperation and in conditions of British decline, the French naval presence in the Mediterranean was sanctioned by a concerted reallocation of Anglo-French naval responsibilities vis-à-vis Germany.

The British interest in remote waters militated against conceding even a local naval superiority or mere parity to any vigorous state in the period preceding British decline. Great as was the interest in remote waters, however, it was secondary to the insistence on a clear supremacy in home waters. Nothing approaching parity in the North Sea could be conceded to a German naval capability, for instance, whose effective radius made it suspect of offensive intent as well as potential. Apart from suggesting an invasion threat, potentially hostile parity in adjacent waters was also a menace to Britain's isolationist option. It compelled Britain to supplement her naval capability with alliances and compromises that were not always attractive on other grounds. Adjustments with Russia in the Egyptian crisis of the late 1830s and early 1840s anticipated those with several others on a vaster scale beginning with the 1890s. Nor was this the worst possible contingency. An unchecked naval diffusion could take the remaining "splendor" out of a British isolation, insofar as it would impose isolation from the outside on the strength of navally backed hostile diplomatic alignments.

As a result, it was next to impossible to evolve tacit or explicit parity agreements either in the naval sphere alone or by means of tradeoffs between naval capability, colonial possessions, and continental alliances. The difficulty was manifest in the several naval races with the French in the nineteenth century and in the even more conspicuous one with Imperial Germany in the early twentieth. With brief exceptions coinciding with their self-limitation, Great Britain would not concede continental preeminence to the land powers; nor would she concede, depending on the distance from British shores, naval near-parity, parity, or superiority in regional theaters. She remained wedded instead to the eighteenth-century strategy, as it had been formulated among others by the Duke of Newcastle with regard to France. Under that doctrine, mobilizing continental alliances was the mandatory means for diverting the superior resources of the major continental power from building a navy to expanding the territorial army, and for maintaining thus Britain's maritime supremacy. Conversely, the leading continental powers continued and, in response to the British doctrine, could not but continue, France's seventeenth-century strategy. This meant seeking to absorb key coastal positions and maritime capabilities on the Continent (such as those of the Low Countries) as a partially compensating asset and a preliminary to near-equal confrontation with Britain on the seas. The result was a vicious circle. Any residual or exceptional British readiness to make concessions in either the continental or the maritime arena was undercut by the suspicion that the conceded assets would help equip the rival for an eventual global climacteric from a position that would be more-than-preeminent on the Continent and be too close to equality on the seas. The risk seemed greater than the prospect of concessions initiating a lasting accommodation for stability on the basis of mutually acceptable parity-mix. At the very least, even supposing immediate good faith, it was always possible that the continental rival asserted overseas claims and interests as so many leverages for successful bargaining over positions nearer home—or else saw local or regional reinforcements as mere springboards for a global leap at a later stage. Comparable methods had secured such vital naval points as Calais or Corsica for France and Heligoland for Germany, while larger near-home targets of Bourbon France were in and off Italy and, secondarily, in Spain, and at a later stage in North Africa, and Germany's were in the center of Europe and extended to Asia Minor.

Like the earlier historical situations raising the issue of parity, the land-sea power relationship was also subject to both uneven and divergently evolving capabilities, to attempts to circumvent the inseparability of the two spheres, and to injections of multiple "third" elements into the two-power parity contest.

Capabilities-in-being were the most immediate problem. The French fiscal commitment to a strong fleet alongside a sufficient land capability was not sufficiently consistent to uphold the implementation of an Anglo-French parity agreement had it been possible; even more probably, other threats to such an agreement would originate in the divergent rates of savings from a temporary reduction of tensions. In the case of Imperial Germany, and contrary to the impression of a massive economic strength and drive, the capital available to her was inferior when contrasted with the British and the politically managed French financial markets. The capital insufficiency militated against the implementation of tradeoffs between German naval and British colonial concessions. One such tradeoff, on the eve of World War I, anticipated an equal Anglo-German participation in the exploitation of the Belgian Congo, another in the railway- and oil-related activities in the Ottoman Empire. They represented a promising, if belated, beginning to formal parity agreements or actual reapportionment of world power. The same financial weakness removed political support in Germany from under the Tirpitzian objective of a 2:3 Germano-British naval ratio, as the presumed minimum for the purposes of bargaining, deterrence, and a fighting chance in conflict. If immediate assets favored Britain, long-term expectations and projections favored the German late-comer, however, making provisional agreements unreliable for the British and "final" ones premature for the Germans.

Divergences between actual and anticipated capabilities were compounded by antagonistic ideas about the separation or separability of the continental and the maritime spheres. This was critical for attempts at parity agreements to comprise a reciprocally agreeable mix of naval strengths, colonial or near-colonial positions, and links in continental alliances. Outright separation of the two spheres was most patent on the operational level, in the British Admiralty's prewar indifference to planning for territorial warfare and in the hostility of the German General Staff to its naval counterpart. A high degree of separability, if not outright separation, was implicit in policy ideas favoring barters that would hopefully produce rearrangements limited in scope but stable in duration. Such was the German governmental idea to barter German self-restraint in the naval sphere for British neutrality on the Continent, tantamount to a free hand for a self-containing German preeminence. German obsession with British continental neutrality bore witness to an inadequate comprehension of the dynamic and the dimensions of "complementary imbalances," as well as to an inadequate assimilation of the few instances in which Britain conceived of such a short-term *modus vivendi* with regard to either a temporarily weakened France (e.g., following the War of Spanish Succession and, again, at one stage of the Seven Years' War in the eighteenth century) or a yet nonconsolidated Imperial Germany in the early Bismarckian era. The corresponding and no more realistic British idea of parity entailed a version of "parallel balancing" or equilibration, in the form of only relatively minor colonial concessions to Germany to be matched, next to naval modesty, by virtual German acquiescence to be lastingly constrained in a relatively deteriorating situation on the Continent by the Anglo-French-Russian entente.

An insufficient separability of the secular and spiritual spheres helped defeat the implementation of parity agreements in the investiture contest between emperors and popes. Operational and policy concepts positing separation or separability of the continental and the maritime spheres worked against a serious effort to evolve an overall parity formula between empires. The immediate consequence was negotiations that were inconclusive because they were in one part unrealistic and in another part less-than-candid. Their futility enhanced receptivity to an all-out military resolution of an intractable dilemma that was, moreover, increasingly superimposed upon comparable ruling-class disgruntlement with the rising forces of "social democracy" on both sides. The pursuit of an Anglo-German parity formula was finally subverted, however, only by the concurrent multilateralization of the dominent land-sea power relationship. This occurred when Britain's understandings and commitments introduced into the Anglo-German relationship several third-power naval and, incidentally, also territorial military capabilities as an alternative to a parity-promoting third party inspiring ambivalent feelings in both principals. The move was reminiscent of, where it was not literally comparable with, Britain mobilizing European allies for subsequent "total" wars against France as the ostensible aggressor in the wake of fleetingly successful negotiations for the peaceful partition of the Spanish empire with Louis XIV and for a global power distribution at Amiens with Napoleon.[3]

Yet another, and not the least, obstacle in evolving a land-sea power parity formula was in the reciprocal perceptions of the insular and the continental powers. They compounded, where they did not cause, their individual and separate misconceptions. The disparity in the "objective" situation or environment of the two kinds of powers constituted a rational

---

3. Pertinent historical data on Britain's relations with the land powers can be gathered from Alfred T. Mahan, *The Influence of Sea Power on History 1660-1783* (Boston: Little, Brown, 1890); M.S. Anderson, *Europe in the Eighteenth Century* (London: Longmans, Green & Co., Ltd., 1961), ch. xii; and C. J. Bartlett, *Great Britain and Sea Power 1815-1853* (Oxford: The Clarendon Press, 1963), next to previously cited works by Graham and Fischer.

basis for largely contrary definitions of needs and interests. But, insofar as the powers also projected upon each other their respective experiences, the thus distorted perceptions and exaggerations of requirements, attitudes, and behavior tended to convert an intrinsically manageable disparity into seemingly irresoluble dissension about key aspects of individual security and the encompassing balance of power.

Exaggerations will be nourished by differences in the basic conditions of security. Security for the land power rests primarily on intrinsic material capability, to be increased by additions; for the sea power, security rests primarily on its natural and diplomatic advantages to be improved by manipulation. Each approach produces different degrees and kinds of immunity, and each approach to security has its different utility for being exploited offensively vis-à-vis other powers. The typical continental statesman will attribute to the seapower-based empire either inordinate strength or likewise excessive vulnerability. He will have only partial understanding of the requirements of control, material returns, and resilience of maritime power structures, and of their differences with continental ones. As a result, strains in the cohesion of maritime conglomerates and the costs and causes of conflict on the maritime peripheries of the international system will be equated as to their gravity with those in the more familiar and exacting central or territorial balance of power. Thus the eighteenth-century French Minister Choiseul assumed a fundamental incompatibility between the small size of the British insular nucleus and the vastness of the overseas empire even in the short run; and Bismarck and his successors posited an extreme vulnerability of Britain in peripheral colonial conflicts and her likewise absolute intransigence vis-à-vis navally competitive France and the United States. The combination of weakness in the face of endemic peripheral trials and resolution in the face of traditionally irksome maritime challenges were expected to make Britain receptive to German views and alliance. The assumptions were correct, when at all, only in a long-term perspective. It was but a step from them to exaggerate the short-term capacity of the continental state to decisively affect Britain's security by acts of commission or omission, mainly in the naval armaments field, as a means to securing her nonintervention on the Continent. Such a neutrality would, still as seen from the *terra firma*, be fully consistent with the security of an imperially augmented offshore island.

Other perceptions underlay the insular, British statecraft. They inclined to attribute to the dominant land power an unbounded and self-generated urge and capacity for hegemonial expansion. A prudent continental anticipation on an implacable British opposition to even moderate gains could thus assume the hue of pathological aggression. In the process the British focused attention and emphasis on assertive methods, which could actually express no more than the zest of a still immature Louis XIV, the felt inadequacy of a Napoleon as a legitimate ruler, or the mercurial temperament of a William II. And they tended to draw facile inferences from assertive methods to actual material capability, and from material capability to manifest goals. The intellectual mechanism was comparable to a matching tendency of the continentals. They inclined to conclude from the propaganda directed by mercantile interests at the government of the maritime empire to its actual policy and profit, and to correspondingly underestimate the rewards of fully exploiting the economic potential of the large continental domain. If the continentals saw the overseas empire as the source of limitless wealth, to be spread more evenly, the managers of the insular sea power attributed to the major land power the drive for what they themselves both possessed as a gift from nature and sought to extend overseas by the arts of policy: total security behind an impregnable boundary.

What is perceived as excess depends on what is seen as sufficient. Accordingly, the maritime state will define the land power's sufficiency in terms of its own needs. limited as they will be by the capacity to restrict military involvement to the maritime sphere or to any one chosen territorial theater. The limit on needs applied to Britain, even after first dynastic and later technological factors had linked her more closely to the Continent and abridged somewhat her freedom of choice. Conversely, the land power will tend to project on most contingencies the requirements of a central war, to be waged concurrently in two or more theaters. Whereas the sea power can dispose its mobile reserve after delayed or gradual mobilization in ways that are commensurate with the revealed scope of the challenge, the land power must ultimately rely in even peripheral or diplomatic conflicts on a central capacity-in-being, knowing full well that the reverberations of that capacity will diminish with the growth of physical distance from the stakes and with the consequent shrinkage of the stakes as a credible concern. Nor is this all. Continental statesmen will easily view as required for security a naval capability that they actually seek mainly for reasons of status, as a token of equality in terms of category rather than capability and as a means to being "taken seriously." Conversely, the masters of seapower will discount the status requirement. They will construe as bluff or blackmail, as expressions of national conceit (in the case of France, by Lord Palmerston) or of an innate spirit of domination (in that of Germany, by Sire Eyre Crowe and others) that which the continental power regards as the innate privilege (France) or necessary prerequisite (Germany) of great-power condition; a privilege, moreover, which the sea power can contest only as a matter of inveterate presumption and a prerequisite which to misconstrue is a token of ineradicable perfidy.

Security and self-aggrandizement, sufficiency and status, converge in divergent perceptions of what constitutes the balance of power. The land power is typically slow in perceiving the long-silent and long-invisible workings of maritime supremacy. It will overreact eventually all the more into regarding sea-based power as the decisive advantage that compels imitation. Continentally confined thought will assume that the sea power can or will behave with the utmost "maximizing" rationality, and will exploit its ascendancy to control access to overseas markets, raw materials, and naval facilities to the point of excluding the land powers. It will thus see the merely continentally preeminent state as irremediably consigned to the second rank, unless it should seize upon any weakness of the maritime empire to revise the continental balance of power into a fit basis for securing maritime equality. The tendency will be heightened if, as is likely and was true for Imperial Germany before World War I, the same continental statecraft runs up against a discrepancy between its material potential at the center and the policy results that it can secure therewith at the peripheries.

An insular sea power like Britain will reciprocate. It will impute to the leading continental states both the inclination and the capacity to convert coercion into a combination of continent-wide resources for claiming a share of overseas prizes. This perception will impel the sea power to interpose itself among the continentals so as to channel their many discords toward conflict and their fears of the strongest one among them into submission to the leadership of the sea-based arbiter. The unacceptable alternative is the resolution of conflicts and the diversion of anxieties into a joint continental enterprise against the common, insular, enemy. In being so quick to attribute ruthlessly coercive aims to the preeminent continental power, early British statecraft may have been also projecting onto continental interplays its experience with compressed, more than commonly violent, insular politics before it was contained internally and drained off outward. Regardless of any deeper motivation, however, a rational insular statecraft will strive to gain universal acceptance for its attribution of boundless expansiveness to the leading continental power. It will, consequently, play down any self-containment of such a state, and see in its moderation an undependable accident or a weakness unfit for gaining compensating admission to global sharing and codetermination. Rather than globalize the balancing of viable powers, the sea power will possess itself of even negligible assets or outright liabilities if this is required for withholding any and all acquisitions from the navally ambitious land power.

British statecraft exaggerated at crucial junctures the costs and risks of recasting a global balance of power in scope, structure, and standards of evaluation into a new equilibrium. In the instances of both France and Germany the result was reciprocal stimulation in action and exacerbation in sentiment. Either divergent or perversely parallel perceptions consummated the difficulty to evolve a shared idea of parity. Moreover, sooner or later, an increasingly hostile assessment of conflicting aspirations would be rationalized into presumably basic ideological and ethical differences. The choice would become, from the continental perspective, one between materialism and idealism, hypocrisy and heroism, in the service of honor; from the obverse perspective, one between pragmatism and dogmatism, peaceableness and militarism, constitutionalism and arbitrary or totalitarian misgovernment. The conflict escalated as the insular power fought fair or foul to avoid being excluded from the Continent for good, while the continental power strained every nerve and muscle to break through the oceanic barriers to the outlying regions. And the mutually destructive resolution of the schismatic conflict was pursued in an atmosphere in which fears of invasion were matched by the terrors of encirclement; charges of continental dictatorship were met with denunciations of maritime tyranny; and the assertions of a design to unite by force were countered by warnings against the practice of divide and rule.

III

EMPIRES MILITARY
AND MARITIME. *Concert
or Catastrophe*

A contradiction defines the relation between the maritime empire and the continental military empires. The contradiction is one between their ultimate interdependence for an order that would transcend bilateral adjustments and proximate misperceptions that foster hostility. An acceptable parity mix involved habitually a naval-colonial-continental reapportionment to be considered in the context of basic policy or strategy options and preferences. The options would be brought to a head for both protagonists by quandaries regarding third powers; and they consisted in the last resort of the extremes of close alliance and total conflict to the exclusion of the middle term of mere and indefinite coexistence.

Each side to the Anglo-German relationship disposed of a number of basic options, more or less compatible and conducive to accommodation. Their specific identity was and is less important than is the recognition of more basic phenomena. One concerns the interplay between priority and sequence. At issue for Britain was whether to assign priority to positions supporting the empire or to her security in Europe. It was possible to uphold empire against Russia and France, and naval ascendancy in the major oceans, in cooperation with Germany as much as with the aid of Japan and the United States. By contrast, if emphasis was placed on the classic balance of power in Europe and the adjoining waters, that priority fostered accommodation with Russia, France, and the United States against Germany. It did so even at the cost of naval adjustments that would go far toward a belated acceptance of maritime equilibrium. Actual delays in choosing —and, possibly, a "wrong" final choice—encouraged developments that endangered both maritime empire and continental equilibrium in the end. Britain's problem of priorities was matched by Germany's. It bore on correct sequences in both functional and geopolitical terms. Functionally, the quandary was whether to seek "world power" in a sequence proceeding from assured military predominance to political ascendancy and on to economic equality with the world powers. That course was advocated by the German political right, the military, and the heavy industry. Or, as argued the "liberal imperialists," could it be reliably assumed that economic activism with but discreet military backing would engender in due course also political influence on a global scale and without war? The geopolitical dimension overlapped with the functional. One possibility was to start with a military-economic (or only economic) organization of the middle-European region, to be extended to the Middle East-and-Asia Minor and Central Africa. The regional platform could serve as leverage for securing global parity with one or both of the Anglo-Saxon powers. Another option was to start with the world arena, and then to do so either relatively peacefully (i.e., commercially) or by way of a direct naval contest with Britain. The assumption then was that the European and related geographic arenas would automatically go to the winner.

Britain's problem with priorities resulted in policy pragmatism and relativism. And especially the geopolitical aspect of the two-stage quandary produced vacillation between policy absolutes for the land power. The pragmatic British bias grew out of the two-wing structure of an empire comprising the overseas colonial and the European hegemonial sectors, as much or more than out of deliberate ambiguity; similarly, the contrary absolutist bias of the continentals reflected their two-element (land and sea) situation and their two-front predicament on land, as much or more than betokening any ingrained duplicity.

The differently conditioned biases evolved on both sides into choices between options. The biases themselves were, however, to a large extent a function of anticipations rather than actualities and, furthermore, of domestic actualities rather than foreign. Moreover, the choices themselves mattered less as indicators of immediate intentions or sources of immediate results than as commitments ruling out alternatives and entailing uncontrollable long-range consequences. The consequences for diplomacy were more often incurred than intended, and the consequences for the issue of peace and war were to be ultimately accepted rather than wished for. Thus the continental diplomatic strategies originated by Bismarck were intended to insure Germany's independence as a great power and were not markedly anti-British in bias. But they did entail a measure of diplomatic isolation for Britain. Similarly, Britain's initial responses to the danger of isolation in the direction of the United States and Japan were not single-mindedly anti-German in immediate intention. But they entailed a choice against alternative "European" strategies to contain both the United States and Japan in the world markets and oceans under Anglo-German leadership. Just as Britain's policies came to postulate Germany's hegemonial and world-imperial ambitions, policies and policy-advocacies in Germany reacted in part to the prospect, rather than the extant reality, of a Greater Britain-in-Imperial Federation or a protectionist U.S.-centered economic bloc in the Western Hemisphere. They also reflected assessments of how efficacious the different foreign-policy alternatives and strategy sequences would be to shield the autocratic and hierarchical German regime against change into liberal-parliamentary or socio-democratic modes. Liberalization of all sorts was believed to follow from the economics-first type of global imperialism, as well as from versions of the *Mitteleuropa* concept favoring intraregional free trade.

Finally, choices were made by more or less consciously eliminating alternatives that had been previously held in reserve. Thus the makers of Imperial Germany's foreign policy suffered bankruptcy when they progressively eliminated two key options that Bismarck had held in reserve in order to enhance German security, at some cost in status, while he actively pursued alternative strategies more propitious to German standing as the preeminent continental power free to exploit the colonial quarrels of other states. One such option was a far-reaching agreement with Russia on spheres of interests. Since the option entailed Russia's aggrandizement it was deferred, but was also reserved by German self-restraint in the Middle East and the restraints placed on Austria-Hungary in the Balkans. The other option was a firm adhesion to Britain. It was likewise repugnant because it entailed a junior status for Germany, but it was reserved by Bismarck's self-abnegation in the naval and colonial fields. Beginning with 1890, the eastern option succumbed to the abandonment of treaty ties with Russia, competitive penetration in the Middle East and Asia Minor, and partial "unleashing" of Austria-Hungary. The British option was at first only jeopardized by German naval and continental strategies, which were conceived largely to promote a later accommodation with Britain on favorable terms. The option was in effect eliminated after the demonstration of the Anglo-French entente in the Moroccan crisis of 1911, in favor of a military response to the feeling of exclusion from worthwhile gains. British political concessions were deemed insufficient, as was Germany's financial capacity to open up real prospects for a substantial reapportionment of world power before the anticipated relative decline of Germany on the Continent would set in. Similarly, British statecraft avoided accommodation with Germany while keeping it in reserve for some time by procedural explorations, and possibly also in mind for a while thereafter as the substantial end-object of alternative alignments. Both sides preferred, if at different points in time, to postpone the inevitably costly and hazardous attempt at a grand solution to the land-sea power dilemmas and to pursue limited, apparently open-ended and unprejudicial, adjustments with other powers instead.

Against this background only is it worthwhile to view the specific options that were available to the rival continental and maritime powers. Each option implied the choice of the principal adversary. Option and adversary alike were actually "chosen" by elimination as much as by deliberate election in the context of controversial priorities and sequences, long-range implications and immediate tactical preferences.

The principal options available to the dominant continental power can be identified as regional and global, next to a third, national option. The regional option consists of a bloc immune to the dominant sea power and serving as a military-economic basis for an eventual climactic contest. It was identified in the German case with the much-discussed *Mitteleuropa* concept. Although it had been latent in the policy of preferential trade treaties favored by Bismarck's immediate successor as chancellor, the fuller concept came near official adoption only after the outbreak of World War I. It was never clearly defined as to the envisaged spatial scope and degree of economico-political integration. *Mitteleuropa* could be conceived as an informal framework substituting for German political hegemony and economic protectionism; a relatively narrow, but compact, material base for a military assault on either Britain alone or both Anglo-Saxon powers; or a broad, all-European customs union including Britain and serving as a basis for effective bargaining with the United States over terms of admission to world markets in the context of protective imperialism. In different scopes, conceptions, and contingencies, *Mitteleuropa* could be construed to include also France (next to Austria-Hungary and the Scandinavian countries) as either partner or satellite, and to either counterbalance a rising Russia indefinitely or help reduce her to dependent status. Correspondingly, if the German leadership invoked "Europe" against the United States in a pragmatic economic context, it also affirmed in an emotional context the affinity of the "Anglo-German peoples" against an ideologically and racially alien Russia, while Pan-Germanism could be set up against both Pan-Slavism and Pan-Americanism as well as against the "hereditary" French enemy.

The regional strategy was a step to global results, by way of extra-European extensions (in the Middle East) and the reduction of non-European opposition. The partly contrary global strategic option had in turn continental implications. In the German case the world strategy had two main versions. A liberal-commercial version would imitate Britain's free-trade imperialism

along with shaping a maritime capability to protect access to overseas markets and raw materials. The more conservative-coercive version meant
direct conflict with Britain as the first (rather than possibly second) step and
a twice-necessary one. The conflict was mandatory to release Germany,
after delays required for a build-up of strategic naval power, from an increasingly restricting and unfavorably evolving continental frame. And it
was unavoidable in view of Britain's interference in continental relations,
which was inimical to any clearly separable two-stage approach to world
power. Implicit in the version stressing commerce was a domestically liberalizing alliance with Britain, aimed at the United States and Japan.
Germany's initial status in such an alliance would be that of a junior partner.
How pronounced and permanent was such a status would depend on
whether it would be part of a Europe-wide customs union under Anglo-
German aegis or would link to England a Germany less broadly influential
on the Continent.

The third, national option stood for only a provisional or intermediate approach. It reserved the definitive choice of one of the more fundamental approaches and was, therefore, aimed primarily at improving tactical leverage
for the effective implementation of either. It consisted of alliances that
would preserve Germany's freedom of action as an "independent," and in
effect preeminent, continental great power. The principal aim was to neutralize the critical major land powers (Russia and France) by preemptive
alignments (with Austria-Hungary, mainly, and Italy) or by preventive
military action in the last resort. An incidental gain was to add secondary
(Austro-Hungarian and Italian) naval capabilities to Germany's continental
power base. The intention behind the combined effect was to give Britain a
taste of isolation and induce her thus into alliance or at least nonintervention.

It was tempting to combine or juggle the options within their several
ranges for maximum effect, and to soften their individual liabilities and mute
conflicts among their domestic proponents. But their very variety confound-
ed the formulation of a consistent German foreign policy in peacetime and of
her aims in wartime. The tensions were intensified, along with pressures for
choice, by developments in military and related technology before World
War I. These increased the importance of space for survival and defense in
depth. Space had to be secured for the centrally situated continental state by
preclusive expansion, if necessary; and for the offshore island state, as
readily as possible, by preemptive alliances with the continental wing powers. Germany's defeat in World War I paradoxically improved her strategic
situation relative to the in-depth capabilities of her wartime adversaries. But
her fundamental options remained unchanged and were intensified by the
tenets of the official National-Socialist ideology. The new German decision-

makers and the largely continuous influence groups carried on the earlier options, preferences, and misperceptions relative to Britain and to the Anglo-American relationship, after a brief postwar shift of emphasis from the Anglo-German parity issue to a Franco-German understanding about the practical meaning of equality between land powers. Nor had both options and outcomes been qualitatively different in the more elementary military-technological context, and economic environment, involving Britain with France as the dominant land power. Such recurrences impart to the intricate factual content of pre-World War I Anglo-German relations a continuing analytic significance that matches their epoch-making (or epoch-undoing) historical importance.[1] Moreover, the continuities secrete lessons for policy which, if appreciated, might have spared German statecraft some illusions if not mistakes.

The French variety of the regional-to-global strategy in two stages was intimated by Louis XIV's drive for a French-dominated "Westeuropa." This was to comprise, next to the reacquired Dunkirk, ascendancy in South and West Germany, the two Netherlands, and parts of Italy. The area was to be ultimately controlled either by France alone or through dynastic association with a Spain that had been invigorated and integrated by way of economic and technical assistance in return for the commercial exploitation by France of the Spanish overseas empire. In this connection, Louis' youthful pursuit of the Holy Roman Emperorship matched William II's quest of leadership in a "united Europe." When frustrated, the relatively moderate west-European scheme of the *ancien regime* was surpassed by the Napoleonic all-continental system, just as Imperial Germany's *Mitteleuropa* expanded into the Third Reich's "New Order" for all (continental) Europe. Likewise, long before Germany, France experienced the incapacity to neatly separate the "European" phase from the "global" in a two-stage strategy. An increasingly British-influenced diplomacy and warfare obstructed Louis' early European policies keyed, with a debatable persistence of purpose, to the anticipated issue of succession to the global Spanish empire. And in the climactic global phase French military operations had to be "misguidedly" extended on the Continent in order to fend off the threatening reencirclement of France by British-sponsored Habsburg rule in both West (Spain) and East (Austria).

1. Next to the previously cited sources by Dehio and Fischer, an important succinct source on German foreign policy is Andreas Hillgruber, *Kontinuität und Diskontinuität in der deutschen Aussenpolitik von Bismarck bis Hitler* (Dusseldorf: Droste Verlag, 1969). The British side is discussed in Kenneth Bourne, *The Foreign Policy of Victorian England* (Oxford: The Clarendon Press, 1970). On eighteenth-century France see, next to the books by Soltau and Anderson, also Arthur M. Wilson, *French Foreign Policy during the Administration of Cardinal Fleury, 1726-1743* (Cambridge: Harvard University Press, 1936). Also Basil Williams, *Stanhope: A Study in Eighteenth-century War and Diplomacy* (Oxford: The Clarendon Press, 1968).

It was for later French statecraft to capitalize on Louis' exertions when it revived the regional-bloc strategy on the basis of dynastic family alliance with a curtailed but Bourbon Spain. The effort was hampered by the irreversible decline of the but intermittently, and then disturbingly, energetic ally; and it was ultimately thwarted by the concurrent transformation of a former French ally, Prussia, into a powerful continental rival. The later analogues were Germany's connection with Austria in the Dual Alliance and her estrangement from Russia, while the increasingly unmanageable Austrian issue supplied the connecting continental link. As French statecraft lost control, and its priorities got confused in terms of both opportunities and dangers, its efforts were repeatedly pulled eastward on the Continent to a degree that exceeded the requirements of the "regional" strategy. Thus Cardinal Fleury tried, in the briefly promising conditions of 1740, to concentrate the French military effort on the sea in alliance with Spain while stalemating diplomatically the continental balances in Germany, Italy, and against Russia. But the effort was brutally pushed back from the second-stage to the first-stage position by the eruption of an acute crisis (over Austrian succession) in the center of Europe. The duke de Choiseul tried again in the next round of warfare to manage the concluding phase and the sequelae of the Seven Years' War over the intra-German balance in such a way as to free France and her Spanish ally for a decisive contest with Britain. His efforts were likewise frustrated by continental distractions. As they were to be in the later case, these distractions were focused on Poland and the Ottoman empire as the stakes in the Austro-Russo-Prussian competition. The fiasco of Choiseul's two-stage strategy was repeated when Napoleon failed to eliminate Russia either forcefully or diplomatically, as a preliminary to either an accommodation with Britain (in the peace of Amiens) or Britain's reduction (by way of the Continental blockade). The omens were thus unfavorable for the later efforts to separate the two theaters even temporarily; and likewise for the preoccupation of the German Chancellor Bethmann-Hollweg with Russia as the key target, to be eliminated before employing the fleet for fighting or bargaining with previously neutralized Britain in the second, global stage.

Nor was France successful when she applied the global strategic option in direct contention with Britain and in both relative and temporary isolation from continental distractions. The *ancien régime* scored successes in the direct competition with Britain over the Americas, mainly economic in regard to Spanish America and political in regard to North America. To do so, its objectives had to remain the limited ones of commercial access in the first case and be confined, in the second case of the War of American Independence, to no more than prestige success over a Britain that had been temporarialy isolated in diplomacy and weakened on the seas. And even then the material costs of the global effort, to be mounted on top of prior and routine current continental obligations, contributed significantly to the internal erosion of the *ancien regime* and to the subsequent revolutionary explosion. A different kind of failure befell Napoleon's efforts to destroy the British empire by a direct thrust, by way of Egypt or subsequent invasion schemes. The fiascos boded ill for the comparable Tirpitzian scenarios, envisaging the conquest of northern French ports for a decisive sea war against Britain while compensating Russia with unenclosed, or warm-water, maritime exits.

And finally, the French efforts to develop and exploit a loosely allied Spanish empire commercially had some similarity to the economics-first global strategy of the German liberal imperialists, while some domestic "liberal" overtones adhered to the series of unequal alliances into which a succession of weak, unstable, or doubtfully legitimate French regimes entered with Britain. Such alliances were possible only when France was free of both the west-European and any other regional complex, and the British alliance was an alternative as well as an impediment to resuscitating one in either Spain and Belgium and the other in the Mediterranean and North Africa. Yet the British alliance entailed, as both a condition and a consequence, considerable diplomatic isolation of France from other continental great powers. But, and this was yet another possible lesson for Germany, the alliance carried with it the only possibility of enjoying Britain's neutrality while seeking and securing a continental aggrandizement. Cardinal Fleury won such for France in Lorraine, as a result of the War of Polish Succession in the 1720s, in exchange (whether tacit or explicit remains questionable) for self-limitation in the development of naval resources.

British neutrality was to be futilely pursued by Bethmann-Hollweg before the First World War and furtively eyed by Hitler before the second. In addition to the larger preconditions, it was contingent on achieving success in quite deliberate tactical operations. One requirement was to generate economic considerations that would deflect Britain from participating in the war. To that end Fleury released Britain's Dutch competitors for wartime trade by assurances of military inaction against their "Belgian" underbelly. The relatively self-restrained German posture on the Middle Eastern economic issues just prior to 1914 was not sufficient to create a comparable disincentive to British involvement in the bigger, later war. Another requirement was to avoid placing the major continental state in a position of an unprovoked aggressor. Even though France was the first to declare war, Fleury met the condition by allowing the (Holy Roman) Emperor to commit all the tactical mistakes. Germany's waiting for Russia to in effect mobilize first was not sufficient in view of her prior diplomatic imprudence. A third requirement was to avoid naval provocation. This consideration led Fleury to abstain from attempts to relieve a damaging Russian blockade off Poland in deference to Britain's claim to supremacy in the Baltic. Germany did not match this token of determination to limit the conflict, its stakes, and her possible gains, in the moves to keep Russia out of the Austro-Serbian controversy. Finally, the French were markedly moderate during the peace negotiations, and went so far as to defer possession of the territorial gain. No such self-restraint was prominent in Germany's prewar stipulations for British neutrality, and restraint as to war-aims was wholly abandoned under the pressure of war. Most importantly, however, only in the setting of French eclipse could Fleury's tactical skill exploit the hesitations of his British counterpart, Walpole, and the divisions of British politics to stalemate the decision-making process this side of intervention. The deferred cost was intensified British interventionism when the next continental crisis came about in 1740.

As an alternative to "Westeuropa" and either global confrontation or liberal alliance with Britain, France could have merely maintained herself as a power. She could do it most appropriately in association with conservative eastern powers, be it rising Prussia or relatively declining Austria or fluctuating Russia. This third possible, national strategy was comparable to the Bismarckian alliance diplomacy in its conservative bias domestically and in its foreign-policy objective oscillating between moderate continental preeminence and sheer diplomatic independence from Britain. When Prussia and Austria had been eliminated as potential allies of France in 1866, a connection with Russia became essential to relieve French inferiority in the henceforth indispensable link to Britain for security against Germany. Germany herself sought similar relief from junior status in a strictly bilateral Anglo-German association when she vainly sought to affiliate Britain with Austria and Italy next to Germany in the Triple Alliance.

Britain's own strategic options and preferences corresponded closely to those of the continental powers. The most limited, national, strategy for great-power independence elicited likewise limited British adjustments, notably in the naval sphere. They were designed to offset particular consequences of diplomatic isolation in less-than-critical conditions for the balance of land power. Here may be included strategies to preempt the Scandinavian and Russian connections from France and against her in the seventeenth and eighteenth centuries, so as to secure the North Sea and the Baltic naval stores. And the Japanese alliance was incurred in the first years of the twentieth century to offset the Franco-Russian entente in the Pacific and German activism in China. A grand-coalition approach to the European balance of power was the more comprehensive British response to more far-reaching land-power strategies for a regional bloc or to a direct assault on the maritime bases of Britain's global supremacy. The first full-blown aggregation of continentals by virtue of British diplomatic initiative and material support was directed against the French bid for the Spanish succession. Conversely, extreme caution (originating in the Walpole-Fleury experience of the 1720s and '30s) would be the British attitude toward a "liberal" alliance with a (temporarily) reduced or reasonable continental hegemon. Such an alliance had to insure for Britain a foolproof preponderance of both influence and gains, lest the supreme good (of a both advantageous and pacific land-sea power accommodation) turn into the supreme evil of alienating the continental states that might become again indispensable for a countervailing grand coalition at a later date. A Holy Roman (or Austrian) Empire and Russia in the French phase, and France and Russia in the German phase, might react to Britain's apparent abandonment of the "common cause" by coming themselves to terms with the preeminent land power. Such a turnabout would enable the leading continental actor to exchange an insufficiently productive or unduly constricting British connection for the opportunity to resolve intra-continental differences as part of a concerted spoliation of the British empire. British statecraft would not run the least risk of being thus "neutralized," even without assenting to neutrality. In the German phase, this posture virtually compelled a British accommodation with Russia that was preemptive as well as protective. To preempt was the danger that a rejected Germany would gravitate toward a receptive Russia in anticipation of a long-term decline relative to the Tsardom, and bring helpless France along into an anti-British continental combine.

To forestall even a remote possibility of such supreme evils, Britain "chose" first Japan over Germany against Russia in the Asian imperial-oceanic context and then Russia in the European land-sea context. France was a precipitant, but materially only a secondary, factor in Britain's continuing retreat from "splendid isolation," being initially at least more salient as Russia's maritime ally in the Middle and Far East than as a territorial actor to be shielded from further abridgement by Germany. The choice was final when Britain's Asian ally had pushed Russia as the principal continental challenger with colonial-maritime ambitions behind the imperial enlargement of Britain's one-time favorite Protestant ally.

The failure of the British and German protagonists in the land-sea power drama to reach concert resulted in the advent of a partially preventive conflict and a wholly disruptive catastrophe. The rights and wrongs cannot be even tentatively assessed without regard to the basic attitudes that reflected the situational dilemmas of the two parties, first in relation to one another and then to Russia as the key third party.

On the surface, Britain's pragmatic policy of partial measures (largely alongside Imperial Germany until the onset of the twentieth century and against her thereafter) clashed with Germany's urge for a total solution on an all-or-nothing basis in regard to Britain in particular. The tentative approach reflected the dilemmas of a two-wing, Euro-global empire in decline. British policy-makers were uncertain as to what priorities to assign to threats to global-maritime assets, to interests on the European continent, or to the physical security of the islands themselves. Consequently, they were unsure with whom to align for limited purposes and against whom, so as to avoid being duped by Germany or drawn into premature irreversible commitments without or against her. In their contrary dogmatic attitude, the German policy-makers reflected in turn the position of a temporarily ascendant land power wedged between two potential fronts militarily and within two elements (land and sea) for more comprehensive strategic purposes. They were anxious to choose and be chosen so as to turn into an irreversible advantage in continental security and world status one of their main options, with or against Britain, before the narrowly national German assets had begun to be devalued.

If Germany's structural dilemma found expression in diplomatic as-sertiveness, Britain's was reflected in a combination of ambivalence and ambiguity. The results were emotionally aggravating for both. Thus a foremost British statesman (Lord Salisbury, in the 1880s) could speak of a "close union" between Britain as the greatest naval power and Germany as the greatest military one,[2] while British statecraft remained actually long unable to decide whether to favor German military might to tie down Russia's (and France's) in the overseas realms, or fear it as capable of eliminating France and Russia as vital counterpoises on the Continent. Likewise, while the British sought to confine Germany to her "military" role as against a naval one, the lack of long-range naval capabilities could not but limit Germany's much-pondered utility for Britain at large (e.g., against the Franco-Russian naval cooperation in the eastern Mediterranean and the Far East). Ambivalence resulted in ambiguity when Britain finally did choose (in 1901-1904). At least for a time it could be questioned why she opted for France and, through her, Russia. Was it to placate the two as rivals and relieve Britain's naval weakness in the eastern Mediterranean (which got underway in the 1890s) and her imperial position in the Persian Gulf area? Or did British statecraft act in the last resort in order both to preempt France and Russia as allies on the Continent and relieve them against Germany, perceived as a threat to both the empire and the British Isles since the South African war and the concurrent discovery of her growing short-range naval capability? In reality, by deliberately abandoning that which she no longer could defend (her imperial interest in the Straits and Constantinople against Russia), Britain perhaps only half-consciously en-

2. See Bourne, *The Foreign Policy of Victorian England*, p. 425 (documentary section).

hanced the need along with the capability to defend her security in the more northern seas and on the Continent.

Britain's delays in choosing represented so many dangers for Germany if the choice finally were to go against her. These dangers were reflected in German actions of a kind causing alarms in Britain and confirming the incontrovertible rightness of the choice when it was finally made. Because of the delays, the choice as it was finally made could not be subsequently either reversed or significantly revised. It lost thus most of its potential for dissuading or deterring Germany from last-resort reaction. Unlike in the 1880s and 1890s, by 1900 the German imperial regime could not retract its world-power ambitions in the face of an "encircling" coalition without drastic internal repercussions. Nor could Britain thereafter risk the appearances of "surrender" as part of a policy that would effectively ration or reverse her commitments within the Triple Entente, along with adjustments on the colonial and naval fronts. The reciprocal inability to appreciate each other's structural dilemmas could not but grow and introduce emotional hostility into a situationally conditioned rivalry. The worsening climate reduced the advocates of Anglo-German accord to either impotence (in Britain, where Germanophobes became ascendant in and outside the Foreign Office) or to unrealism (Bethmann-Hollweg, with his groping for British "neutrality" in the face of hostile German heavy industry and both military and naval pressure groups). In the event, for purposes of deterrence, the de facto British commitment to France (and Russia) had been more decisively late in 1904 than its final ratification was in 1914; and the prewar alliances precipitated the global conflict not so much because they polarized the international system as because they were themselves superimposed upon previously hardened structural foundations of policy dilemmas in turn inspiring an attitudinal drift. Regardless of the "rightness" of the choices made, the reversibility of both commitments and trends fell victim to bad timing. This nullified the potential that an earlier clarification could have imparted to reciprocal dissuasion and deterrence from extreme courses and commitments alike.

The time-span that was available for decision making was fatally shortened, and the dilemmas rooted in configurations were intensified, by the active reinvolvement of Russia in Europe following her repulse in Asia by a Japan backed by England. The introduction of a second major land power transformed a problematic bipolar situation between inversely amphibian Britain and Germany into a pressing challenge to statecraft. It also converted a situation irresoluble to equal mutual satisfaction in depth into one with a definite limit in time for any kind of resolution. In isolation, the Anglo-German issue did not compel in the then prevailing economic and military conditions a mutually undesired climactic confrontation. It took the spectre of a Russia capable of overpowering Germany to turn multidirectional drift into an irreversible one-way chain reaction. In the earlier era, the many factors that forecast the impending supersession of France as the preeminent continental power underlay the changeover from the essentially limited, if global, Anglo-French contentions to the apocalyptic clash between Albion and Napoleon. Now, the highest German circles came to see Russia as irresistibly rising on the Continent to the detriment of a henceforth provisional German ascendancy. This perception made a "self-protective" German enlargement in middle Europe abruptly more vital as a safeguard against Russia than as a regional springboard against England. Crisis grew with the urgency to make decisions; and both were intensified by the dwindling prospects for a compensatory British guarantee of Germany's continental position or a British grant of an offsetting naval-colonial enlargement in the global sphere.

The vicious triangle was completed by Britain's near-parallel decision against a serious attempt to consolidate her empire into a power aggregate that could alone withstand Germany in the worst conceivable future contingency. A thus weakened Britain was unwilling to incur the risks of either a condominial alliance with Germany or of a provisional separation of the maritime-colonial and continental theaters that would follow from her neutrality in Europe. Instead, the British moved in 1907 to preempt the Russian alliance in a setting that was defined by the accomplished maritime decline of Britain (compelling some devolution) and the anticipated continental decline of Germany (increasing pressures for a decision). The Anglo-Russian entente completed Germany's virtual diplomatic isolation (save for the burdensome Austrian and unreliable Italian alliance) and added overland-military to maritime encirclement. Speculation about long-range relative material inferiority vis-à-vis Russia fell in place behind the near-certainty of a henceforth deteriorating overall German position relative to the Triple Entente and its peripheral Japanese associate and American well-wisher.

Russia's key role as the second leading land power was obscured by the high drama of mere events centering on France, such as the Moroccan crisis. It had been in evidence, however, in the preceding Anglo-German flirtations before placing a time-fuse under Anglo-German alienation. Thus Germany would not enter into only partial understandings with Britain aimed at Russia in the Near and Far East, for fear of arousing Russian hostility in her own East Prussia and adjoining parts of Poland. Moreover, the Bismarckian tradition of not accepting a "junior" role in an Anglo-German alliance, except as the supreme recourse to avert an impending Anglo-Russian alignment, was a safe position to take so long as the Anglo-Russian conflict exceeded Anglo-German differences. On her side,

Britain shied from alignment with Germany so long as good Russo-German relations threatened to make Germany into a "senior" ally and bad Russo-German relations made a British commitment appear redundant. While the British calculated that Germany would help against Russia in her own interest even without an alliance, the Germans were adamant in refusing to antagonize Russia by Anglo-German cooperation overseas before securing a both total and equal, ironclad alliance with the insular state.

The final collision occurred in function of the temporarily dominant land power's urge to do something, almost anything, rather than see live options decay into wasted opportunities; and of the decreasingly dominant sea power's preference to wait out events as long as possible and avoid commitments longer than desirable, rather than see premature decisions turn into final disaster.

Compared with the structural constraints and resulting imperatives and inhibitions, specific acts and omissions were derivative and endlessly debatable. Germany's diplomatic stance was more correct on substance than in style, whereas British statecraft deserves higher marks for initial procedure (by turning first to Germany for accommodation) than for the final product (reflecting indecision and in the last stages also bias). Regarding substance, an economically ascendant and militarily superior Germany could hardly remain satisfied with an essentially landlocked position and only symbolic naval and colonial adornments. She was bound to seek a bigger share of world power including a "guaranteed" access to global markets, and to exchange support for British interests outside Europe for no less than British undertakings in Europe. In short, given the norms of the past and the apparent imperatives of the present, Germany could not but pursue both parity and security, and seek to promote by political transactions both economic strength and diplomatic status. And she was entitled to do so, so long as she was not shown unready to have either a far-reaching agreement or close association with Britain work as restraint as well as a reassurance. As things turned out, the increasingly postulated German insatiability was not subjected to a conclusive test; and both the appetites and the ineptitudes of German statecraft appear less peculiar or self-generated in the light of the French precedents. The latter disclose adamant British opposition to the overseas aims of both a clearly conservative and visibly decadent legitimist regime in the 1760s, and of a both friendly and liberal Orleanist regime in the late 1830s and early 1840s. Equally precedent-setting was the cost of British reluctance. It consisted of pressures in France for a preventive war on England in the first case, to the initial advantage of the American rebels and the ultimate one of revolution in France herself; and, in the second, of the substitution of a more restless and ambitious ruler for a relatively moderate regime. Just as the first imperial Bonaparte superseded the only fitfully activist *rois fainéants*, so the Second Empire of the third Napoleon took over from the bourgeois monarchy in France and the Third Reich replaced the Second in Germany. The "radicals" followed the "moderates" in the wake of internal collapses originating more or less exclusively in foreign policy setbacks or overexertions; and these latter causes of trouble were in turn inseparable from a continuous British bias to identify the insular with the European interest.

As the critical agent, British statecraft was locked within its own fears and traditions. These were engendered by insular position and bred by the habits of a prideful sway overseas and a more precarious and less readily avowed hegemonial spell within the European balance. Thus inspired, the British were reluctant to concede to Germany *her* succession to Spain, in the twin guise of an authentic world power and of the acknowledged premier or foremost continental actor. The latter status was a habitual one for the European system of states, and one that the system had managed to absorb while England was only one and not especially prominent or privileged of its members, just as the former corresponded to the emergent outlines of the global system. So long as British preoccupations were chiefly imperial, British statesmen inclined to ask solely what Germany was able to do in either the Middle or the Far East *for* a Britain that was safe with respect to the Continent. They abstained from speculating what Germany might be able or disposed to do *to* the British position in the world if she was too long ignored. Only at a later stage did they shift abruptly to the latter alarms. One of the British notions was to have Germany shield the defense of the Indian empire in exchange for a guarantee of Germany's (still very limited) colonial empire in the case of consequent European complications. The exchange could hardly meet German ideas of diplomatic parity while being predicated on the assumption of continuing nonparity in the colonial and naval realms (at least until the point of no return was reached just before the outbreak of World War I). At its best, British readiness to make colonial concessions was limited to Africa (before the South African war swung British public opinion against all concessions) and to the hard-to-visualize areas where German gains would not conflict with British global interests (increasingly including Anglo-American harmony). In a similar vein authoritative British opinion professed tolerance for a German naval capability requisite for the "defense of German national interests." But it subjected the size of a tolerable German short-range capital-ship capability to the criterion of British insular invulnerability, while the scope of tolerable long-range commerce-supporting naval capability for Germany would be regulated by the sensitivities of self-governing British colonies, by American imperviousness to anything that might remotely challenge the Monroe

Doctrine, and by Britain's opposition to the creation of a "German India" in Asia Minor. Applying such criteria and restrictions made naval parity for Germany in any one region or area take on the menacing hue of outright maritime supremacy fatal to British national independence as much as to her imperial interests.[3]

At the back of British attitudes was rigid adherence to geographically fostered and historically tested traditions. These soon set doctrinal limits to Britain's famed pragmatism in foreign policy and, upon becoming unexamined articles of faith, were translated into as many commandments for the continentals. The tradition of insular self-dependence linked opposition to a dictatorial aggregation of power on the continent with the unilateralism of a diplomatically free hand for England herself. And whereas the tradition militated usefully against tolerating German hegemony, the underlying tribal-insular mentality found anything approaching a global Anglo-German duopoly by way of alliance no more tolerable than it did cogovernance of an integrated empire with the "white" dominions. Another tradition posited an intimate tie between the Royal Navy and British domestic liberties on the one hand and external independence as a great power on the other. This association set emotional barriers to accepting naval proliferation in favor of other beneficiaries than "blood-related" Americans, dependent and thus friendly weakened French, or remote and in appearance submissively imitative Japanese. Insular self-dependence and single-minded dependence on the naval arm were habits acquired from experience. They were buttressed by retrospective contemplation of the inability of antecedent sea-based empires, the Venetian and the Dutch, to compensate for lost naval supremacy with either financial sources of economic strength or territorial sources of political and military strength. The historically tested vision stood in the way of either seeing or adapting to fast-approaching inadequacy of merely national self-dependence; of reliance on the navy alone to underpin scattered overseas dependencies and insular independence; and of both to do duty for ensembles aggregating insular-maritime assets with continent-based resources, be they German *or* Australian and Canadian, into a new order of economico-military power.

Insular condescension overestimated the value of British nationalism and made light of its continental counterparts. Fear lest France and Russia submit or defect to Germany as a result of an Anglo-German accommodation implied an underestimate of the force of French and Russian national feelings. This in turn led to overrating the irreversibility of such accommodation and its attendant risks. Britain's peculiar perceptions strengthened, moreover, the penchant for a grand-coalition response to a continentally

3. This spirit pervades the influential Crowe Memorandum, for instance. See Bourne, *The Foreign Policy of Victorian England*, pp. 481-493, for text.

preeminent power that had last proven itself against Napoleonic France. In yielding to the tradition-bred reflex, British statecraft discounted the meanwhile enlarged global dimension and failed to consider intervening changes in circumstance within Europe alone. Thus while in a prenationalist setting Napoleon could hope to subvert resentful Russia diplomatically into cooperating with the Continental blockade of Britain, he had in a preindustrial setting no alternative to direct physical conquest and control if he was to consolidate preeminence also economically against first dynastic and later also national resistance backed by Britain. By contrast, short of a "struggle for existence," Imperial Germany had neither the ready means nor (and more importantly) did she lack alternatives to forcibly combining the two (military and economic) key elements into the one real threat from the Continent to British security and position.

To be sure, technological innovations placed a premium on initiative and preemption. They prompted forcible expansion when Germany came to feel both encircled and insecure on the Continent, and denied overseas. But they favored a precautionary grand-coalition approach only if German continental expansionism was treated as a primary or original fact anchored in national peculiarity or perversion. British statecraft ignored technological changes, moreover, to keep alive yet another British tradition: the intangibility of Belgium. The tradition of keeping that area out of potentially hostile hands had been upheld against declining France in 1830, with ruinous consequences for her later defense (and thus Britain's) after precipitating action against Germany in 1914. In reality, the neutralization of the Belgian space had lost its elemental value as an impediment to a hostile invasion of Britain with the advent of naval steam-propulsion earlier in the nineteenth century, and it became even more irrelevant when submarine and aerial warfare generated other military and economic pressures on the British Isles.

British preconceptions combined with Germany's restless probing to make the war appear to both rival powers as the lesser of evils. The greater immediate danger for Britain was a further decimation of France; for Germany, the collapse of Austria-Hungary and the resurgence of Russia abroad and Social Democracy at home. A leftward movement was expected to follow stagnation or setback in the international arena and was judged incompatible with the survival of the imperial political system under such external conditions. Similarly, a belief in the incompatibility between ascendant *parlements* and a strong royal power in France underlay Choiseul's advocacy of a domestically healing preventive war against Britain in 1770. It was to be grafted on a lesser quarrel engaging undependable allied Spain, just as Germany's supreme bid was superimposed on Austria-Hungary's dissension with Serbia.

It did not prove impossible to convict Imperial Germany in retrospect of having self-consciously initiated a preventive war.[4] Outside the court of one kind of moral judgment any such verdict is meaningful, however, only if it has survived exposure to the dynamics of land-sea power relations and international-system transformation. The verdict, that is, must be accompanied by a demonstration that the policy of Britain and the Triple Entente was designed and implemented not only to contain Germany, but also to draw her safely out of continental confinement; that a progressive recasting of the world balance of power from positions of strength was accepted both as necessary and necessarily entailing a reapportionment of access to the assets and outlets that were considered inherent in great-power status at the time. Though not ideal, conditions prior to World War I had been infinitely more propitious than they were to be in the 1930s. The verdict would have to be substantially qualified, therefore, if no sustained attempt was made to see whether Germany's financial weakness and the powerful compensatory forces in Europe (Russia) and reserves overseas (the United States and Japan) made it possible to satiate the ambitions of official Germany with concessions that would activate the reserve powers and still stay within the bounds of the new global balance of power; and to mete out the concessions in ways and in installments calculated to promote a new intra-German balance of political forces favorable to constitutional rule consequent on nonforcible politico-economic expansion. It would seem instead that (in part on the since discredited moral grounds of an exceptionally inhumane German colonial administration) additional overseas and seaborne assets were denied Germany at a time when British governments professed reluctance to expand further their nonproductive colonial responsibilities; and that the German encirclement complex was derided as fictitious while British statecraft treated as sacrosanct its invasion complex and strategic fixation on India.

The several bids by France to match Britain on the sea broke the *ancien régime* under the effort required from the continental challenger in a global system that had been enlarged at a faster rate than were individual capabilities. British empire and national power alike went down finally under the effort of the maritime defender to perpetuate a European system that was by itself no longer sufficiently capacious to contain the capabilities of the continental challenger in war any more than in peacetime strategies for obviating the need for war. In the last resort, British statecraft sacrificed accommodation with Imperial Germany to British imperial and global interests, at least as much as to the peculiarly British view of the European

---

4. This is the burden of Fischer's conclusion in *Krieg der Illusionen* (Dusseldorf: Droste, 1969).

balance of power. It did so among other things while deferring to the anticipated distaste of the fully self-governing colonies and the incipiently remote-controlling United States[5] for a British alliance with globally activist Imperial Germany. Britain preferred Japan and the United States to Germany, only to abandon the Japanese alliance subsequently to American displeasure and release Imperial Japan, like Germany previously, for self-help through forcible expansion to the detriment of Britain in Europe and her empire in Asia.

5. Cf. Bourne, *The Foreign Policy of Victorian England*, p. 470. In a "very secret" memorandum, dated November 11, 1901, the Conservative Foreign Secretary Lord Lansdowne identified, "The risk of entangling ourselves in a policy which might be hostile to America" as "a formidable obstacle" to an Anglo-German alliance. For parallel views on the Liberal side see Keith Robbins, *Sir Edward Grey* (London: Cassell, 1971), pp. 129ff.

Part Two

AMERICA AND BRITAIN

IV

THE UNITED STATES,
BRITAIN, AND IMPERIAL
RIVALS. *Balance and*
Alliances

The relationship of the United States to the European balance of power was a biased one. Not only was the United States favored, on an enlarged scale, by the tendency of the continent-centered European balance of power to operate one-sidedly to the advantage of the offshore sea power. It also escaped the regulatory impact of flexible interallied relations upon the balance of power, which tends to limit the gains of the ascendant party to conflicts.

In enjoying the first-mentioned advantage, the United States resembled Great Britain; following the period of American nonalignment, the second-mentioned one was reinforced by the fact that Britain was the principal partner of America in peculiarly nonflexible (and thus nonregulatory) alliances. These alliances reflected not only the kind of conflict: total war, which inhibits interallied transactions culminating in separate-peace strategies; they also conformed to the kind of connection: one between powers that were not only culturally cognate, but were also, and more importantly, divergently rising and declining maritime-mercantile states. Such powers will tend to constrain the centrifugal pressures of naval and economic competition, straining toward monopoly, within a particularly close political alliance in the face of threatening major land powers, aspiring to parity or better. The bias to close alliance between maritime-mercantile powers was to affect also American-Japanese relations in due course, but only after World War II had purged the intense conflict that (witness the Anglo-Dutch sequence) normally precedes intimacy between such powers. The failure of the "normal" conflict phase to take place between Britain and America in full was a function of the triangular Anglo-American-German interplay. The interplay surfaced prematurely, as it were, the "schismatic" tension between the navally ambitious German land power and the fitfully expansive American sea power. In the process, the American impact on the global balance of power centered on Europe resembled Britain's on the European system anchored in the Continent, just as the policies that the United States was to choose came from among the available diplomatic-strategic options or alternatives, which largely survived from the preceding phase. It was an open question whether, once developed, an authentically global system of equilibrium would sustain a stabilized and withdrawing or declining United States more effectively than the European had constrained America while she was ascendant.

The central—European or Eurocentric global—balance of power promoted American aggrandizement without enjoying reciprocity in either operation or effect. As part of its one-sided operation, the European balance-of-power system had thrown up either opportunities that permitted or pretexts that justified American expansion before generating the threats that would compel it. Tempting occasions commingled with threats to an unequal degree. In function of both, the working of the European balance drew the United States out of and beyond the compass it had provisionally assumed at any one time. The drawing-out mechanism supplemented any immediately operative inherent American drive to expand, just as power vacuums in the world at large replaced in two separate periods the pull or suction exerted previously by an empty continent at home.

The balance of power worked for the United States from its beginnings. Thus, in 1795, a Spanish regime at odds with Great Britain in a precarious European constellation made concessions to the United States over the Mississippi navigation and the southern boundary, for fear of a joint Anglo-American action against Louisiana. In 1812, by contrast, American hawks stepped up the drive for Spanish Florida on the grounds that Spain was an ally of Britain—against Napoleon, whose primary concern with related evolutions in the European balance had by then secured Louisiana for the fledgling Republic. Nor was Spain the only individual victim. A strong Britain's foreign-policy principle of keeping rival European influences out of the Americas was eminently propitious for the young United States. The principle expressed Britain's capacity to act unilaterally in the maritime sphere, and the two combined in Britain's reluctant underwriting of the Monroe Doctrine against the "Holy Alliance" in regard to South America.

Likewise favorable to the United States were to become the fears of a less confident Britain. A key one was of the United States acting either jointly with or parallel to one or several of Britain's European rivals, or even merely creating a favorable context for such rivals in any way whatsoever. If American license had derived at first from Britain's penchant for unilateralism, it evolved with Britain's fear of isolation. And it was to climax with the setbacks for British imperialism over South Africa, which raised the possibility of a German-inspired European combine. Yet another advantage for the United States was that it could and did profit from Britain's preoccupations as both a sea power and, in regard to India and South Africa as well as Canada, a power vulnerable on land as well. There was one possible danger for the United States. Before Russia and Germany became Britain's chief rivals, Britain and France as the two original European adversaries evolved from a radically adversary starting position in North America toward shared opposition to continuing American expansion. But their likewise continuing and greater divisions over stakes within and outside the Western Hemisphere served the United States well. So did the diversion of the rare cooperation by the two powers to non-American stakes, in the Crimean war against Russia.

In a general way, the European balance-of-power system favored America in all circumstances. When the system enjoyed competitive vitality, the conflicts and distractions of individually strong powers could be exploited for advancing America's expansion in her "natural" geopolitical orbit. And when the system came to suffer from protracted militant deadlock, insufficiency of indigenous resources to either stabilize or tip the balance enhanced America's role and status by presenting the United States with occasions for exploratory involvements in the larger arena. Thus, after providing initial (French) support and subsequent (British) safeguard, the war-studded workings of the Eurocentric balance of power favored American aggrandizement in both space and status. In sum, the European system neutralized systematically effective opposition to American expansion; it supplied throughout plausible security rationales for that expansion; and, having first provided both unexpected occasions and patiently awaited opportunities for expansion, the system eventually produced also incentives to an expanding and expansion-legitimizing involvement in the European balance of power itself.

The balance of power worked "both ways" for the United States. But its relation to America and the Western Hemisphere was not a "two-way" street. The balance promoted American interests when turning Spain into an ally of Britain as well as when converting her into Britain's enemy; when it was dynamic as well as when it was deadlocked. But its scope failed to spread conjointly with American expansion. Thus France had supported the

American Revolution in order to restore a balance of power system in the New World as well as to redress the balance of forces in the Old. In the event, the newly independent United States was actually both hostile to remaining British positions and weaker than had been the unabridged British empire-in-America. But the change also meant that France lost the leverage she had previously enjoyed over the key North American actor in the guise of continental-European combinations and contentions, without re-creating on the North American continent their counterparts for influencing the new creation. Nor were the rudiments of a South American balance of power (comprising the ABC powers—Argentina, Brazil, Chile—in particular) ever sufficient to equalize somewhat the interplay between the Eurocentric balance-of-power system and the Western Hemisphere. While a succession of powers and conflicts linked the European balance of power to the Americas in ways that were favorable to the United States, important forces separated the Western Hemisphere from Europe. They included the Royal (and, intermittently, the U.S.) Navy as a midocean barrier; the inability of translating monarchical or any other solidarity into a transoceanic bridge for concerted European action; and the disparity between the great and growing dispersion of power outside the Western Hemisphere and the progressive concentration of control within it under the regional "caudillo." An equalized two-way traffic between the two theaters would be promoted by one of two developments only. One was a matching concentration of power or concertation of policies in Europe or Eurasia, sufficient to deconcentrate control in the Americas; another was replacing European presence in the Americas with permanent American involvement in Europe, as a source of possible leverage on U.S. action and position overseas. The first contingency was the more pressing danger for the United States; and it was the only one so long as it could be dealt with without producing the second situation.

Meanwhile, indecisive efforts by European powers to change the equations in North America and in the Western Hemisphere by positive action were as futile as were intermittent expectations, before and during the American civil war, to see them change of themselves. The continental United States did not disintegrate from overextension and did not, consequently, reexemplify the classic alternative to containment by external balancing in cases of rapidly and inorganically expanded agglomerates. The European powers acted uniformly only in 1898. They did not do so, however, to contain the United States within the hemisphere but, instead, to competitively condone its extrahemispheric expansion into the Philippines. The incentive was not only their competition in the Far East and Africa (pitting, by and large, the continentals against Britain). It was also because they (Germany as much as Britain in particular) placed the level and balance of trade with the United States over the balance of power between the United States and Europe, about to be tilted further by Spain's final expulsion.

The lack of reciprocity between Europe and America was compounded by the net effect of the United States on the Eurocentric balance of power itself. There were positive effects. They were in evidence when America's approach to Europe's wars and shifts of power veered from exploitation to equilibration following the consolidation of the U.S. core-empire. They were to be noted when a limited and relatively disinterested American involvement diversified and moderated somewhat the Far-Eastern theater of the Eurocentric balance in Asia and when interventions to contain or arbitrate intra-European conflicts by diplomacy (Theodore Roosevelt) and subsequently also by military force were followed, between the world wars, by efforts to reintegrate the thwarted German would-be hegemon economically into a working equilibrium. Less propitious were the inconclusive bids by American statecraft after World War I to replace the balance of power outright with cooperative institutional and economic techniques for system maintenance. The more positive efforts or effects were counteracted, however, and the need for them was enhanced even if not created, by the negative effects of the American impact. Most obviously, actions by the United States either helped confine or directly confined the operational scope of the Eurocentric balance by eliminating the Western Hemisphere as a reservoir of interpower compensations and outlet for intrabalance tensions. More subtle and less determinate was the very existence of the United States in the periods preceding both world wars and especially the first one. It distorted intra-European adjustments to shifts in national capabilities and energies by constituting a too-interested, if too-long uninvolved, and an overly powerful, if merely potential, party to European rivalries. Both negative consequences—confinement and distortion—converged in the German problem and, secondarily and in part derivatively, in the Japanese one, by way of critical British choices.

The German problem was brought into focus both indirectly, by way of British choices, and gradually as regards American-German parallels and interactions. The United States and Germany came to perceive one another as ultimate rivals well before the issue between them was joined in overt conflict. And the mutual perception was the delayed consequence of a coincidence: the prevalence of both the German and the American "norths" in the two epochal civil wars of the 1860s. After subduing the Austria-led German South, Prussia-Germany was not likely to confine indefinitely her growth in industrial and international power to the early-Bismarckian continental compass. Her naval and commercial extension was bound to raise issues for the parallel consummation of post-bellum industrial growth and subsequent naval-commercial expansion of the United States, once the unequally complete preeminence of the two powers in their respective continental frameworks came to be judged insufficient by contemporary standards. For some time, the Eurocentric balance of power obscured this seemingly ultimate conflict by interposing the more spectacular Anglo-German one. The fact that the Anglo-German contention also merely interrupted the more broadly based Anglo-Russian rivalry became fully apparent only when that conflict was resumed in its updated American-Soviet version following Germany's disappearance and Britain's decline as principal players. So long as it kept the United States out of sight as the primary and primarily interested party, the Eurocentric balance of power operated thus as a screen between the United States and the implications of its growth after ceasing to be the source of virtually cost-free American expansion and a shield against interference with American ambitions.

Cleveland and Bismarck had stood for modified continentalisms, un-evenly resistant to the appeals of overseas imperialism. The following era of the first Roosevelt and the second William initiated the collision course between the two rising world powers in full. On the one side was the Kaiser's inept contingency planning for an assault on the U.S. security system, his advocacy of European unity against American and Russian expansionisms, and the presumed German designs on the Philippines. They were widely noted, even while being either less immediately pertinent factors or less authentic facts than were German efforts to exchange goods with the United States and outcompete Britain for American good will in the war with Spain. Regarding specifically the Philippines, the Germans were merely anxious to step in should the United States decide against taking the archipelago. On the other side was the nascent emotional and naval-professional hostility toward Germany and distaste for the Emperor, fed by the imbroglios over Samoa as much as by the myth about the Philippines. They had long-range significance, although operationally kept in check by Theodore Roosevelt's desire to be diplomatically effective because even-handed among the world powers and by Germany's basically favorable disposition toward an "open door" to China. An eventual collision was immanent both in the tactically pertinent inferences that leading Americans drew from wayward events and in the strategically significant constructions they placed on trends in capabilities. And German statecraft, disappointed in hopes for both an Anglo-German alliance and an Anglo-American conflict, came to view the United States as the principal example of the kind of continent-wide economic-industrial system that Germany had to match, or was certain to succumb to if she remained constricted between the materially awakening Russian mass and a but internally restructured Anglo-Saxon naval-mercantile mobility.

The official German assessment was fully developed by the outset of the twentieth century. It was, if anything, preceded and thus in part precipitated by the disposition and the determination of critical American elites with interest in foreign policy. These were initially more unambiguously Germanophobe than they were Anglophile, and were more antagonistically disposed to Germany than were the British themselves for some time. They were consequently determined to impede an Anglo-German accommodation or, at any rate, diminish the British need for it, inasmuch as any such accord would enhance Germany's ability to foster secessions from the American system in the Western Hemisphere and to compete with the United States for succession to the British empire in due course. The anti-German bias rose with rising German naval power and deepened along with the American conviction of Britain's imperial decline. That such a decline was in the offing was the one perception dominant American and German circles had in common. In this perception, the British empire was evolving from principal adversary into a virtual buffer between the two rising claimants. While it lasted, the buffer kept possible accretions to either side inconclusively within tolerable limits and helped thus to postpone the incidence, confine the scope, and moderate the intensity of American-German conflict. The empire was, consequently, to be provisionally spared and only gradually eroded by association. Association with Germany would point against Russia in Europe and in Asia and, *if* necessary, against the United States; association with the United States would work against Russia in Asia and, *when* necessary, against Germany. A growing tendency to define the ultimate conflict as one between America and Germany stimulated informal exchanges among Anglo-American foreign policy elites. It reinforced, moreover, independently existing British prejudices against an in-depth composition of the accelerating differences between Britain and Germany at the turn of the century.

The Anglo-French-American triangle had been determining for the continental and hemispheric expansion of the United States. By 1900 it was superseded by an Anglo-German-American triangle as one critical for the global phase of American foreign policy. The shift coincided with the recession of Anglo-French (cum Russian) naval rivalries to the Near and Far Eastern theaters. The American part in the first triangle was profitable for the United States and helped deliver the French Monarchy to the third estate. In 1900 it was not yet formally decided whether the well-established record of the United States as the beneficiary in conflicts between two or more European powers would induce Britain to legitimize the global aspirations of Germany within the second triangular configuration, or would help exacerbate the aspirations at a risk to both of the European powers. Nor was it yet clear how British statecraft would cope with its growing incapacity to uphold the two-power naval standard (applicable to France, the United States, and other rising naval powers) and to wage simultaneously two-and-one-half wars (with a European power and the United States, in addition to a small colonial conflict). An outline of a decision could be gathered from an official British conviction,[1] which was reaffirmed on the eve of the Prusso-French war in 1869. For Britain to be entangled in a major continental-European conflict would precipitate a U.S.-wrought military débâcle in and for Canada so long as Britain withstood pro-American devolution in the Western Hemisphere. The conviction had previously helped keep Britain aloof from any attempt to obstruct or oppose the overthrow of the old European balance in the last phase of German unification. If German national unity benefited at first as a result, the next question was whether Britain could accommodate or appease an ascendant imperialistic Germany at the later stage without antagonizing the United States and jeopardizing the increasingly vital American good will. The close and complete alliance that Germany demanded was apt to insure the continental state in Europe more reliably than it would guarantee Britain against the consequences of alienation from the United States.

The issue was postponed by the informal Anglo-German division of influence in Europe and overseas in the major part of the Bismarckian era. The division involved a complementary imbalance, favorable to Germany on the Continent and to Britain overseas, the consolidation of which in Europe and rectification overseas was to become the elusive objective of all later German statecraft. The year 1901 signalled the beginning of Britain's shift away from "splendid isolation" toward the "special relationship" with the United States. If the first had still emboldened a Lord Salisbury to equate the United States and Germany as potential (and Russia and France as the more pressing) enemies, the second was to consummate in the hands of a Winston Churchill the previously accelerating responsiveness of British calculations and decisions to the United States as the key factor, not least dominant when seemingly dormant. The parallel transition was from perceiving Germany as Britain's best hope for assistance in the Far East (against Russia) to viewing her as a threat to amity in the Far West (with the United States) and, by a not immediately appreciated but nonetheless necessary consequence, a threat also to Britain's survival as the insular kingpin of imperial cohesion and European balance.

Substantially one against Germany, the British decision was technically against accession to the Triple Alliance including also Austria-Hungary and Italy. And although far-reaching, the decision was taken in an immediate

---

1. Cf. Kenneth Bourne, *Britain and the Balance of Power in North America, 1815-1908* (Berkeley: University of California Press, 1967), p. 203, for the restatement, independently of the European context.

and narrow context of the Far East only. But the British decision-makers weighed painstakingly both the adverse effect of a German connection on France and Russia and the comparative advantages of immediate German and longer-term American support in the Far East. When viewing Asia, the British leaders did not ignore the consideration that Germany could aid Britain against Russia with respect to both India and China, and could help more directly than could either the United States or Japan and more essentially from the viewpoint of the empire than the United States either could or would at that late stage harm Britain in Canada. Since specific pros and cons were inconclusive, the decision was taken on the basis of a principle: that of avoiding everything that might engender hostile relations with the United States. Concern for amity with the United States was not the only grounds. It was self-sufficient, however, also because it was the only one on which the key British decision-makers were in full agreement. The choice between the United States and Germany was viewed as necessary because of the reciprocal animosity of the two powers, and because the animosity was likely to endure.[2]

As an immediate consequence, the British coupled naval devolution in favor of the United States in the "American seas" with making effective diplomatic or other action dependent on American initiatives or feelings. The feelings (e.g., against British cooperation with Germany in the second Venezuelan crisis over debt collection) were all the more intense because the initiatives were long lacking (not least in the Far East in and after 1903 as much as in the 1930s). And if the choice was seen as final, its ultimate consequences were less clearly conceived of and less firmly controlled. Whereas the Conservative cabinet had calculatingly exercised a diplomatic option in favor of the United States, the succeeding Liberal Ministry drifted into a rigid posture of nearly ideological opposition to Germany. The determinant of British actions evolved in tandem. It had started out in Salisbury's mind as a mere distaste for the disparity of initial payoffs, from an Anglo-German arrangement, supposedly more favorable to Germany against Russia in Europe than to Britain against Russia in the Far East; by Edward Grey's time, the determinant had decayed into the fear of an untimately uncontrollable imbalance of power on a polarized Continent. By her decision Britain renounced the attempt to use alliance for steadying influence, if not moderating control, over the expression and extent of German preeminence on the Continent and of German diversions in the colonial realm. Between comparable but unequally forward powers, moderation by alliance will be the alternative to constraint by an adversary posture. In the absence of one and failing an adequate use of the other, a both exasperated and un-

2. Cf. George Monger, *The End of Isolation: British Foreign Policy 1900-1907* (London: Thomas Nelson and Sons, Ltd., 1963), pp. 66, 105-6.

channeled German naval-continental expansionism realized, in 1914, the implications of the British choice in 1901. And in the ensuing war for a new equilibrium, the perennial balancer himself was partially balanced against Germany by Woodrow Wilson's initial neutrality policies, until constraints of time and resource drove Germany into methods of maritime warfare that lifted the latent biases of American foreign policy makers above the concerns of electoral mass politics into active involvement on the British side.

An event occurring in the first year of the twentieth century[3] prejudged in effect the course of the century's remainder for both Europe and the United States. The British decision and subsequent German conduct can be evaluated both in themselves and in the perspective of an alternative past. In terms of Anglo-German relations alone, Britain's interest in only a specific understanding limited to the Far East was at variance with Germany's interest in nothing less than a total alliance, guaranteeing her against the European consequences of anti-Russian policies in China. The problem for the naval-imperial great power was to decide how and why to assume an unaccustomed peacetime commitment to a great continental power; for Germany, why to underwrite the British empire piecemeal, starting with land-type threats in China and, by extension, India (increasingly exposed by Russian railway-constructions), while remaining if not encircled then confined by the Franco-Russian alliance on the Continent and overseas by British animosity for the German *Weltpolitik*. If the original British argument was that the costs of alienating Russia and France on the Continent and elsewhere by making common cause with Germany everywhere would exceed the benefit of any immediate aid that Germany could, and actually would be willing to, render Britain in the Far East, the counterargument was that since British interests in critical overseas areas including China were inordinately greater than Germany's, she had to be compensated elsewhere. The structurally rooted clash of perspectives could be resolved only at an immediate, albeit limitable, cost to the preestablished power. As their foreign policy was continentalized by accession to the Triple Alliance, the British would have had to agree to extending Germany's reach beyond the Continent. There was no other way to reduce the disparity of incentives and the inequality of interests and stakes in the arenas at issue: continental and maritime, European and colonial. So long as they did not have substantial and recognized overseas interests of their own to defend locally, the Germans were unlikely to feel anxious to defend the existing distribution of power and interests across the board. And they needed a secure home base for involving themselves contentiously on the British side overseas. Ger-

---

3. For excerpts from key memoranda by British statesmen, see Bourne, *The Foreign Policy of Victorian England* (Oxford: The Clarendon Press, 1970) pp. 462-474.

many's posture could be globalized at the least immediate cost to the British in an area from which Britain was being extruded in any event—the southern part of the Western Hemisphere. This fact alone highlights the triangular nature of the critical relationship, the grounds for the British choice, and, indeed, the identity of the principal (if ostensibly absentee) party to the decisive turning point in world affairs.

The deepest reason why the British rejected alliance with Germany was their growing belief that her diplomatic restlessness demonstrated territorial insatiability. This conviction dispensed them with exploring objectively both the structural inhibitions to an Anglo-German entente and the costs of an alternative policy. The fact that subsequent German conduct and aims substantiated the original conviction imparted to it the authority of correct prevision and to ensuing events the aura of fatal inevitability. The contrary, and more general, "fact" is the difference between the conduct of a denied aspirant and the behavior of an even only partially satisfied possessor. The unquestioned German aspiration to equal status with Great Britain could not but be exacerbated (on the classic European pattern) into the quest for predominance by Britain's rejection of a form of parity in a complementarily structured continental-colonial or land-naval mix of assets and responsibilities. An Anglo-German accommodation would have come close to a de facto condominium in Europe while setting the stage for partnership in action overseas. The accommodation failing, the land-sea power schism could not be resolved within the European framework; but, barring naval superiority over the Anglo-Saxon power or powers, Germany could find only on the Continent the capacity for resolving structural disparities and consequent dilemmas in an interempire as against an interstate configuration.

Germany followed in the footsteps of France. In a longer perspective her basic predispositions resembled Macedon's in antiquity. Before she, too, incurred comparable wars and ultimate partition, Germany shared with that state a two-faced naval and continental orientation toward an overmature state-system on one side and an ascendant world power on the other. She was likewise undecided whether to fear most Russia (Syria for Macedon) in the short run or the United States (Rome) in the long. The unifying disposition for the ancient and the modern Macedon was a blend of assertiveness and anxiety, characteristic of an ambitious power disposing of relatively inferior resource and beset by dilemmas that resist solution by routine diplomacy. The only, but formidable, question for Germany was whether she would neutralize Russia and confine America in concert with Great Britain or clash with Britain as part of an overt conflict with one and covert competition with the other of the two (Russian and American) continent-wide wing powers. Inherited British principles embalmed into tradition by contests with France pointed toward the latter outcome. Any contrary bias would have had to inhere in the contemporary global distribution of power and recent British weakening. It was offset by the likewise traditional preference, strengthened by decadence, to decide in terms of immediate and known costs rather than long-term hypothetical consequences. The surest immediate costs of Anglo-German accommodation were to be found in deteriorated Anglo-American relations; while the immediate risks of Anglo-German alienation seemed less than the dangers from association. In the last resort, both the German and the American options meant a change for the worse from confident British unilateralism. But the hope of substituting an Anglo-American for British supremacy in due course was sufficient to highlight the immediate liabilities of an essay at Anglo-German condominium.

The principal threats perceived by the Germans were Russia, to physical security, and the United States, to relative economic standing and (consequently) social stability. The same two big powers figure as likely allies of one another in an "alternative past" that unfolds as a speculative consequence of an Anglo-German accommodation. An Anglo-German entente would have aimed at Russia on both her European and Asian frontiers; it would have placed France under British protection in Europe while diverting her definitively from any thought of revanche—and thus from the Russian alliance—in Europe to compensations in Africa and the Near East within bounds compatible with the established British and developing German positions and interests there. Outside Europe, in addition to confining the possible scope of the French colonial empire, an Anglo-German entente would have accelerated progress toward Russo-Japanese accord (actually reached in 1907) to the probable exclusion of the prior war (in 1904). Such a rapprochement was an alternative to the Anglo-Japanese Alliance of 1902, which the entente with Germany would have made unnecessary to Britain and either unattractive or unattainable to Japan. It would also constitute a basis from which the two local Asian powers could have offset the free-trading European, Anglo-German front in mainland China and the adjacent seas. For the same reason, Russia would have had additional reasons for wooing the United States. She could have done so by way of offering special access to the Russian part of China, which she actually agitated as a prospect in the relevant time period, as an alternative to an open door to all China trade. Suspicions regarding the consequences of an Anglo-German entente for the Western Hemisphere would have inclined the United States to soft-pedal irritation with Russian policies in Asia, in favor of the "traditional" American-Russian friendship. Any link to Russia would have been also a reinsurance against Japan exploiting the newly exposed and vulnerable American positions and interests outside the continental United States proper. As an overall result, land- and sea-based power might have been diffused more equitably, and between Britain and Germany more concertedly. Tendencies to polarization would have been defused. The United States would have been challenged in its core-empire. But it would also have been given a timely impetus for reaching out of the regional cocoon in peacetime as one of the near-equal world powers, instead of depending on wartime pressures for movement beyond regional dominion to world empire.

Real British options between Germany and the United States meshed thus with America's hypothetical alternatives to her actual conduct. At issue was the role of the United States as a globally active power, and its scope. One possible strategy for the United States was to actively help perpetuate the stalemates within the Pacific and the Atlantic regional balances of power along with the degree of their existing separateness from one another. The two, equipoise and distinctness, conditioned the lull in American expansion after 1898, next to the partial autonomy of the regional systems from the central or strictly European one. Another possible, and the less active, strategy was to adjust defensively to the intraregional balances breaking down in regional hegemonies on the pattern of the American dominion in the Western Hemisphere, and to accept the implications of an interregional equilibrium.

The active strategy required a more sustained and evenhanded American involvement in the two regional balances of power than was actually in evidence. Such an involvement could have been initially more direct in the Pacific theater than in the Atlantic (and, by extension, European) one, if only because the United States had greater immediate interests there (the Philippines, China) and because it was there that American statecraft could act more impartially and efficaciously between the critical European powers (Britain, Germany, and Russia). As an evenhanded American activism spread from the Pacific to the Atlantic theater, however, it was likely to transmute American identity. From entrenching itself within a regional core-empire, the United States would evolve into being one among the great powers pursuing worldwide interests within a balance-of-power and concert system that was being at once simplified or unified and fully globalized. The shift would imply greater reciprocity in access among the powers, as also the (southernmost) Western Hemisphere was reopened to outside influence and compensations by a United States that had ceased to be defensive-isolationist and operated on an equal basis in all the other world areas.

As either a core-empire within the Monroe Doctrine or a world power emancipated from it, the United States was eligible to occupy—but only in the second identity was it likely to perform—the role of a balancer or moderator anxious and able to preclude a polarization and conflict in Europe of the kind that eventually occurred with help from the actual American attitude if not policy. Some such polarized conflict was the likely or even necessary prelude to creating conditions that would exact from the United States the other hypothetical, more passive or defensive, strategic response. The conditions would be those of an interregional balance-of-power system among comparable core-empires in Europe around either Germany or Russia, in Asia around Japan if not yet around China, and in the Western Hemisphere around the United States in addition, possibly, to a reduced British Empire reorganized into a more compact entity. In such a structure of power, the American core-empire was less likely to be an automatic balancer or moderator than a mere centerpiece by virtue of its geopolitical position if nothing else.

American foreign policy before World War I had neither the time nor the incentive to promote inter-great power equilibrium along the lines of the more active first option, and helped thus move the second interempire option into the realm of real possibilities. Thereafter, both during and after the war, American policies failed to either adjust to the regional-empire variety or reestablish the bases of a system of great powers. The failures laid instead the foundations for the pressures that would propel America into a third alternative, that of world empire.

Once the First World War got underway, a strategy of interregional equilibrium required the United States to combine neutrality in the war with being prepared for one that might follow it. Such neutrality had to be indifferent to the immediate results of the European war (i.e., accept in advance a "hegemonic" outcome) and, therefore, also to the subjectively assessed merits of the contestants. Beyond that, such neutrality could mean either complete self-isolation or an adjustment of supplies to the rival continental and maritime powers that would promote a balance of resource assets while ruling out direct intervention and acts of partisanship apt to precipitate intervention. Simultaneous military preparedness would enable the United States to deal with the collapse of the European balance into a polarity of power between the United States and either an immediately hostile or only eventually competitive European victor in mid-Atlantic. As a matter of fact, American naval planning prior to U.S. intervention had been actually aimed solely at securing the core-empire against a German victory after the end of the European war. The other, active great-power option reflected America's status as a wing power rather than core-empire and would implement her identity as a major nation-state with latent membership in the geopolitically expanding central balance of power. It entailed an early and near-automatic American involvement in the European war, though not necessarily an immediately or unreservedly belligerent one. And it required an unchanging purpose: to promote a "balanced" outcome, favorable to continuing postwar involvement in a pluralistic great-power system.

The differences between the two strategies were real as regards American self-perception, the time sequences in the unfolding of either strategy, and the resulting structures of power. Actual wartime American policies had started out with the first strategy, and were then inflected in the direction of the second by a pro-Allied bias that subsequently rendered impossible an integral and consistent implementation of the balancing approach. America evolved from being an aloof moderator to becoming a partial associate, from having unlimited leeway to assuming limited liability. And the evolution was due to stimuli of a kind that had made other regional core-empires resume expansion in the past. The Anglo-Saxon elite in charge of U.S. foreign policy was committed in the last resort to Britain's survival and, in fact, victory, as a matter of its own position within the interethnic group dynamics in the United States itself. Moreover, the need of a lagging American economy for outside outlets during wartime had engendered a material stake in Allied victory, which alone could insure eventual reimbursement. And finally, American intervention was precipitated by Germany's infringing upon the American *imperial* frontier in both the maritime and the continental zones. Germany's intensified and indiscriminate submarine campaign, in part a response to prior American discriminations in favor of Britain, along with the proffer of German alliance to Mexico in the "Zimmermann telegram," went far to substantiate the dual, maritime and continental, dimension of the by-then traditional perception of German threat to American predominance in the Western Hemisphere. It was left to subsequent rationalizations of the American involvement to stress the danger that a German victory (and consequent power concentration) would represent for American *national* security regardless of the means employed toward attaining such a victory.

What the consequences of a German-managed power concentration in Europe would have been for American role and security in a global balance of regional empires or ensembles is a subject for speculation. Less hypothetical are the pressures and the consequences of the pressures that were unleashed by the erosion of the European balance of power, and by America's failure to continue dealing with the consequences of her intervention in the European war. Since that intervention was unplanned in advance of involvement and uninformed by a steady strategic concept after invovement, it was far from immune to prompt disenchantment and soon-to-follow disinvolvement. Just as the American involvement in the world war had been essentially for Britain, the disruptive effects of American disengagement from world order worked themselves out through Britain. As American aloofness from actual issues for policy deepened, it only intensified British reluctance to contravene in any way declared American principles and preconceptions while discharging, from a dramatically lowered material basis in national and imperial resource, an actually enhanced postwar role in global stability. Britain's unreal posture was bound to cause standing irritation for an inversely misproportioned defeated Germany, even before her real passivity on critical occasions created an opening for revived Germany to pose again the Anglo-German question under incomparably worsened conditions in the second round.

Speculative possibilities and actual developments did likewise coexist in relation to the Pacific area generally and Japan specifically. Japan was Germany's counterpart in Asia, liable to be influenced by Anglo-German estrangement as much as she (and her relations with America) would have been by Anglo-German entente. Great Britain chose Japan self-consciously over Germany as the principal, if initially junior, ally in the Far East, also because the United States subordinated both Russia and Japan to Germany as the key strategic threat in that area.[4] Whereas the British choice and its implementation was to affect critically the terminal phase of the British empire in the Second World War, America's assessment was crucial for the thrust and timing of the emerging American empire. Such an empire could be solidly established on an Asian base only so long as Japan was still relatively weak, China malleable, and Russia decayed, while the European powers were paralyzing one another. Yet if key Americans had either anticipated upon or agreed with British assessments of Germany before 1902 (the year of the Anglo-Japanese alliance), they were to concur only later with the German assessment of Japan as a rising major military-industrial power to be matched and rivaled.

Japan profited in her rise just sufficiently from conflicts among the Europeans in Asia and from the British shield against Russia to qualify for overland expansion. She conformed thus to the precedents set by many another offshore island, including medieval England, in the past. Only when the island power has been repulsed or outgrown on the mainland will it concentrate on far-flung commercial activities overseas and seek physical immunity in a more or less active adjustment to a balance of power on the adjacent land mass, which stultifies the more directly or continuously participating continental states. In consequence of the British choice, the triangular Anglo-American-German interplay, which spanned the Atlantic and Pacific theaters and merely affected Japan, was joined in the Pacific by one among the United States, Britain, and Japan herself. The Pacific interplay was to become comparable to the earlier global one as regards the

4. The provisional choice of Subic Bay for U.S. base in the Philippines by American naval planners reflected that identification. Cf. J. A. S. Grenville and G. B. Young, *Politics, Strategy, and American Diplomacy: Studies in foreign Policy, 1873-1917* (New Haven: Yale University Press, 1966), p. 312. On American-Japanese relations see Akira Iriye, *Across the Pacific: An Inner History of American East-Asian Relations* (New York: Harcourt, Brace and World, 1967).

American attitude to a developing Anglo-Japanese accord. Its impact over the decades helped convert the latent symmetries in drives and values between Japan and Germany into association in climactic action against the two Anglo-Saxon powers. A combination of modern technology and largely overlapping ambitions on the part of insular Japan and continent-wide but near-insular United States nullified the moderating effect that the absence of a full-blown land-sea power schism ought to have exerted on their conflict, and exposed the conflict instead to a spell of ferocity peculiar to creatures of the sea. Conversely, the geographic distance between Japan and Germany and their unifying grievance obscured provisionally their qualitative difference as continental and insular states.

The obsessive preoccupation of British statecraft with American attitudes toward Germany and later Japan and with securing American aid in the Far East, first in support of Japan and finally against her, gave the United States a hold over the Anglo-Japanese alliance and relationship at all points. A variable American viewpoint was controlling at the inception of the alliance (when Japan was chosen, and the United States had been advised even before the treaty was finalized); in its implementation (after the British Cabinet set the tone for the future by concluding as early as 1903 that it could not face a war with Russia on Japan's side without American aid); and in its eventual termination (at American insistence, after single-handed victory over Russia in 1904 and assertiveness against China and Russia before and in World War I had transformed Japan from a junior British ally into a senior antagonist for America). Initial British hesitancy about implementing the alliance implied Japan's inferiority to Germany as an effective anti-Russian ally; when inferiority vanished with ascendant strength, Japan, like Germany before, was cut loose from the restraints of a British connection.

The American-Japanese collision course after 1905 matched the Anglo-German one after 1901. The two English-speaking countries would have either the European or the Asian power contain Russia in Manchuria and in China generally, without commensurate aggrandizement there or elsewhere. In United States relations with Japan, that original pretension was compounded by a plethora of secondary confusions and complications culminating in conflict. Among the confusions was the American failure to foresee and subsequently to appreciate the fact that Japan's exclusion from the Philippines in 1898 would divert her expansive energies to the Asian mainland; that Theodore Roosevelt's design to balance the two powers while mediating the Russo-Japanese peace could not lastingly nullify the consequences of Japan's victory for the scope of her continental diversion; and that the pursuit of legitimate American objectives in the area—a regional balance of power that would shield the Philippines and help secure commercial access to China for the United States—had to combine sustained containment of Japan with concessions sufficient to prevent amplifying periodic scares into a systemic threat to larger-than-Philippine security. While pursuing its legitimate objectives in Asia, American statecraft may be taxed with first directing Japan's ambitions away from the Philippines to China. Subsequent American misassessments of fundamental local givens and perceptions transformed that debatable misdirection into a critical Japanese misunderstanding as to the supposed American willingness to concede a Japanese sphere in China in exchange for Philippine immunity. That misunderstanding was dispelled only by an ostensibly patternless and ultimately costly alternation of efforts to appease Japan and acts to restrain her. Appeasement was tried mainly, but not only, before the 1912 revolution in China. The restraints provoked their target most when the implied insensitivity to felt Japanese needs posed as opposition to the means employed to meet them.

More markedly even than the British policies toward Germany, the American strategy vis-à-vis Japan would confine the ascendant power in subparity conditions by way of an ill-assorted combination of denial, deterrence, and defense. Denial of the right to territorial expansion (through either a northern continental or a southern insular strategy) was not adequately compensated by concessions of a different kind. It quite probably could not be in a collapsing world economic order. But neither was the denial attended by either adequate deterrence of Japanese excesses or timely defensive aid to the targets of Japanese expansionism. German-Japanese convergence in the Second World War implemented thus a shared experience with the two preestablished Anglo-Saxon powers. That experience was made all the more affecting by the fundamentally ambivalent attitudes, admiringly imitative as much as competitive or antagonistic, that the two aspirants harbored toward the English-speaking counterparts.

Both Germany and Japan had been initially promoted in their ascent by their respective Anglo-Saxon sponsor, only to be subsequently debarred from parity as world powers combining formal status with its substantial dividends in naval-colonial posture and economic access. If oceanic expansion was denied to both, so was a compensatory diversion on the mainland away from the most sensitive assets of the two Anglo-Saxon powers. And if the Anglo-Americans became convinced that the two "aggressor" powers were insatiable, the Germans and the Japanese developed a complex about being willfully "encircled." Ambivalence evolved into hostility not least, and perhaps especially, among those who had believed longest in the possibility and desirability of accommodation: the Japanese Navy, the American Secretary of State Lansing, A. J. Balfour in England, and Chancellor Bethmann-Hollweg in Germany. There were indubitable structural or systemic biases toward eventual conflict. It took policy, however, to convert them into strategic necessities and moral obligations. Whereas the United States was free to join or not to join in the first, essentially European, war when consulting its immediate security alone, it was forced into the second war as a preliminary to the second and global phase of the American imperial expansion. The necessity arose as Japan and Germany staged devastating parallel drives to overthrow the *intra*regional Atlantic-European and Pacific-Asian balance-of-power systems in favor of a new, *inter*regional global order.

The flaws in the American performance affecting the Eurocentric balance of power, in the period following the one-sided operation and exploitation of that balance to American advantage, were ultimately rooted in insufficient political aptitude, in moral ambiguity, and in intellectual confusion. The insufficient political aptitude was embedded in the too-easy expansion in the formative period. It was aggravated at a later stage by the lack of continuity in basic orientation between Theodore Rooseveltian as compared with Wilsonian globalism and Cleveland's as compared with Hoover's kind of continentalism, between Wilsonian and (less consistently) Franklin Rooseveltian collectivism and Lodgean unilateralism. The hiatus in American involvements was most notable between the world wars. It permitted a maladjusted European and a truncated Asian balance of power to collapse as a consequence of de facto vacuums of power in Eastern Europe and in Eastern Asia (China), and of partially artificial disparities between mobilized power (French in Europe and Japanese in Asia) and potential power (German in Europe and American in Asia). From formally neutral and then associate status, the United States moved up to grand-coalition leadership in the last stage of World War I. Thereafter, the United States left the European balance of power in a worse condition than it had been after Britain's earlier withdrawals from continental involvement in the aftermath of the wars with Louis XIV and Napoleon.[5] Since World War I established American laggardness as the ultimate balancer-intervener, moreover, the anticipation of inevitable American delays shaped especially British responses to the newly gathering crisis in the 1930s. When described in terms of options that were becoming largely fictitious, the crisis unfolded as the British reenacted and extended to Japan-in-Asia their hesitancy between accommodation with upthrusting powers and acquiescence in American vetoes. Whereas the United States vetoed adjustments of which it

---

5. This is true even if Britian is made principally responsible for the discontinuous extension of Prussian territory toward the Rhine at the Vienna peace congress, as a check on France, and if one regards that extension as the original cause of the subsequent difficulty—once again manifest at Versailles—to either confine German power effectively or to assimilate it into Europe painlessly.

disapproved without making them redundant by timely and effective substitutes, appeasement of Germany and Japan was contingent, next to revision of the political and territorial status quo, on developing "preferential" economic blocs that would contravene the general principles of U.S.-favored open-door economic "liberalism" while injuring specific U.S. interests in Latin America and elsewhere.

Insufficient American political aptitude merged thus imperceptibly with a moral ambiguity which, as political skills matured, was chiefly if not only rooted in an exorbitant pretension to a privileged status among nations. That claim had found an early expression in the perception of other powers as the provisional custodians of particular territories that the rising United States had adjudged to itself. It was amplified into the presumption of opposing a more-or-less explicit veto, with typically less-than-effective backing, to any major-power policy or constellation that threatened to foreclose or even only impede America's accession to world leadership at some future time of her choosing. An ideology such as this could readily and alternatively either interplay with or be mistaken for a balance-of-power strategy. And because the ideology was not sustained by continuously active diplomatic strategy, it rendered even more ambiguous morally the American equivalent of a particular British tendency and impact. The deliberate bias or actual effect of British strategies had been to either promote or only intensify the warlike frictions on the European continent to be subsequently resolved, or the aggressions to be checked, by the forcible intervention of the insular originator-balancer. The United States contributed comparably to conflictual situations by its very existence as a background factor, and by its actual or only presumed expectations as a forward-moving power, while it reserved unto itself the role of either a distant critic or the ultimately nonresponsible arbiter. The chain of causation between act or attitude and consequence was more involved and prolonged in America's impact on Europe and Asia in the decades preceding the Second World War than was the case for Britain's impact on the Continent up to the first. But, in the last analysis, the United States was no less coresponsible for the upheavals that its arms somewhat reluctantly proceeded to pacify at a later date.

As Britain vis-à-vis France and Germany at different points in time, so the United States vis-à-vis Germany before World War I and Japan in the period preceding World War II. In both or all instances, competitive economic preliminaries with naval overtones were reinforced by at least partially interested propaganda to stimulate crisis-prone diplomatic developments and constellations. The momentum deriving from both structural conditions and policy considerations transformed mere competition gradually into conflict between increased fears for security by the "satisfied" states and augmented claims and aims of the "dissatisfied" states. The process colored perceptions of what constituted key threats; of balance-of-power needs; and of the means for redress. If it was never particularly attractive, it became speedily impossible to persist in attempts to determine "objectively" whether denying finite expansion and alternatives to larger-scale expansion to the identified expansionist would not drive him to overassert himself. And a "mercantilistic" setting and outlook was peculiarly apt to make the possessor-powers underestimate the capacity of the international system itself to expand and assimilate even substantially enlarged claimant states in a new equilibrium. The temptation was instead for both of the Anglo-Saxon balancer-powers to commit a vulgar intellectual error, precariously suspended between self-deception and deliberate misrepresentation. They would posit radically enlarged or reoriented new powers on one side and an unchanged scope of the international system and unaltered shape of constellations on the other side, and view the two seeming givens as radically incompatible. They would thus posit a tendency to cumulative disequilibrium in the system of states, rather than entrust unavoidable risks to the tendency to limit damage by reconfigurations of forces both within and among states.

V

THE UNITED STATES, BRITAIN, AND RUSSIA.

Parity and Preeminence

The Anglo-American relationship was superficially defined by its beginnings, in the relatively easy conquest of American independence, and by its climax in the still more readily conceded transfer of imperial primacy. Yet, behind the distorting screen of an apparently preordained outcome, the relationship had a more equivocal anatomy and, in terms of consequent "might have beens," elicits not altogether benign analogies.

If the role of the British empire in the American political experience is to be placed where it belongs, it must be restored to its original salience and stripped of the sentimentalities with which it has been invested in retrospect. The salience derived from the menace that, on sound strategic and systemic grounds, the two English-speaking nations represented for one another's interests, at all times potentially and quite often acutely. Specific issues varied, but the underlying concern was with reciprocal parity or one-party preeminence, at first regionally. The sentimentality gained the upper hand when the threat to one another appeared in hindsight as unreal. It did so for the simple, if superficial, reason that it had never found expression in a climactic conflict, in view of the definition of vital interests that was finally preferred over the other possible one.

The barest anatomy of the Anglo-American relationship is that of two initially unequal and thereafter unevenly evolving antagonist powers, uncomfortably harboring the latent identity as sister nations. They competed over shifting stakes against the background of competitively usable, and also changing, third parties in conditions that were relieved by physical distance between the seats of formal authority and by asymmetry in material capabilities and policy priorities. Physical contiguity was eventually limited to Canada in North America. It sufficed to provide an emotional stimulus to acute antagonism for a time, along with historical memories of coercion and conflict and the influx of Anglophobe ethnic groups. In due course, the initial territorial incentives to continuing contention were to be supplemented by the two countries' conception of role in the wider system. As some saw it in America from the beginning, and at a later stage others in Britain, there was not room enough in the Western Hemisphere and eventually in the world at large for coexisting British and American empires. In principle, it was possible to allocate the continental parts of the Western Hemisphere and the closely adjacent islands on the Atlantic and Pacific sides into juxtaposed and balanced American and British spheres of influence. The theoretical possibility faded, however, once the originally dominant continental perspective of American foreign policy surrendered control over policy attitudes to offshore concerns and, with them, to the monopolistic biases of naval power. It then became more difficult or even impossible to distribute influence and control in the several local sectors in a way amounting to overall parity between the two powers in the absence of an equally threatening common enemy.[1]

The "normal" consequence would have been a progressively widening, system-encompassing conflict. It could have been averted only by one of two means. One was for the British to contain the United States on the North American continent in a position of strength well short of continental hegemony. This would have confined the American resources that remained available for the maritime Atlantic and Pacific spheres. To this end, Britain's relations and antagonisms with third, European powers would have had to be treated as no more important than those with the United States quite early in the game. This meant further that the balance-of-power doctrine, evolved by the British to impede the near-equal or coequal maritimization and globalization of the momentarily preeminent continental power in Europe, could be applied to the expanding continental United States

1. See R. G. Neale, *Great Britain and United States Expansion 1898-1900* (E. Lansing: Michigan State University Press, 1966); Howard K. Beale, *Theodore Roosevelt and the Rise of America to World Power* (Baltimore: The Johns Hopkins University Press, 1956); John A. Garraty, *Henry Cabot Lodge* (New York: Alfred A. Knopf, 1965); and Frederick B. Pike, *Chile and the United States 1880-1962* (Notre Dame: University of Notre Dame Press, 1963). For a much later period see Ian Colvin, *The Chamberlain Cabinet* (London: Gollancz, 1971). Also, as previously cited, Kenneth Bourne, *The Foreign Policy of Victorian England* (Oxford: The Clarendon Press, 1970); idem, *Britain and the Balance of Power in North America, 1815-1908* (Berkeley: University of California Press, 1967); George Monger, *The End of Isolation: British Foreign Policy 1900-1907* (London: Thomas Nelson and Sons, Ltd., 1963); J. A. S. Grenville and G. B. Young, *Politics, Strategy, and American Diplomacy: Studies in Foreign Policy, 1873-1917* (New Haven: Yale University Press, 1966).

only at the cost of applying it less stringently to the continental-European powers. Most British statesmen desired the result of America's containment. And some, such as Lords Palmerston and Clarendon in the middle period and Lords Salisbury and Lansdowne in the final phase, seemed to understand its requisites. But none was prepared to assume the immediate risks or costs in the few critical contexts. Thus France was not coopted in the mid-nineteenth century for effectively blocking the United States in California on the mainland and in Cuba off it; and, as time was running out at the turn of the century, neither was Germany brought into common action in support of, say, Chile as the indigenous resister to American hegemony in Latin America. This left the second, and spurious, means for avoiding a climactic Anglo-American conflict over regional and global primacy. It was to surrender effective balancing for the mirage of a concert and joint Anglo-American supremacy. An unopposed American navalization would, in the more optimistic British view, replace the original land-sea power asymmetry between the two nations with a new solidarity, based on symmetry first in naval capabilities and eventually on that basis also in global concerns.

In terms of bare structures, the continentally expanding power of the United States "ought to have" come into collision with the maritime-mercantile power of Britain. Reenacting the Rome-Carthage relationship between a land and a sea power, the collision would have occurred in Central America, the counterpart of the Sicilian land-sea area, and produced a matching amplification of American naval capability while Britain fell back on alliance with a continental European power just as Carthage had allied with Macedon in the earlier setting. If the Anglo-American relationship is viewed as one involving increasingly two sea powers, the proper historical analogy changes. It shifts to the seventeenth-century Anglo-Dutch contest preceding the passage of naval supremacy to Britain as the maritime state with a more substantial base in territory and resource. In their relative decline, the seafaring Dutch, too, had only a continental power, France, as the potential (if actually spurned) counterpoise to the ascendancy of their maritime-mercantile competitor in conflict and, later, in the "union" drawing precariously on religious affinities and similarities in political institutions. Analogies such as these inspired expectations, not least in Europe, of a climactic Anglo-American clash. They may have contributed to avoiding the collision when prompting the continentals to neglect an apparently unnecessary effort to either back Britain more (France in the 1840s and, to a degree, 1850s) or demand from her less (Germany in the 1890s).

In the event, there were to be only periodic scares and preparations for war on both sides of the Atlantic. Actual war with the United States came to be regarded in Britain as undesirable and, eventually, as unthinkable. It was either or both, because it was likely to be somehow conjoined with hostilities engaging Britain with some other European power or powers, as either the American or the European antagonist seized upon Britain's prior involvement with the other for acting against her. Such a conjunction would tie down the British resources, and might even replicate the original Franco-American alliance. While she was the strongest single naval power, therefore, Britain had to avoid conflict with the United States unless she was able to carry the lesser European powers into war with America on her side and neutralize their nuisance potential. This implied conceding to the continentals in regard to anti-American policies the kind of effective veto power that the British had once felt obliged to concede to the Dutch in regard to conflicts with France unless they were ready to let Netherlands at peace recover from an England at war the trade she had wrested from Holland by war. When she had weakened at a later stage, Britain feared being herself carried by a European ally such as Germany into a larger conflict with the United States than she had reason to desire. The Anglo-French alliance in the Crimean war offered the most propitious occasion for joint European action extending coalition-type containment from Russia in the Black Sea to the United States in the Caribbean sea. Divergences in the priorities of the increasingly war-weary allies impeded the execution, however. The prime British concern lay with the Central American land bridge and the related canal project, while France's was with Cuba and even Hawaii pending the later infatuation with Mexico attended by coolness in Anglo-French relations.

Thus, when power was still sufficient to deal with the United States, British priorities pointed elsewhere. When priorities might have been reversed into focusing on U.S. expansion into South America, shifts in the wider power distribution insured that they could be revised in practice only at a cost and a risk that a defensive, incremental statecraft of a self-consciously declining empire could no longer weigh serenely and consider seriously. Concern with the Indian land frontier (and commercial access to China) against railway-building Russia outweighed by then apprehensions over the Canadian land frontier, just as preoccupation with the balance between British and American naval power in the West Indies and of commercial access to Latin America had paled gradually before the combination of railway and naval constructions by Imperial Germany. The long-range consequences of the German civil war between Prussia and Austria made Britain welcome in due course the ultimate implications of the once-impeded outcome of the near-simultaneous American "war between the states."

The actual and, given British choices, unavoidable dénouement unfolded over two world wars. Previous to them, America had progressed to ascendancy at first intermittently on land and then in the maritime domain, within the for-long asymmetrical setting of an Anglo-American stalemate. Both sides were ready to attempt subversion of the other: the Americans, when the Canadians were restless under British rule; and the British, when the South rose against the North in the United States. And both sides resorted repeatedly to bluff and counterbluff in periodic scares, in lieu of applying effective force and counterforce. Until the end of the nineteenth century, the stalemate rested upon Britain's naval supremacy on the high seas, usable against the principal American coastal cities, and on America's ability to deploy against Canada a superior potential on land in prolonged hostilities and instant superiority on the Great Lakes. The military-strategic asymmetry was not the only source of stalemate. It was complemented by an evolving, and likewise lopsided, structure of economic interdependence and of politico-strategic priorities. The interdependence discouraged both the New England traders and the English creditor-investors from favoring economic or any other Anglo-American warfare; the priorities were regional for the United States and global or eastern-hemispheric for the United Kingdom.

Structural asymmetries were neatly reflected in highly ambivalent attitudes toward one another on both sides of the Atlantic, and of the American elites toward England in particular. Since no climactic struggle over hegemony was to take place between the two English-speaking nations, they were deprived of a medium for catharsis in perceptions and attitudes as much as of the supreme catalyst for reordering interests and objectives. The consequences were not wholly beneficial.

It was reserved for less-potent wars to condition the evolution from Anglo-American stalemate to American superiority. The last to pit America against Britain directly, the war of 1812 both set off the Anglo-American contention over the North American balance of power and presaged its outcome, while the war of the United States with British-favored Mexico decided the continental issue to American advantage. Thereafter, the blighting of the promise of the Anglo-French partnership in the Crimean war and the outcomes of the American and German civil wars swayed in the same direction the issue whether a balance of power might crystallize in Central America and the Western Hemisphere generally. None of the military side shows in Latin America proper was able to modify, let alone able to reverse, the earlier verdict. Before the process ran its course, the Anglo-American relations had covered the entire spectrum. The continental-maritime hostility of 1812 was transmuted first into Britain's only unfriendly neutrality in the American Civil War and then softened further into benev-olent neutrality in America's war with Spain. The benevolence was reciprocated by the United States when interpreting neutral rights on the seas in favor of Britain in the First World War, pending the ultimate step of alliance.

The stakes of the minor wars shifted geographically from Canada and California in the North American theater to Cuba and the Isthmian Canal in the Central American one; and they shifted operationally from continental and only secondarily mercantile rivalries to the issue of maritime and commercial supremacy and extraneous "caudillo-ship" in South America generally and in Chile specifically. The shifting stakes denoted the receding line of Britain's efforts to contain the United States as well as the shrinkage of her usable military capability and practicable diplomatic options. The caliber of Britain's protégés, too, declined from Mexico to the Mosquito Indians, and from Chile (in the War of the Pacific) to Guiana (against Venezuela and her American protector), coincidentally with the rising tide of American capabilities. The new power underpinned a long-standing assertion of right to expand so absolute as to rule out any American reciprocity for British concessions, in Canada or elsewhere. As a result, when the Monroe Doctrine was finally applied to the Canal issue, British naval and diplomatic withdrawal was as uncompensated as had been Britain's naval protection of the Doctrine when it had first been enunciated. No more was reciprocity forthcoming in the intermediate period, when the relatively pro-American Lord Aberdeen sought in the 1840s an easement on Oregon, in exchange for renouncing California and accommodating the United States in Maine.

Even as attitudes were being formed, roles were being transformed. During her initial primacy, Britain was a species of provocative protector of the rising United States: just as British naval power shielded, so her continental presence stimulated, American expansion in North America. In that phase, the two unequal powers were overtly antagonistic tacit allies against the real or suspected ambitions of the "Holy Alliance" powers in the Western Hemisphere. The British merely adapted thus to peaceable relations in the 1820s the strategy they had applied when terminating the two preceding Anglo-American wars by peace treaties. The 1840s and 1850s witnessed intensified, if half-hearted, British containment efforts, correspondingly more tolerant of third-power (notably French) involvement, while the 1860s witnessed speculations about a possible balance of power to arise from the fragments of the Union. Beginning with the late 1880s, British statecraft abandoned indecisive containment of the United States for initially reluctant concession of regional naval parity to America in the Caribbean, as a tribute to third-power challenges outside the Western Hemisphere. No longer a target of containment, the United States became a partner in devolution and the U.S. Navy a surrogate for the Royal Navy in

West Indian waters and the Eastern Pacific. The Hay-Pauncefote Treaty of 1901 formally reversed in favor of the United States the compound of local parity and regional British naval supremacy that had still been implicit in the earlier attempt to regulate the canal issue (by the Clayton-Bagot Treaty of 1850). At that point, the earlier efforts to contain the United States within tolerable limits on land were only faintly echoed in a British effort to delimit the areas of primary naval responsibilities. The real British objective was henceforth to involve the United States imperceptibly in Far Eastern issues. The effort proved to be only provisionally abortive, as the United States evolved from being a devolutionary substitute for Britain regionally into a savior and, finally, successor of Britain's empire globally.

America's mere existence as Britain's material and diplomatic support of last resort propelled Albion in the direction of her greatest dangers. By contrast, Britain protected an expanding American empire against threats from the seaborne capabilities of continental Europe which were barely real, as when France was mandated to act for the "Holy Alliance" in Spain and, presumably, her defecting Latin American colonies in the 1820s. If and when the dangers were more than imaginary, they were as much provoked by the larger policies or, at least, the dazzling example of the British protector as an impressively successful overseas colonial and commercial power, as they were prevented by his efforts. Since it rested on such fragile and equivocal foundations, the Anglo-American relationship depended from an early date heavily on the state of economic interdependence. Interdependence mitigated, just as later spells of trade competition intensified, the antagonism implicit on one side in the rational political assessments of the British ruling class and its superiority feelings relative to the young United States and, on the other side, in the irrational moods of much of the American public regarding things British at least partially rooted in a complex of inferiority. Consequently, as the critical period of transfer of primacy approached, it was necessary to rediscover and press into service the once-divisive affinities between the two branches of the Anglo-Saxon race. The affinities had to be overstated as well as reaffirmed if they were to redress, in public opinion and policy alike, the adverse weight of the many disparities in interests and, increasingly, power between the two countries.

Britain's regional supersession was completed by the Venezuelan crisis in the mid-1890s, after her diplomatic defense perimeter had regressed to South America from the Texas-Oregon-California triangle in the 1840s and from the Mosquito coast in Central America in the 1850s. The crisis marked a shift from Palmerston's fitful bellicosity, laced with aristocratic contempt, to Salisbury's yet less consistent firmness, assorted with patrician condescension toward the pushy overseas cousin in line of succession to the family entail. It also marked the transition from France to Germany as the critical continental-European power. Salisbury's "aggression" against Venezuela in behalf of British settlers in Guiana was supposed to place the Monroe Doctrine on trial; and it enabled Secretary of State Olney to assert America's virtual sovereignty in the Western Hemisphere. But all this added up to no more than a symbolic climax. The contest had been materially resolved when, in 1879 and immediately thereafter, Chile failed to conclusively repulse U.S. interference in the War of the Pacific with British (and German) support. The Chilean drive into the Bolivian and Peruvian low-efficiency areas matched, and in effect collided with, the American drive into Mexico and beyond. It represented for a time the strongest potential indigenous counterthrust to the United States in the Western Hemisphere. In the language of the theater, Secretary of State Blaine's militancy in 1881 in behalf of American supremacy in the hemisphere against the threat of British-Chilean preeminence in the Pacific had thus been the dress rehearsal for the American performance over Venezuela in 1896. And measured against the first act in the 1890s, the second act of the Venezuelan drama, in 1903, was an anticlimax following as it did the catalyzing Spanish-American war of 1898 and Britain's capitulation over the canal issue in 1901.

More significant than the most conspicuous events were the background factors. Thus Britain and Bismarckian Germany extended only weak diplomatic support to Chile, and even then in parallel rather than jointly, in view of their diverse economic and (for Germany) colonizing interests. Conversely, Argentina and Brazil supported the United States in the confrontation. This fact alone showed that, in the period before it either ceased or ceased to matter, the working of the inchoate Latin-American balance of power was no less favorable to the expansion of a regionally involved United States than the operation of the highly developed European one had been and was yet to be for an otherwise self-isolating America. After shielding the continental expansion and before drawing the United States into world empire, the European equilibrium helped decisively the cause of American regional imperialism when it was briefly relieved of Britain's supervision by her South African entanglements culminating in the Boer war. Continental-European and, particularly, German reactions to those entanglements (beginning with the Kruger telegram) isolated Britain in effect from both of the major continental alliances. Isolation in Europe encouraged the British to respond with near-unconditional and uncompensated surrender to American unilateralism in the Western Hemisphere, as illustrated by the first Venezuelan crisis and the second canal treaty.

The very nature of the British surrender required, as a matter of psychic compensation and political justification alike, the injection of positive sentiment into Anglo-American relations. The necessary obverse was to further intensify negative British emotions in regard to Germany, helping to transpose onto the politico-strategic plane a competition that had previously been manifest mainly or only in commerce. As the first, immediate consequence in the Western Hemisphere, Britain deserted Germany in the second Venezuelan crisis (over joint forcible Anglo-German debt collection) in the interest of placating an American displeasure unevenly distributed between the two European interlopers. A more delayed consequence was to found Canada's security from the United States on Anglo-American solidarity within an Anglo-American-German triangle superseding the narrower, and contentious, Anglo-American-Canadian one.

Other, related features denoted trends more than they determined their thrust. One such feature was the futile replay by British military planners during the 1896 diplomatic confrontation, on the drawing board, of the strategy that had been put into effect in 1812. The two military contexts had actually about as little in common as had the two Venezuelan crises in diplomacy. By the later date, the technological factor, associated with coal as source of energy, had turned against Britain in North America as decisively as the political factor, associated with coalitions as source of leverage, was deflected from the United States by British global priorities. While the price to be paid for German support in China seemed too high for the British to warrant American displeasure in the Americas, the cost of a war with the United States in North America was more than imaginary if losing it would deprive the steam-propelled Royal Navy of the vitally required coal supplies from Canada. Thus decisively supported by the strategic and material factors alike, the United States was able to treat formal status as being the primary issue in the Western Hemisphere and British concession of it as a sufficient result, conforming with the American concept of the Monroe Doctrine. Consequently, once the British accepted the claim of the United States to be the principal ''American'' party to Britain's dispute with Venezuela, and subscribed thus to the U.S. pretension to suzerain status in the Western Hemisphere, the substance of the issue could be, and was, resolved on specifics in Britain's favor.

America's successful assertion of proprietary interest in Venezuela gave her a de facto protectorate over that country. The same American pretension was to be applied to Cuba. Thus the Cleveland administration and, initially, the McKinley administration identified acceptance of American mediation between the rebels and Spain as being *the* key issue. So defined, the formal stake was distinguishable from the material satisfaction of maximum rebel claims; and compliance with the American definition of the stake would again have effectively placed the territory in question under a virtual American protectorate, even without prior recourse to war. Being able to confine diplomatic emphasis to status demands was the clearest possible

sign of the emerging American naval supremacy in the "American seas."
By 1901 that supremacy was well-established on both sides of the projected
canal. The new reality made the British surrender not only uncompensated,
by the United States, but also virtually free of meaningful cost to Britain in
terms of any remaining capacity to effectively oppose American control and
fortification of the site.

An imperious insistence on forms symbolized the transfer of empire. It
could be followed by imperial insouciance about substance on the part of the
securely entrenched successor. In the event, the United States favored the
British settlers in Guiana over the Venezuelans. A similar tradeoff might
have worked against the Cubans had the more deeply decayed, and thus
more punctilious, Spanish empire seen fit to match British flexibility about
forms. In the same vein, strategic naval supremacy permitted the United
States to wait out confidently the transfer from Britain of the economic
supremacy (though not uncontested monopoly) in Latin America in the early
twentieth century as part of an informal American empire there along
British lines.

The failure of Great Britain to uphold a balance of power on the North
American continent cleared the way for American regional preeminence, in
the wake of an abortive prior British quest for parity with the United States
in the Western Hemisphere at large. Britain's concession of regional
preeminence was in large part a function of her will to effectively sustain the
conflict with Germany on the still larger, global stage. When Germany had
been eliminated as a world power by two wars, this fact alone seemed
sufficient to restore the previously unresolved Anglo-Russian rivalry to
dominance. But Britain was by then no longer able to sustain the conflict on
her own. Her inability made it in turn impossible for the United States to
avoid contention over either parity or preeminence with a major power on a
global scale. The United States could not withdraw again into only regional
hegemony, a degree of exclusive sway going beyond "mere" preeminence,
as it had done when refusing to continue involvement in world affairs after
World War I.

The First World War was for America's global role a source of portents.[2] They were unrealized because the postwar external pressures
were not sufficiently acute to overcome domestic inhibitions. It remained for
the external conditions surrounding the Second World War and its aftermath to make the earlier portents mature into a propensity to act. Particular

2. See Arno J. Mayer, *Politics and Diplomacy of Peacemaking: Containment and Counter-
revolution at Versailles 1918-1919* (New York: Alfred A. Knopf, 1967). Also Arthur S. Link,
Woodrow Wilson the Diplomatist: A Look at His Major Foreign Policies (Baltimore: The Johns
Hopkins University Press, 1957), and Julius W. Pratt, *America and World Leadership 1900-1921*
(New York: The Macmillan Co., 1967).

differences and similarities between the two world wars contributed in unequal degrees to the basic differences in outcomes. In both wars Germany was perceived as the principal threat, reflecting the primacy assigned to the Atlantic theater. But in World War II it was Japan who actually precipitated hostilities for the United States and was the source of contention over strategic priority as between the Atlantic and the Pacific theaters. Japan globalized thus both threat and response well beyond the extent of her ambiguous role in the first war. In the second, two-ocean war America's clash with two major military powers was compounded, moreover, with a profound weakening of the European colonial empires in Asia and Africa. It was increasingly plausible to anticipate this to be a major postwar problem. Consequently, if the level of mobilized conventional resources, to be complemented by a revolutionary new military technology in the form of the nuclear weapon, was enhanced and intensified from one war to another, so was the impending problem of antiempire revolution and postempire reconstruction. The crisis was to be more complex and more extensive following the second war than had been the comparable one of succession to the Austro-Hungarian, Ottoman, and Russian empires in the first. The new quantitative and qualitative dimensions of the 1940s and '50s were well-designed to interact, and thus amplify one another, in the American perception of Russia. The Soviet state loomed large as both a military threat (replacing that of the defeated Axis) and a revolutionary agent (anxious to replace the defeated empires of the first war in Eastern Europe before turning to the enfeebled West European "victors" of the second). This completed the outline of the enlarged challenge. After World War I, Germany had been perceived as a possible, but also possibly unnecessary, counterpoise to a just sovietized, but militarily weak, Bolshevik Russia. Henceforth, Western Europe as a whole, including the better part of Germany, would be necessary to counterpoise a meanwhile militarized and industrialized Stalinist Russia, while being insufficient unless supported from the outside. The outline began to be filled out when the problem child of the first war's aftermath, fragmented postempire Central and Eastern Europe, was superseded by the entire non-European East as a likely, and sooner or later unavoidable, target of both revolutionary infections and politico-military interventions.

Even before the expansion of the challenge became fully manifest, a complementary difference between the two wars came into evidence in the area of response. The key European issue in both wars was the postwar German-Russian relationship. Some of the fundamental options remained likewise basically the same. One was a moderate treatment of defeated Germany, so as to deflect her from becoming a communized brain of a Russo-German complex, and to both induce and enable her to serve instead as a conventional military-political barrier against Communist Russia. An alternative to this primarily if not consistently Anglo-American approach was the primarily French preference for a strong Russia, participating in Europe as an essential counterpoise to even a weakened Germany. By the end of World War II, however, it was no longer possible to either evaluate these options in consonance with earlier beliefs or manipulate them by previously available actions. One such post-World War I belief was the British one that Bolshevism would weaken Russia, notably in Asia; one such action was military intervention against Bolshevism for either a non-Communist Russia strong in Europe, to suit France, or one weakened mainly in Asia, to suit Britain. Moreover, if it became impossible to reduce both Germany and Russia by a policy of severity applied to both, it came to appear equally impossible to inhibit the fusion of Germany with Soviet Russia by doing no more than showing moderation toward one of the two parties.

Offsetting such drawbacks, the change in the scope and diversity of the threat was met by an improved, concentrated capacity to respond. The earlier sharp divisions over peace strategy among the near-equal British, French, and American allies were reduced to the differences between unequally weighted British and American positions. In the realm of high policy, the differences concerned wartime strategy (and reflected then Britain's special concern with the East Mediterranean-Middle Eastern-Asian sector); postwar economic and related imperial-colonial order; and (less sharply) treatment of defeated Germany (with the British merely anticipating American disposition to clemency). These and other divisions (e.g., about nuclear sharing) between the two Anglo-Saxon powers were contained in their actual range of permissible intensity by growing disparity in material resource, compounded by the virtual disappearance of France as a contributory element in the European viewpoint. However divided over World War I peacemaking, the two principal European allies had been still able on the previous occasion to presume to supply the guidelines for the settlement with Germany and the disposition of the Russian problem while assigning to the less-exhausted United States the prime role in implementation. The unintended result had been a paralyzing disjunction of concept and capacity. The gap was replaced in the second war by the gradual fusion of military and diplomatic leadership in American hands, which consigned any remaining disparity between ends and means to American failures in coordinating concepts and initiatives for peace with evolving military conditions in the final phases of the war.

The waning of interallied pluralism had a supporting counterpart within the United States itself. Whereas both American war entries were preceded by the fading of both the promise and the prospects of major domestic programs, first the New Freedom and then the New Deal, both American military interventions abroad were followed internally by a withdrawal reflex. The American recoil from sustained international involvement following World War I was delayed somewhat by Wilsonian rhetoric; but it became complete when Wilson's rigidity frustrated the internationalists and reinforced the practical effect of the several component strands of isolationism, some of them socioreformist. A similar initial recoil from the second war was responsible for an abrupt demobilization. But it was weakened from the start by the wartime demonstration of the uplifting effect of "collectivist" internationalism on the economic depression that had climaxed the age of isolationism. As a result, an ideologically colored pluralism in foreign-policy outlooks, converging into isolation from the central balance of power in the post-World War I era, was replaced by bipartisan coalescence of the meanwhile pragmatized pluralism, responding to ideological polarization in the international arena.

The identification of a palpable external threat saved the association of domestic prosperity with the propensity-to-intervene abroad from either explicit formulation or open controversy. As the military power of Soviet Russia was observably translated into political gains and was being presumptively related to still more far-reaching political ambitions, it was seen as posing a greater and more concrete threat to American liberal values than diffuse Bolshevism had been able to represent for a buoyant capitalist America in the aftermath of the first war. The consensus taking shape behind the need to organize peace and security in response to the new threat was consequently free of the ambiguities and inconsistencies of the earlier era. Then, perhaps paradoxically, the internationalists of the Wilsonian persuasion favoring collective security were more disinclined to intervene against the Bolshevick source of international disruption in Russia than were the conservative-nationalist and positively militarist opponents and detractors of the League and its covenant.

The principal difference between the two wars was thus in changing perceptions of the Soviet Russian threat. From being a danger to domestic stability of remote countries in Central and Eastern Europe, it became one to international security impacting on the United States by way of Western Europe and, secondarily, the Western Pacific. The shift accounted sufficiently for the eventual militarization and amplification of the strategy of containment, which had been only adumbrated after the first war. After World War I, the Allied and Associated Powers had explicitly rejected a military integration of the border states detached from the Russian Empire into the allied system, as entailing a too passive posture and too extreme dispersal of resources. And only a few advocated a military role for Germany in the containment of Bolshevism, and even then only in the form of locally deployed mercenary contingents. Agreement did not form around any of the alternative containment strategies, whether overland or maritime, aimed to secure access to material resources in West Siberia and the Caucasus or inflict territorial abridgement behind a *cordon sanitaire* in Eastern Europe. Consequently, there was no effective implementation either. The different situation following World War II was characterized by the displacement of the containment line westward, while the different state of mind was eventually symbolized by the Atlantic Alliance and German rearmament within it. A one-sided and exclusive American military occupation of Japan had denoted initially a difference in approaches to Asia and to Europe. That difference was soon effaced by the American military entrenchment in Western Europe. The unprecedented presence marked a break with the purely economic American approach to peacetime influence and order abroad, such as still manifested by UNRRA carrying on the post-World War I strategy to stabilize Europe and assuage Bolshevik Russia by dispensing food as the substitute for applying force.

Before the perception of the Soviet threat as both real, major, and primary became dominant, similarities between the two wars had made the second conflict appear as something of a replay of the first. This appearance helped carry over into the later, enlarged context the by then traditional objective of American statecraft, definable as one of status preeminence, to be extended from the regional hemisphere to the global plane. The pretension to act as moderator-arbiter was distinguishable, in the American conception, from being a continuous balancer. In the regional compass, the claim had been successfully asserted in the 1890s under the auspices of the Monroe Doctrine (in the British-Venezuelan and Spanish-Cuban issues), and the role's conversion into acknowledged right had legitimized America's rise to naval supremacy or near-monopoly in the area. The posture was globalized in the late phase of World War II as part of the reluctance to take sides and "gang up" with the British against the Russians; and it was placed under the aegis of a nuclear supremacy or near-monopoly that would be raised above suspicion by the essential disinterestedness of its possessor. As long as the British side held up, American preeminence in upholding world order could be had and kept on the cheap. It would be institutionalized in a new international organization, while the nuclear asset would be demonstrated to the Soviet Union (in ending the war in Japan) after it had been denied as much as possible to Britain following the shift of research and development to the United States. In such a setting, an evenhanded American moderation between the two unequally close allies would keep a ceiling on the resurgent rivalry between the declining colonial-imperial sea power and the rising land-power empire in Europe and in the adjoining Middle East and West Asia. The rivalry would not prevent the United States from advancing its own interests selectively in the Middle East and beyond, if only as the unavoidable side effect of its opposition to classic forms of colonial imperialism. Last but not least, the Anglo-Soviet conflict would augment the weight that American material superiority would bring to bear on both war-enfeebled contestants in the service of a liberalized economic order, inherently favorable to the comparatively advantaged power.

Such a perspective was in large part merely implicit in attitudes and situations and was only fragmentarily expressed in particular tactics and strategies. It was not intrinsically different in kind and aspiration from Wilson's vision of a United States that would be at once dominant in moral authority and insulated by the legal-institutional device of the League of Nations from contentious and corrupting power politics. All that is necessary is to substitute the anticipated Anglo-Russian for the superannuated Anglo-French rivalry, the United Nations for the League, American nuclear monopoly for naval primacy, and a superficially different Rooseveltian for the authentically Wilsonian mode of the will-to-power in conditions under which only the United States escaped material decimation.

The quantitative change was one of scale and scope. It was bound up with the enlargement of the relevant stage and with the intervening growth in the absolute power of the United States and its relative superiority over the capabilities of other states. A qualitative change, tantamount to a new kind of involvement, occurred only with the collapse of the postulate combining overall American preeminence with the dominance of the Anglo-Russian conflict. Once Britain and the surviving British empire revealed themselves materially deficient for "superpower" status, the United States became automatically the key litigant with the rising empire, even before fully succeeding as residuary legatee to a declining one. Some contest over the many positions of power that had been evacuated as a result of World War II was unavoidable. But if succession to Britain globally had long been anticipated in the United States as a sequence to superseding her regionally, and may even have been half-consciously fostered in the economic and nuclear-technological fields during and immediately after World War II, the actual timing and setting of the *translatio imperii* may still have come initially as a not altogether welcome surpise.

In the critical first year of the "American century," Britain turned away from what was to be the last real opportunity to reverse by a diplomatic revolution the process of naval devolution in the Western Hemisphere. Such a revolution would have linked the future of Britain as an overseas empire to a predominant European land power, at first in Asia. The British chose to assess in their way the different structural impediments and sentimental complexities of an Anglo-German as against an Anglo-American entente. The assessment insured that their displacement in the Western Hemisphere would carry within it the makings of imperial devolution to the United States also on a worldwide scale. The British Empire continued to appear for some time and over two world wars as a prime actor. But it was henceforth more significant as a mere screen or buffer interposed between, and either battered or eroded by, the rivals for the next world empire combining continental land mass with industrial mass production. The rivalry between the United States and Germany was largely concealed when it was not being enacted in two brief spells of open warfare. By contrast, the contention with Soviet Russia soon became overt, and was to unfold within a more intricate pattern of modes and stages over an indefinite period of time.

VI

THE UNITED STATES, RUSSIA, AND GERMANY.
Catastrophe or Concert

A key difference between the two world wars turns on the nature of the threat arising out of each, and its bearing on the United States and American-Soviet relations. The difference embraces the two meanings of the word "revolutionary" in international relations, as entailing the pursuit of radical change in the distribution of either "national" power among states or "class" power within states.

In the aftermath of World War I, Allied apprehensions were over Bolshevism's threat to the social order in Central and Eastern Europe. Bolshevik Russia herself offered no immediate military threat to Western Europe, while military dangers resided less in an immediate imbalance of power and more in an asymmetry between two classes of great powers. On one side were the effective but internally eroded military capabilities of the "satisfied" powers in Western Europe (mainly France and secondarily Britain); on the other side were the artificially, and thus only temporarily, eliminated superior potential capabilities of the "dissatisfied" powers in Central and Eastern Europe (primarily Germany and secondarily Soviet Russia). The corresponding juxtaposition at the end of World War II was one of a genuine vacuum of indigenous power in Central and Western Europe with the both mobilized and apparently readily usable effective military power of the Soviet Union. In terms of European capabilities alone, and discounting the American military capacity for its demobilization, the situation following the Second World War was thus on the face of it even more precarious than it had been after the removal of restraints on Germany and the Soviet military recovery following World War I.

The military imbalance in Europe in favor of an ostensibly revisionist state worked to reduce or altogether nullify the practical significance of another reversal, as regards social revolution. In the aftermath of the first war, social upheaval was relatively authentic as both a force and a threat in important parts of Central and Eastern Europe. It was much weaker and virtually nonexistent as a preponderant and autonomous political force following the second and more destructive war in any part of a Europe that had been depleted of all spontaneous mass energy, including the revolutionary one. The post-World War I revolutionary ferment was gradually absorbed within the affected countries, aided by the stalemate between external encouragement (by the Soviets) and external opposition (American and Western European). Thereafter, Europe was mainly subject to a delayed threat of forcible territorial revision, whenever asymmetry in the makeup of power would yield to imbalance of usable power in favor of an unshackled German (or fully deployed Russian) potential. The more immediate threat following World War II resided in the capacity of mobilized Soviet power, if unchecked by countervailing strength, to go on filling in an ever-widening orbit the vacuum of authentic popular revolution with its surrogate in the form of militarily backed putschist subversion. That danger faded with effective American reinvolvement, which spurred Western European economic recovery, while the resulting polarization of forces converging on Europe from the outside kept in check any temptation to reactivate indigenous territorial revisionisms in her central and eastern parts.[1]

The Soviet threat, as perceived in the West, could be disputed. But, as a determinant of actions and events, its perception was independent of the threat's genuineness. And since the ensuing Soviet-American conflict is comprehensible in terms of existing structures independently of apparently precipitating manifest events, the problem of responsibility for its initiation is further downgraded.

---

1. The political results fomented in due course an academic species of revisionism that would downgrade postwar Soviet capabilities and intentions and upgrade both the sociorevolutionary potential in Europe, mainly by equating resistance to German occupation with revolution, and its status as the primary threat in American end-of-war perceptions. This branch of "revisionism" was largely an effort to reinterpret World War II events in terms of World War I categories, themselves informed by the awareness of later events. It differs from an attempt to compare and contrast the two sets of events with a view to both similarities and differences. For the "revisionist" thesis see Gabriel Kolko, *The Politics of War: The World and United States Foreign Policy 1943-1945* (New York: Random House, 1969); its World War I foil is Arno J. Mayer's *Politics and Diplomacy of Peacemaking: Containment and Counterrevolution at Versailles 1918-1919* (New York: Alfred A. Knopf, 1967).

The so-called Cold War between the United States and the Soviet Union was both a prolongation of World War II and a mechanism for dealing with the issues that the global conflict had either failed to resolve or itself engendered. As such, the Cold War was an essentially unavoidable event in the prevailing circumstances. Two late-developing and finally ascendant huge wing powers were drawn into contest over intermediate vacuums of power and control as part of a formally unregulated succession to the older and more narrowly based, either defeated or nominally victorious but declining, powers at the henceforth passive center of the enlarged international system. The conflict was thus rooted in the basic and fundamentally simple structure of power and of its absence. It was aggravated by more particular disparities which constituted the second-higher structural plane and undergirded, at mid-range, the third or surface level of specific actions and events. The second-level disparities aggravated the conflict by impeding its resolution by a policy that is as simple conceptually as it is hard to evolve in practice. Such a solution is an agreed-upon partition of a de facto inheritance that would express the rightful claims of the successor powers, based on wartime performance and continuing needs for mutual security, while reflecting their present capacity to resolve the succession issue forcibly.

The two key disparities between the United States and the Soviet Union were only intensified by ideological and other value differences, although existing and acting independently of them. They comprised, one, the latent land-sea power schism, overlaid and modified but not abrogated by airborne technology and related strategic options; and two, the more manifest incongruity between a superior but largely potential power capability and an inferior but comparatively more mobilized (and politically usable) one. Whereas the second-named disparity recalled the interwar equations, the first-named one reactivated the classic and recurrent conflict between differentially situated and equipped states, one of them a continental heartland power and the other an offshore insular power, over the intermediate rimlands. Its updated guise was conveyed, without being analytically and prescriptively clarified, in the contrast between American open-door universalism—or "imperialism"—and Soviet exclusivist—or "defensive/antiimperialist"—regionalism. There were crucial differences with earlier antecedents, however. When compared with earlier offshore insular sea powers—such as Venice in relation to Italy, England to the European continent, or Japan to the Asian mainland—the United States facing Eurasia was also a continent-sized land power in its own right. It was consequently capable of both meeting and possibly outmatching the heartland power on *its* own ground. Nor was the similarity with the interwar asymmetric balance of actual vs. potential military power in any way complete. If the initially more mobilized but inherently weaker Soviet Union was, like interwar France, a victor state, so was, unlike its German analogue, the initially demobilized (or demobilization-prone) but inherently stronger United States. Both new superpowers were, consequently, entitled to "legitimate" self-assertion. Moreover, the Soviet Union was also an indefinitely rising power unlike France and more so than Germany; and it was such both absolutely and, in its self-perception, relative to the United States. It enjoyed, therefore, the freedom to manipulate relevant time-spans and methods for either relaxing or removing altogether any external and internal limits on effective self-assertion. As for the United States, it was—or saw itself as being—a defensive-conservative power rather than (like interwar Germany) a revisionist one, subject only to freely adjustable self-imposed constraints on the full deployment of its material capabilities.

As a result of these differences, the two key asymmetries had different consequences than previously. In earlier contexts, they were conducive to periods of only latent hostility until the uneasy artificial stand-off exploded in violent struggles over primacy and dominance. In the later setting, they favored, instead, a protracted Soviet-American conflict on a fluctuating but essentially middling level of intensity. The earlier objective of irreversible dominance of victor over defeated was correspondingly muted into one of "coexistence" on the basis of mutually acceptable parity of sorts between the two powers. The process of dynamic adjustment did not rule out a provisionally stabilized preeminence of the initially superior power, however, any more than it would incline the inferior party to accept such preeminence indefinitely or make for an easy success of contentious negotiations between the parties at the beginning of the process.

At that stage, both the parity and the preeminence formulas for conflict resolution were subject to near-intractable structural impediments. Parity required most immediately a distribution of spheres of influence that would convey equal status, reflect different but comparable wartime performances, and deal with unequal if comparably assessed security needs of the two victor states. An agreed-upon institutionalization of parity along these lines would be difficult under the best of circumstances and dispositions on all sides. It was actually thwarted by the difficulty to evolve between the two differentially unequal powers a modality for reciprocal access to the critical spheres of preponderant influence of each. This meant concretely political access by the United States to Eastern Europe, as a countervailing and mitigating influence locally and an indirect surety for Western Europe, and both economic and diplomatic-cum-strategic access by the Soviet Union to Western Europe, as a means to material reconstruction and long-term security against German revanche.

In the postwar circumstances, the Soviet Union was, or felt itself to be, too weak to be satisfied with mere preeminence short of complete control in Eastern Europe; and it was, or felt itself to be, too strong (and the internal regime too insecure) to tolerate an overarching "moral" American pre-eminence being achieved and consolidated in all of Europe including the Soviet Union itself by way of economic instruments. Insufficient Soviet capacity to compete successfully in Eastern Europe with the West over degrees of privileged access and influence consistent with assured security militated in favor of seeking and asserting there an absolute control; and the implicit denial of virtually any Western (meaning chiefly American) access to the Soviet sphere made the American side contest the qualitative equality of the Soviet Union as a power entitled to a regional orbit on a par with the United States. On the other hand, so long as the objective of the Soviets was status equality, they could not but contest American preeminence in Europe as a whole, even if such preeminence would actually improve Soviet security in the area between Germany and Russia and reduce pressures for an all-out American military-political as well as economic hegemony in Western Europe, which hegemony was bound to cut the Soviet Union off from an important segment of the new international system for the purposes of a counterpoising that would work both ways between the emergent superpowers.

Insoluble in Europe, the parity-preeminence issue was merely amplified by the problem of Soviet access to extra-European areas of traditional Russian concerns in the Middle East and, relative to Japan, Far East. Nor would the principle of proportionality advance the issue toward resolution. How much of a sphere in geographic scope and degree of control, it might be asked, was justly proportionate to the continuing extent of long-term German threat to Soviet security in hypothetical conditions free from provocative Soviet expansionism westward and, consequently, American backing of Germany? And, what geographic sphere would be proportionate to the overall Soviet status in the power hierarchy which, while acceptable to the Soviets, would neither fatally compromise the principle of an open even if not egalitarian international order nor seriously abridge the American arbitral role and material access as the order's presumed provisional precondition? To pose such questions in the abstract is to indicate the difficulty of securing answers to them by negotiation rather than by prolonged evolution.

If the issue of succession was the very basic "cause" of the Cold War, while asymmetries in the structures of power conditioned its operative unfolding, the ideologically exacerbated subjective perceptions and mis-perception became secondary. They could merely intensify drives and dilemmas on the plane of events and incidents that attended the origins and the aggravation of the conflict rather than causing either. Thus an indictable series of American omissions during the preceding global war included U.S. reluctance to negotiate about the postwar territorial needs of the Soviets in

Eastern Europe, on the basis of Soviet assessments, at an early stage of the Russo-German hostilities; to admit the Soviets, after prolonged delays in Western military initiatives, to a share in the political benefits of Anglo-American military successes in the South and West of Europe; to commit the United States to an unconditional recovery loan to the Soviet Union in the closing stages of the European war; and to share the new nuclear technology at the conclusion of the war in Asia rather than using it to demonstrate American superiority and, perhaps, overawe the Soviet Union.

American actions such as these could be invoked to show that the Soviets had a basis for suspecting the United States of seeking to integrate a materially weakened, diplomatically upstaged, and militarily intimidated wartime ally into an economic and institutional world order shaped to fit America's inherent strenghts and contrived advantages. In the same perspective, the cost of the strategy's failure was a reactive hardening of the Soviet posture into one originally neither desired nor intended by a Communist-Soviet leadership reluctant to put to a test its only limited control over indigenous revolutionary forces in Eastern Europe. However, another set of events, concerning Soviet actions in Eastern Europe generally and in Poland particularly, could be adduced to confirm the contrary and more conventional view. According to that view, the Soviet assertion of exclusive sway in the Eastern European area was an unprovoked, original and self-sufficient, cause of the Cold War. It expressed a deliberate Soviet expansionism into Europe as an immediate fact and into Asia in intention, which could not be assuaged by any reasonable Western concessions on matters of either material interest or principle.

Once the Cold War had begun, its internal dynamic acted to intensify its tone and expand its scope. Initial American-Soviet failure to evolve a consensus on reciprocities (e.g., a common policy on dealing with past enemies and avoiding future enmity among past allies) spawned reciprocal competitive stimulation. As part of that interstimulation, it became perforce a controversial question which of the two contestants began integrating his part of Europe into a exclusive orbit of influence first and aimed at controlling it more fully. Was it the United States with respect to the Western occupation zones in Germany or the Soviets with respect to the Soviet-occupied Eastern Europe? Beginning with the Italian ex-enemy, the Western allies were anything but anxious to admit the Soviets to political influence in Western Europe. Beginning with Bulgaria and Rumania as formal ex-enemies, the Soviet Union proceeded to tighten its control in Eastern Europe as part of end-of-war expansion. Thereafter, the Soviets moved to secure Czechoslovakia and Berlin in 1948, as a reaction to failures (of Soviet designs on the West German economy and of the plans of the local Communist parties for the French and Italian polities) that marked the end to that expansion. The resulting escalation of the conflict eliminated any possibility of an intermediate buffer zone between American and Soviet power, while the ensuing polarization accelerated the conflict independently of other reasons. By 1949 the polarity was institutionalized in the opposition of an inferior Soviet Molotov Plan to the American Marshall Plan in economics and of the Warsaw Pact to a North Atlantic Alliance in the military sphere. The actual interplay was inextricably complex. It was sufficiently so to relinquish to retrospective reexaminations the question whether American actions removed any possible Soviet alternative to all-out dominion in Eastern Europe or ruled out any Soviet occasion for further extending that dominion westward and southward.

A critical enlargement of scope occurred in Asia, when the Chinese Communist mass was added to the momentum of conflict in Europe and undid the previously moderating degree of American-Soviet military disengagement in postwar China and in Korea. The Communist military invasion from North Korea instantly remilitarized the United States as a Europe-centered world-imperial power and, in due course, helped toward rearming West Germany as the key European power within the regional Atlantic Alliance. In its renascence, German military power became once again a key link between conflicts in Asia and the balance of power in Europe. If it was not the spearhead for rolling back Soviet political dominance in the East of Europe, it was to become along with the rising German economic strength a definite background factor in the crises of Soviet control in Eastern Europe that began in 1953 and had their first climax in 1956. At that later date, America's failure to challenge the embattled Soviet dominion in Hungary belied the Cold War rhetoric and began the routinization and deceleration of the contest in Europe. Events such as the second Berlin crisis in 1958 and the second Czechoslovak crisis in 1968 were to heat up the conflict anew, but all such spells of revived intensity served mainly to highlight returns to "normalizing" the status quo and continuing the "relaxation" of Soviet-American tensions.

While the superpowers were feeling their way toward accepting one another's spheres in Europe, they also groped for strategies for encircling one another in Afro-Asia. The acceptance meant that neither imperial power would actively seek to expand in Europe by expelling the rival one: the United States would accept, and thus begin to legitimize, the Soviet Union as the dominant ordering power in Eastern Europe as an alternative to smaller-state anarchy or alternative great-power (i.e., German) ascendancy; and the Soviet Union would accept the American NATO system as the best available mechanism for control and restraint of Germany. With time-lags and interruptions, the attenuation of conflict in Europe was either caused or compensated by the deflection of expansive Soviet activities to the newly emerging postcolonial arena. The first phase of Soviet *Weltpolitik* was as closely associated with the successor to Stalin as the Europe-centered phase of the Cold War had been with Stalin himself. Begun in India, the initial phase of Soviet world policy culminated in the Cuban missile crisis of 1962. Despite appearances to the contrary, the Soviet attitude in the crisis was of a kind with the mild Soviet reactions to both overt and covert American interventions in Guatemala, the Dominican Republic, and Chile, showing the Soviet readiness to reciprocate America's forbearance relative to Soviet acts of authority in Eastern Europe. Outside the Western Hemisphere, an intense American-Soviet competition in the peripheral Third World extended first both American and Soviet penetrations, while Soviet imitation of the U.S.-perfected substitutes for a more direct enactment of conflict in the form of economic and military aid extended the superpower interaction to a new dimension.

The Cold War in Europe was decelerated by tacit agreements between the bloc-leaders on lines of division, while "third" forces on either side had initially only a marginal role in breaking the conflict's inner momentum. In Asia, by contrast, it was the actual break-up of the Sino-Soviet complex in the 1960s that eventually reduced the American-Soviet conflict by depolarizing it into a triangular American-Soviet-Chinese configuration. The precariously evolving consensus in Asia did not at first concern the delimitation of zones of special influences for either superpower so much as it bore on the permissible levels of mutually hostile involvement. The very limited consensus militated against either of the superpowers adopting conflicting goals of a kind and scope that would reduce their capacity to eschew an undesired escalation of conflict, especially if it was to be due to uncontrolled and uncontrollable third parties including Maoist China. Parallel Soviet-American moderation in Asia was demonstrated in Indochina, first and mainly in Laos and later also up to a point in Vietnam. If the United States reduced its goals in the South, the Soviet Union appeared at least to contribute to the reduction of the immediate goals of its ally in the North by failing to challenge American military initiatives in the last stages of retreat.

As self-assertive third actors proliferated, they helped dampen the Soviet-American conflict on both the substantive-geopolitical plane and on the strategic-nuclear plane. The arms race was attenuated first tacitly and later also contractually. Starting with temporary suspensions of nuclear testing in the 1950s, a series of agreements to control or limit armaments matched the declining intensity of the political conflict when they did not serve as symbolic tokens of the will-to-détente compensating for resurfaced substantive frictions.

The diminution of the American-Soviet conflict conformed to the tendency of prolonged but inconclusive hostilities to suffer erosion over time.

Such sustained conflicts produce the wherewithals of their moderation or resolution by assimilating the adversaries to one another, and by generating new forces and problems with a more unifying than divisive effect on the parties to a gradually superseded antagonism. In the case of the Cold War, the general tendency was strengthened by the structural features that had conditioned the conflict from the beginning. One was the fact that both the United States and the Soviet Union were ascendant powers free to choose within an open-ended time frame between degrees of accommodation and active antagonism. This was a difference from the earlier conflicts between ascendant Germany and relatively declining Britain and France, against the ambiguous background of massive Russia. The divergence in organic trends between Germany and Britain offered only a transient and irrecoverable opportunity for accommodation (at the turn of the century), while the still more radical Franco-German disparity barred mutually acceptable accommodation by means short of virtual amalgamation. Yet another structural feature was the initially inchoate character of the emerging new global international system, differing as regards conflict erosion likewise favorably from the crystallized and, in the interwar period, also fragmented and unbalanced, Euro-global international system. In highly structured conditions, any major change in established relationships will set off not wholly predictable chain reactions liable to compound the certain costs of accommodation and jeopardize the achievement of its hypothetical advantages, not least in the pessimistic anticipation of the declining powers. By contrast, the two post-World War II superpowers shaped the new system as they interacted while being able, as its markedly salient members, to afford putting the costs and benefits of their reciprocal interactions above any other consideration involving lesser parties at critical junctures.

While shaping the international system, the enactment of the American-Soviet conflict transformed the structures that had been largely responsible for initiating the conflict. Thus, the regeneration of both aligned and unaligned secondary powers in both Europe and Asia, largely due to the major contestants' outbidding one another in search for support, went far toward eliminating the vacuum of power between the two victor states. The increasingly autonomous, restored or new, powers in intermediate zones recreated a buffer while also giving rise to changing sets of dynamic tripartite or triangular relations on less-than-ultimate issues. The result was to restrain simple expansive or counterexpansive responses between the two major antagonists by introducing concern for the effect of any particular action on the position or attitude of "third" parties.

The recovery of the Western European powers and of Japan was the most substantial material change. But, in terms of politico-diplomatic relations and attitudes, it was the resurgence of China as an independent actor that transformed the American-Soviet conflict most strikingly. Before Communist China in part advanced and was in part promoted to the status of a third "responsible" world power, the United States had perceived the Soviet and Chinese threats as closely interrelated. The challenges of the two Communist powers were either added up in the notion of a monolithic Sino-Soviet bloc or they were treated, at a later stage, as supplemental to one another. That is to say, when the Soviet threat was perceived as declining in Europe, Chinese threat was seen as rising by the same degree in Asia and produced a corresponding shift in the American containment effort. The American perception of the Sino-Soviet threat could (and did) change from an additive or supplemental to a subtractive one only when open Sino-Soviet rivalry found military expression in border hostilities and nuclear tension, and a correspondingly chastened China started becoming or behaving as a conventional power willing to replace internally-motivated ideological agitation over an imaginary security problem with diplomatic adjustments to a genuine one. At that point, the United States would be concerned with only the measure of threat from the two Communist great powers that survived subtracting the immediately smaller from the immediately greater one. The situation would obtain so long as the two Communist powers continued to oppose and thus partially neutralize one another while seeking, as a consequence, to strengthen their respective positions by competing over degrees of accommodation with the United States.

The resulting American advantage was greatest in Asia, with side effects elsewhere. It was partially offset by the fluctuating Soviet capacity to act on the less acute cleavages between the United States and its increasingly autonomous, and in part alienated, Western European and Japanese allies. The even more limited converse American capacity, in relation to Soviet dependents in Eastern Europe, was to a degree supplemented by China's ability to intrude herself into the relationships of the Soviets with both the Eastern and the Western European states. The complexity of relationships and difficulty of calculating outcomes dampened any existing American propensity to exploit the Sino-Soviet rupture for more than routine diplomtic advantages of a tactical nature. Too venturesome attempts, even if successful, were seen as liable to upset political and military-nuclear stability on the great-power level while jeopardizing the emergent possibility of concerted Soviet-American actions in relation to either over-assertions of authority or its breakdowns in the politically and economically less developed world areas, and their possible exploitation by China.

However slow and partial, reciprocal assimilation between the key rivals, and the generation of lastingly uncontrollable third-force elements typical of protracted conflicts, eased both the succession problem related to power vacuums and the disparity or asymmetry in the capacity of the two contestants to legitimately assert interests and both effectively and responsibly uphold them. The convergence got underway when the Soviet Union began to ascend to nuclear status by the end of the 1940s, to the status of a globally active power beginning with the mid-1950s, and to the status of a respectable maritime power beginning with the (end of the) 1960s, while pursuing industrialization all along. As a result, by the early 1970s, the Soviet Union drew closer to the status of the United States as a multiregional power in terms of influence, and as an imperial power in terms of both influence and experience, while failing to decisively narrow its distance from the United States in productive agriculture and in technologically innovative industry within key sectors of the civilian economy.

The evolution laid structural and attitudinal bases for changes in behavior on both sides, as part of essays to reexamine the possibilities of American-Soviet reciprocity. Such reciprocity could bear, in principle, on different (diplomatic and economic) kinds of access to the respective spheres of influence; and two, on assuming the costs and risks inherent in any attempts to reverse interstimulation, which had intensified the Cold War, into conflict-dampening "disengagement," which had been vainly because prematurely propounded in the period of intense competition. Realigning "access" meant augmenting the political risks flowing from both residual old, and emergent new, forms of asymmetry in the respective capacities and opportunities of the two powers to seek and secure unilateral gains; and selectively "disengaging" meant reducing symmetrically military forces in being in Europe and military aid to dependents in the Third World in general and in its conflict-prone sectors such as the Middle East in particular.

Although they were tentative and reversible, the changes modified none the less profoundly the circumstances within which the alternatives of parity, preeminence, and hegemony had previously instigated the American-Soviet contest. A mere preeminence of one power is difficult to stabilize in a polarized relationship of two powers; it will either progress toward one-power hegemony or recede into a more evenly balanced relationship of forces. The American-Soviet relationship has moved toward the parity-side of the alternative as the Soviets have advanced toward quantitative equality in weapons and, more unevenly developing, qualitative symmetry as a naval-industrial-imperial power with an expanding range of interests. This development eased, without resolving, the previously wholly intractable problem of defining and implementing proportionality between an inferior and a superior power, notably in regard to regional spheres of influence, not least by narrowing the gap between proportionality and overall parity.

If preeminence of one power is hard to stabilize in a polarized relationship, it is both typical and stabilizing for a more pluralistic configuration.

Such a system will include a "first" or "foremost" power apt to manage the balance of power or a concert of powers on the strength of its capacity to exercise the greatest range of options among the great-power "equals." The range of options differs from the range of so-called vital interests, to a point where the two can become diametrically opposed to one another. The range of interests increases with degrees of preeminence in a polarized situation, while the variety of options results from a globally salient state having a more limited direct stake in a wide range of specific situations than do other great or middle powers. Accordingly, whatever the United States had lost to the Soviet Union in the two-power relationships could be partially or even entirely offset by developments toward a multipolar situation. China was among the new forces that expanded the range of American options relative to those of the Soviet Union. So long as her basically anti-Soviet stance continued, China played in the global context the role of comparable land powers in the earlier, regional-hemispheric phase of American foreign policy. France and Germany succeeded one another as the land powers weighing on America's first imperial rival, Great Britain, and promoted thus Anglo-American convergence on terms favorable to the United States. Similarly, so long as China weighed on the Soviet Union by herself alone or in possible combination with Russia's European neighbors, she promoted Soviet readiness to move closer to the United States and America's ability to consummate, as it were, its preceding global expansion. It became possible for the United States to assume and exert a stabilized leadership role in the worldwide international system, and to do so because of a reduction in its direct involvements rather than despite any such retrenchment.

America's chance for leadership within a multipower system was the unanticipated, and so far hypothetical, consequence of an original American failure. The failure, as previously noted, was to extend postwar American preeminence to all of Europe, including Eastern Europe politically and the Soviet Union economically. Such a preeminence would have constituted an inherently unstable starting point for a more readily stabilizeable imperial-type hegemony inside and outside Europe as a whole. The first consequence of the "failure" was the hegemonial American entrenchment in Western Europe alone. Hegemony in Western Europe differed from that previously instituted in the Western Hemisphere in that it was due to outside, Soviet, pressure and opposition rather than to the desire for self-isolation. It differed from the all-European and world-encompassing hegemony, which failed to evolve, by taking shape precipitately and being more than usually dependent on fluctuating means and will to exert control by politico-military and economic leverages. The hegemony in Western Europe was precipitate because the American contest with the Soviet Union escalated with great rapidity and intensity; and it was liable to being provisional in its original extent and problematic in its changing supports because the rush of events compelled the United States to construe its self-interest as requiring a both abruptly and unconditionally stimulated Western European revival. The revival tended to weaken America's global imperial position on balance and in the longer run by steadily eroding European support for such a position and role.

The counterpart Soviet hegemony in Eastern Europe was different and had different effects. Viewed from one side, the hegemony secured for the Soviet Union both valuable supplementary resource and indispensable security in the rear of any subsequent global excursions. Viewed from the other side, the inherent vulnerabilities of a coercive regional empire supplied themselves an extra incentive to spread Soviet presence and influence in an environment increasingly hostile to coercion of smaller by bigger nations. Worldwide expansion into areas primarily concerned with Western imperialism promised to win either strategic or political supports in "third" countries for Soviet tenure in Eastern Europe or, at the very least, neutralize aversion for the imperialistic aspects of that tenure. And expansion at large promised also to secure diplomatic leverage against any American disposition to interfere with Soviet positions close to home. Moreover, a widening range of expansion might aid evolution of a range of methods and incentives for exerting influence that could in due course be applied more evenly to both the Soviet core-empire in Europe and to its global extensions. This would enhance Soviet efficacy overall and qualitative parity with the United States at one and the same time.

Soviet Russia's postwar intrusion into Eastern Europe was the provisional culmination of the Great-Russian movement outward. As is typical for imperial expansion, the process began with the successful casting off of a major threat or pressure—in this case the Tartar overlordship in the fifteenth century. The resulting drive, while continuing in the Asiatic East, was subsequently reinforced in the West by preclusive responses to encroachments by a succession of European powers against Russia's security and even survival as a power. The Russian experience of insecurity during World War II set off a response that was also the concluding act in the drama of a certain kind of modern European history, a history that had begun when the final overthrow of the Islamic overlordship in the Iberian peninsula set in train an ideological-dogmatic and conversion-oriented imperial expansion by Spain from the West, comparable to the Soviet Russian one from the East. The intervening events validated up to a point Russia's entitlement to asserting a right-to-security against the West. This earned "right" was not necessarily decisive in inhibiting the United States from attempting to codetermine vigorously or even forcibly the forms of implementing the right in Eastern Europe. But it strengthened the American disposition to come to terms with the unilaterally evolved Soviet forms in due course.

Inasmuch as Germany was the principal factor in the European security equation, the different sources of the American impossibility to act decisively against the Soviet Union in Eastern Europe merged with an ultimate unwillingness to do so. For one, Soviet dominion in Eastern Europe meant an automatic, effortless containment of German power from the East, as well as the "integration" of the better part of Germany in the West. The evolution of West Germany into a major, and at the height of the Cold War in the 1950s the principal, American ally was an acceptable solution of the German problem for American statecraft in general. It was also a sentimentally rewarding one for that school of American thought which was least committed to a special relationship with Great Britain, even while perpetuating latter-day British discrimination between Western and other than the Mediterranean-adjoining Eastern Europe in effective, as distinct from declaratory, policies. Moreover, the situation was at least temporarily stabilized on the German side. A privileged alliance with the United States realized at last the persistent German desire for full and intimate acceptance by the dominant Anglo-Saxon power of the day. Such acceptance had been previously refused and had been therefore sought, in vain, by means of fitful and, on two occasions, forceful attempts to impose such a partnership. In that perspective, the 1950s rectified belatedly Germany's alienation at Anglo-American hands half-a-century earlier.

A German-American alliance-within-alliance enabled Germany to find the psychopolitical foundation for implementing fully her long-standing economic capacity for indirect, nonforcible, forms of influence if not dominance in Europe and outside. Such influence could no longer grow to the point of threatening American interests in the Western Hemisphere, as had been the case earlier. The new situation rested on the new balance of forces between the two countries as well as on the new balance of American interests between regional and global concerns. In a different way, American willingness, however reluctant, to concede to the Soviet Union in Eastern Europe privileges similar in kind if greater in extent than were the ones Germany had been previously denied in that area at the cost of two world wars had also a western-hemispheric dimension. Whereas the Soviet Union was initially even less able to interfere with the American positions in that hemisphere than had been either Imperial or National-Socialist Germany, its dominion in Eastern Europe was apt to be even more vulnerable over time than would have been a German sway leaning primarily on economic strength. Soviet vulnerability supplied the United States with leverages for bargaining over interference in one another's core-empire should the Soviet Union ever develop the capacity to match or outdo German *Weltpolitik* also in the American hemisphere.

If, on the other hand, the Soviet regional sway in Eastern Europe was progressively moderated as a result of interrelated transformations in Soviet domestic and global postures that did not directly threaten the United States, American foreign policy would have ever less moral and political reasons for impeding a wide-ranging East-West accommodation. One method for promoting such accommodation, opposed by the United States in the past, was to convert the initial diplomatic immobility behind the NATO shield in Western Europe into free-wheeling diplomatic initiatives by individual allies rather than by the American-controlled alliance as such. The alternative always preferred by the United States (and, in the last resort, also the Soviet Union) was a process of direct accommodation between the two superpowers. Still impeded by German rigidities after the critical events of 1956, the process was accelerated by German eagerness, following the events of 1968, to build upon and go beyond the intervening French efforts in that direction. Those efforts reflected a historic French concern, suspended by the relatively brief modern climax in Franco-Germanic rivalry. Alliance with the United States may have been a way for consummating German history in relation to the Anglo-Saxon sea powers; but subordination to an Anglo-American special relationship within NATO was the negation of the major theme in the French foreign-policy tradition in that same respect. The resulting strains within the Western "bloc" between France and the United States escalated into an uneven Franco-American contest over the allegiance of West Germany and, derivatively, the lesser coastal Western European states. The contest paralleled, and diplomatically interacted with, the Sino-Soviet one in the Eastern bloc over the allegiance of the lesser Communist parties. Its climax was characterized by French vacillation between efforts to reactivate intimate association with Germany in Western Europe and steps to restore the special relationship with Soviet Russia in and over Eastern Europe. Both strategies harked back to traditionally vindicated formulas for avoiding dependent inferiority to Great Britain while she was the leading Anglo-Saxon insular power. Their ultimate objective, attended by failure, was to resolve the American-Soviet contest over the succession to Europe in favor of Europe herself.

Part Three

THE UNITED STATES AND EURASIA

VII

FROM EMPIRE TO EQUILIBRIUM. *Altered Balances and Alternate Alignments*

For American statecraft to evolve a more flexible equilibrium or balance-of-power approach signaled the search for an alternative to the Cold War and its empirelike outgrowth. If the requirements of balancing depended on still-fluid antagonisms over both classic and updated stakes, the patterns of related alignments were correspondingly problematic. This opened up avenues for speculation about constellations and configurations as much as about the degrees of continuity with immediately antecedent conditions and more remotely rooted principles of conduct.

The new thrust of American policy was a reversion to earlier traditions. For one, it meant replacing Britain in the role of "balancer," which antedated her full growth into world empire. For another, it meant replaying prior American shifts to balancing, which followed spells of conflict and attendant imperial-type expansiveness. There were obvious differences, though. Great Britain had been a fitful balancer among many powers, discriminating between continental Europe and the maritime realm. In multiple contrast, the postimperial United States could be the more constant moderator in a global setting that was less crassly differentiated but included both fewer and less equal major powers. Moreover, the latest shift to equilibrium differed in both scope and setting from the balancing policies that Theodore Roosevelt had adumbrated in the classic manner after the war with Spain, Woodrow Wilson in a peculiarly normative way at the end of the

First World War, and Franklin Roosevelt passingly in a manner combining classic and Wilsonian features toward the end of the second. Thus, one of the Theodore Rooseveltian variants had been a balance among great powers, each controlling orbits of special influence. That particular formula was being made obsolete by the slow but parallel formation of regional balances of power around lesser local states along with the emergence of the global equilibrium. On the other hand, the variant of a concert of powers institutionalizing a balance among them was somewhat premature at best. Furthermore, the modification of the balancing process by the values and principles of collective security was discredited, despite the fact that Wilsonian presuppositions regarding the role of economic interdependence and antiwar public opinion were becoming more plausible and weighty. And, finally, no material basis was left for the United States' acting, with intermittent support from Nationalist China in Asia, as the moderator between the ascendant Soviet and a declining British empire either within or outside international organization.

Being a replay of past patterns with a difference, the latest reversion to the balance-of-power principle also meant repudiating and readjusting other antecedents. Thus the first Nixon administration concentrated on the great powers, while replacing the Wilsonian link of internationalism with self-government and self-determination with an emphasis on the mere self-reliance of lesser states. Simultaneously, the architects of the new balance-of-power policy rejected Taftian isolationism in both its post-Theodore and post-Franklin Roosevelt embodiment. But they gradually revived the emphasis of the first Taft on foreign economic access and trade, in an effort to redress the imbalance between politico-military and economic priorities as they had prevailed in the Cold War/imperial phase. Within the corrected setting, as actual or sought control was relaxed, freely fluctuating exchange rates among national currencies would match fluctuations of power and policy in the political realm. The newly displayed preference for mere manipulation expressed disgruntlement with interventionist management in depth. But it also expressed a continued, in some respects reduced and in others enhanced, American advantage in both the economic and political spheres.

As noted earlier, America had profited in her beginnings "both ways" from contrasting contingencies within the European and Euro-centered global system. And the system's checks and restraints did not operate as a "two-way street" with respect to American self-assertion.[1] In the realm of economics alone, a preeminent United States was still favored relative to others, when exchange rates had been fixed and when they became floating

---

1. Note: See pp. 62–65.

or when the key sources of mechanical and human energy, oil and food, had been cheap or became costly. The advantage was important at a time when the balance of trade with the United States became, again, sufficiently important for many countriès to induce their making allowances for America's position or policy in the balance of power. America's peculiar privilege relative to the balance of power ought to have diminished or wholly disappeared as she moved from absentee exploitation of Eurocentric equilibrium to participant leadership in global equilibrium. Since the early days, the United States lost the systemic advantages, of small role and modest salience, as well as some of the technologically conditioned advantages of geographic distance and near-insular position. Consequently, the ancient boon ought to have reappeared only if and when a fully developed global balance-of-power system came to sustain a declining America, and did so more effectively than the European system had restrained the rising United States; when, that is, countervailing among major powers held up the fading strength and status of one of them rather than acting, as it once had for the young United States more and longer than is "normal," to level down obstacles to the expansion of a minor power and elevate its status beyond its inherent, if rising, strength. In actuality, however, the United States retained major material and positional advantages in the balance-of-power process, with the result that a virtually unearned expansion was—or plausibly could be—succeeded by largely cost-free constriction. A "hegemony" overseas on the strength of a deadlocked mainland was replaced with substantive qualifications for leadership in global, continental-maritime equilibrium.

In spite of the intervening changes, and in part because of the new involvement, the United States remained geopolitically "peripheral" to the continental mass of Eurasia while being centrally located between the Atlantic and Pacific political arenas. It could, therefore, occupy a key role in the balance of power involving less advantageously situated powers. The advantage was no longer based on current insignificance and future promise; but it was buttressed by greater physical power and it continued to be sustained by considerable physical security, as seaborne nuclear deterrence replaced the Royal Navy as a figuratively midocean barrier to direct assault. As the American imperial prominence waned, moreover, the conflicts among other powers waxed both absolutely and relative to their individual conflicts with the United States. This evolution permitted the United States again to exploit the interplays. There was no longer a cost-free privilege. But a solid remaining advantage rested on the positive "net" margin of American and allied or friendly power over hostile power. As the margin declined, it was supplemented by the widening range of American diplomatic options over that of the principal rival or rivals.

In their revised form, the situational, material, and diplomatic key assets still favored the United States when the balance of power was deadlocked as well as when it was dynamic. In the first case, a Sino-Soviet association automatically rallied Japan and Western Europe into dependent alliance with the United States; in the second, Sino-Soviet alienation released China to act as a counterpoise to the Soviet Union and to compensate for any possible defections or dilutions in the American alliance system. The United States was thus still capable of having it "both ways" and, in addition, of being the hardly contestable leader in either multilateral alliance or a three-to-five-power equilibrium. Keeping the balance-of-power system from becoming in key respects a "two-way street" depended on keeping major Soviet involvement out of the Western Hemisphere, the Western Pacific, or Western Europe. America's basic advantage would endure only so long as no superior concentration of power arose in Eurasia. Such a power would be able to either disrupt ultimate American control in the Western Hemisphere directly or act in Western Europe or in the Western Pacific in such a way as to coerce or induce the United States to tolerate the extension of inter-great power equilibrium into the original American core-empire. Neither was likely to happen in full so long as major Asian pressure either complemented the pressure from the West to beset a rival Soviet Union, or diverted the Soviet posture of rivalry into a self-defensive accommodation with the West.

A "mature" United States escaped thus far being counterbalanced externally on par with its capacity to counterbalance other powers, or moderate the relationships among them, within a global balance-of-power system that was reemerging and expanding at the same time. While this external advantage obtained, the principal danger of a major reduction for the United States lay elsewhere. It lurked in something akin to internal disintegration, the perennial alternative to checks from the outside for a dominant or oversized state within a "primitive" balance-of-power system of internally not fully consolidated states. Such a disintegration had threatened the United States in one way in the 1860s, and the danger of it resurfaced in another way in the late 1960s. The possibility remained that such disintegration might beset the United States or, along different lines, its major-power rivals, while affecting still more critically many an emergent regional middle power. It constituted the principal structural uncertainty and a consequent source of unpredictable reactions for the emergent, and in some ways relaxing, global system of power balancing.

However much it was still favored, American statecraft was reverting to the balance-of-power strategy in behalf of a power no longer clearly advancing in relative position. The new handicap was or could be offset by embracing the strategy with greater authenticity and attention to implementation than before. Thus, the effort could now be more sustained and substantial than it could have been for Theodore Roosevelt as either moderator or mediator. At the same time, the unvarying postempire object remained leadership in responsibility for world order "on the cheap" (i.e., by way of manipulating net margins of potentially hostile power surviving from reciprocally neutralizing interactions of third states, rather than seeking to manage the domestic and external policies of even marginal friendly powers). And the equilibrium strategy was now being applied within a wider scope and somewhat more evenly than had been Britain's, although the tendency continued to seek equilibrium on American terms and only outside the reserved domains. The replay (of earlier American policy) and the replacement (of Britain) were a predictable outcome of a certain experience with empire. More a matter of accident than either replay or replacement was the recentering of the new postempire spell of balance-of-power politics on Russia's conflict with an Asian power. The more recent Asian rival of Russia has been China rather than, as previously, Japan *over* China. Coincidentally, America's interest, which had shifted in the earlier instance from the possibility of sharing China with other powers to upholding her territorial integrity as a partner in trade, has evolved more recently from cooperative efforts at containing the "new" China into upholding her diplomatic identity as a valued partner in inter-great power politics.

If the internal cohesion of the major and the middle powers was the basic structural uncertainty in the newly emerging balance-of-power system, the greatest uncertainty in the realm of strategy revolved around America's "choice" between China and Russia and, relatedly, the choice by either of the Communist great powers between the past American and the current Communist archenemy. The fundamental choice in any balancing system of several powers bears on whom to opt for as partner, for what precise purpose, and by what means to implement the alignment and at what rate. In an initial stage of rapprochement and accommodation, the alignment may do no more than establish "normal" relations and entail no more than near-tacit alignment of some policies into parallel courses of action. Such primitive alignment may or may not evolve into closer and more lasting connection. Whether it does will depend in part upon the degree of congruence between the immediate and the ulterior objectives of the parties. The immediate objective is commonly to contain the chosen target state within a diplomatic constellation, while the ulterior objective will be to inflect the course of the target state and of the international system itself toward a preferred structural configuration (i.e., proceed from mere restraint to controlled and concerted reapportionment of stakes and assets).

To be tackled by policy, the abstractly formulated conditions and concerns will have to be concretized by reference to particular powers and their geopolitical location. The actual policies will be contingent on a range of priorities, pretensions, and apprehensions governing the relations of such powers. In the concrete postempire situation of three-to-five major centers of policy, the dominant triangular relationship involved the United States, Soviet Union, and China; and it unfolded within a geopolitical "belt" and a set of building "blocks" both parallel and overlapping. The globe-encircling belt of powers extended from the United States eastward to Western Europe, the Soviet Union, China, Japan, and back to the United States; it could be strategically centered on one or the other superpower. The only partially separate or autonomous regional building blocks in the global balance-of power politics comprised the more inclusive Eur-Atlantic and Asian, and the lower-level Middle Eastern and Southeast Asian, systems. The image of the "belt" conveyed incentives to strategies of reciprocal containment and countercontainment (or "encirclement"), conducted by the three principal powers with the supporting participation of Western Europe and Japan as the two secondary power centers in particular. By contrast, the critical policy issues within and for the regional systems of building blocks were the possible degrees and modalities of constraints on, and compensations for, any specific gains by an individual major power. Overall equilibrium required, and the politics of equilibrium implied, that the policies of reciprocal containment and of constraint-and-compensation supplemented one another and that, specifically, the advantage of any one major power in one region would be offset by corresponding adjustments in the same or a different region with participation of states of all the different categories.

In a complex situation, the simplifying strategic choice for the United States bore on the identity of the Communist great power to contain or constrain "more" than the other in the short run. In principle, the choice could be determined by the defensive priorities of the United States and the presumed offensive pretensions of the Soviet Union. But to the extent that these were inconclusive or hypothetical, the initial choice became a function of anticipations rather than actualities, and would result less from self-conscious election than from the elimination of yet more uncertain or forbidding alternatives. And the "final" choice was apt to be delayed, and might be deformed, by opting for apparently unprejudicial intermediate arrangements and responses.

If the American priority was the defense of the residual world empire, it pointed to a privileged connection with China as the less immediate or effective challenger in Asia and elsewhere. If it was the security of the North American or Western Hemispheric and Atlantic (including Western European) domains that had priority, even a technologically retrograde China again was the only available military counterpoise to Soviet Union in the Eurasian heartland. Insofar as America's priorites were a function of presumed Soviet pretensions, the answer to the question regarding which segment of the residual American empire was exposed most depended on the presumed sequence of the Soviet strategies for global primacy. The sequence would reflect Soviet capabilities and objectives and react to American ones. It was no more given for the Soviets than it had been for either pre-Republican France or Imperial Germany at the height of their global ambitions in relation to the island- and sea-based British empire. The Soviets had already implemented the option of a regional bloc (in Eastern Europe), as either the stepping stone or a safeguard. But they could still seek to expand the regional domain overland, be it westward, southward, or eastward; and they could first shape it into either a politico-economic, racial, or ideological unit, before fully embracing the global strategy for overseas sway by either economic means imitative of American policies or by forcible means directly challenging positions held or denied by the United States. And, preliminary to pursuing either the "regional" or the "global" strategy with full effect, the Soviets could concentrate on more narrowly "national" great-power strategy by way of tactical bilateral adjustments and alignments with such countries as France in Western Europe, India in Asia, and the United States in the arms arena and globally.

In the earlier historical instances, a global strategy imitative of the dominant maritime state entailed for the ascendant continental power the prospect (and implicit risk) of corresponding long-term liberalization in its internal political order. By contrast, either an initial or temporary tactical accommodation with such a state was liable to induce internally risk-minimizing or counteracting conservative policies within such a power, while an externally resisted forcible strategy of regional or global hegemony risked to reintensify domestic totalitarian constraints. The biases have not necessarily changed since. Simultaneously, the external technological and material environment conditioned strategic preferences by placing, once again, a premium on space and control: space, for worldwide seaborne deterrence in strategic depth; control, by partially restoring the hypothetical attractions of regional alternatives to a global, liberal or other, order in economics. In such circumstances, it was tempting to implement one optional strategy as a leverage or stage in the pursuit of objectives inherent in a different option. Thus economic pressure could be applied to Western Europe by way of the Middle East to reduce the capacity of West Europeans to either inhibit Soviet "resistance" to China regionally and Soviet "offensive" in the Third World globally, or to effectively second the United States in bilateral accommodation with the Soviet Union. Conversely, a provisional Soviet strategy to secure recognition of world-power status by way of American-Soviet accommodation could be designed to circumvent the stalemate between the NATO and the Warsaw Pact systems by way of an all-European "unity" under preeminent Soviet auspices, as a basis for a decisive global bid in the second stage. The full impact of the dilemmas posed by the increased difficulty of separating the basic options when defined geopolitically, was suspended only by the reduced range of the Soviet options when defined functionally. Whereas Imperial Germany had been able to opt between economic and military-political instruments with some and for a time increasing freedom of choice, the Soviet Union was only haltingly developing comparable economic instruments and inducements. Its chief strength continued to be military, as an armed power and supplier of arms alike.

Widespread uncertainties combined thus with the provisional certainty that Soviet politico-military capabilities were vastly superior to economic ones. This state of things made China into an attractive partner in countervailing and pinning down Soviet military might, in a manner that complemented unevenly effective and evolving American and allied Western European (and Japanese) resources ot the same kind. The need for such counterpoising will perversely interact with the claim of a continental power, such as the Soviet Union, to relative military superiority as long as continuing continental scissions face it with threats or pressures from two or more fronts. Only "superiority" can give such a power an effective security that is "equal" to that of the more favorably situated insular empire. If encirclement was the ultimate or worst evil for the Soviets, America's was a recoalescence of Soviet Russian and Chinese power that would gradually convert Western Europe (and Japan) into a captive of the Eurasian complex; it paralleled Britain's one-time fear of a Russo-German combination with France in the captive position. So long as the policies of the insular power risk conciliating ostensibly irreconcileable continental neighbors-antagonists, the offshore state must seek to win over and keep detached one or another of the continentals. To avert Russo-German fusion, Britain chose Russia. In so doing, British statecraft overcame its historical ambivalence toward the Tsardom as intermittently useful in the central balance of power (e.g., against France) and pervasively threatening in one or another periphery (e.g., the Baltic, the Near East, India, and China). The American attitude towards Communist China was identical overtime, while the immediate problem made American statecraft relinquish the "isolation" of China for a tentative form of association. The immediate choice was not necessarily the final one, however. In the long run it was subject to the implications of the "worst evil" for the Soviets, not necessarily desired by the United States, in the form of a West-supported "conquest" by Asia of the Soviet Union in one way from within and of European Russia in another from without.

To emphasize the China connection as the immediate course within the limits of Chinese capabilities and responsiveness, and American ambivalence, appeared to be simpler and safer than to enter upon a far-reaching composition with the Soviet Union that would either exclude China or markedly downgrade her significance. It was simpler as a matter of short-term containment of indubitable Soviet military power. And it was safer in the light of currently calculable risks for both medium- and long-term purposes. In the middling time range, it placed the American accommodation with China either ahead or abreast of Japan's. This forestalled for the time being any marked drift toward exclusively Asian solidarity, and a new form of East-West polarization. An externally undiluted Sino-Japanese entente would mean that Japanese economic and security interests were being sacrificed to racial-cultural affinity with China in the context of practical resentments against the United States. In the longer time span, emphasis on the China connection appeared to be safer, inasmuch as it could evolve either into a consolidated safeguard against a continuously ascendant and assertive Soviet Union or into an inducement for more fundamental Soviet accommodation with the United States on terms that would be equitable and acceptable for both. In either case, it was possible to provisionally downgrade West Europe and Japan to supportive roles, as discreet pro-China weights against the Soviet Union in Europe and Asia, commensurate with their limited readiness to either employ or expand their capabilities. Only as either or both evolved more independent capabilities and postures, could they act as moderating "balancers" between the Soviet Union and the United States (Western Europe) or Soviet Union and China (Japan). Or, they could become in due course the either consenting or constituent parties to a larger unity under the auspices of a meanwhile moderated larger power, the United States or the Soviet Union in the enlarged West and the Soviet Union or China in an expanded East.

If an immediate stress on China came plausibly out of the more readily calculable diplomatic and politico-military equations, it was also subject to more elusive and potentially incalculable risks. One risk was that China's military and material capabilities would not be sufficient, and grow sufficiently quickly, to sustain the role assigned to her in a balancing strategy; that, as a consequence, the strategy would provoke the Soviets more than it would promote overall security and global stability. The risk is reduced by the consideration that, at all times and in a nuclear environment in particular, the dead weight of a centrally located "weak," but impregnable, power may be as stabilizing as is or can be the live interventionist energy of a peripherally located "strong" balancer-power. The difference, illustrated previously by the Holy Roman Empire and Britain in different periods of the

European system, manifests itself in the fact that the relatively immobile central power will weight the system down, as it were at its bottom, whereas the peripheral balancer will tend to first stimulate the surface convulsions into which he remedially inserts himself at a later and critical stage. Another, apparently lesser but potentially serious, risk concerns not so much capabilities as intentions. It resides in the possibility that the choice of China over the Soviet Union would be swayed by favoritism, and discount as a result the continuing uncertainties of China's internal and external postures. Partially sentimental in origins, such favoritism had inclined the British toward America and, subsequently, toward France and Japan against Germany. It swayed significant American opinion toward China against Japan, in the past and to a reemerging residual extent in the present, and against Soviet Russia. In the British case, Japan had come to represent an equal or greater if more remote danger than did Germany. So may China for the American system, even if her revolutionary potential is subdued by practical concerns. The fundamentally understandable and understood motives and objectives of Soviet Russia, as of Imperial Germany before, centered on the issue of parity vs. preeminence. They created the manageable problem of response. The equation may not be so relatively straightforward in relations with China any more than it was in those with Imperial Japan before, inasmuch as the technical issues of parity and preeminence are in a clash of civilizations beset by complicating "superiority" and "inferiority" feelings. Any such historically and culturally conditioned complexes could not but qualify the predictability of the Chinese (as before the Japanese) readings of the precedents and analogies implicit in the "European" systemic tradition, however culturally neutral the precedents might be in their essential dynamic.

Yet another, and longer-term, risk would inhere in the inequality of needs. This would apply in a situation in which the United States "needed" China for the central or global balance either more or less than China needed the United States for the regional one with Soviet Russia, while the United States continued to "fear" China's objectives in the emergent peripheral balances of Asia and, perhaps, Africa. The risk could materialize into threat or catastrophe in two possible ways. One would obtain if the United States were to decay from being a balancer-moderator between a Soviet Union too strong (if not contained) and a China too weak (if not sustained) into occupying between the two Communist powers the position of a passive and eroded buffer, weakened by the concessions and adjustments attendant on successive contentions and conciliations with each. Another would arise if China herself evolved even more abruptly from a countervailing third power into the benefiting (or "laughing") third party, not so much by deceiving the United States about her basic identity and objectives as by drawing America into a conflict with the Soviet Union that was sharper than was America's need and interest. With all due differences, China would then graduate from being the equivalent of what Great Britain was or was expected to be immediately after World War II (i.e., the principal third power in the containment of the Soviet Union) into replicating the impact that the United States itself had had prior to the two world wars, when it intensified Britain's conflict with Germany and Japan to unequal advantage. If China's power was inferior so far to even enfeebled Britain's in the first contingency, her far from unprecedented role in the second would be less that of the uncontrollable ascendant partner and more that of the unsatisfiable junior partner, impelling the senior one to embrace the junior's particular quarrels and ambitions to the full.

To parry such risks, it was prudent on the American side to delay the formulation of final objectives and to decompose their pursuit into phases. Delaying irreversible choices with profit requires the fine art of avoiding commitments that are premature without indefinitely postponing the adaptations that have become necessary. If one risk is to be drawn by the preferred partner into undesired conflicts, another is to alienate the neglected power into last-resort reactions to configurations that it perceived as both unacceptable and unalterable by peaceful means. The propensity to delay critical choices is tactically desirable within limits; since it was in keeping with, and was rooted in, America's character as a near-insular power and empire, it was susceptible of being indulged beyond the opportune limits. It is in the nature of such a power, as it was in Britain's, to favor partial measures and open options. The "pragmatic" tendency is enhanced if the uncertainty as to the identity and location of the principal danger is compounded by a sense of relative decline, justified or not. By contrast, the ascendant continental power, such as Soviet Russia became in the wake of Germany, will seek "total" and "final" adjustments in order to consolidate ascendancy while it lasts. Ambivalence and ambiguity were manifest in America's competitive-cooperative relations with both Russia and China. They were most specifically revealed in the combination of concessions on some issues and intransigence on others in the accommodation-détente interactions with the Soviet Union. The American attitude had its counterpart in the Soviet drive to formalize postwar gains in Europe and in the probing for further gains in the global arena as a way to clarify and concretize the practical meaning of American-Soviet accommodation. The divergence of attitudes is a source of conflicts. But it will engender explosion only when the continental state, whose commitment to a world role was allowed the time and leeway to become final, comes to perceive its ascendancy to be precarious relative to another and adjacent continental state gathering strength from a still larger material or demographic base.

Such a development will shorten the time-span available for global adjustments with the overseas empire and for the conversion of the enlarged regional springboard into a safeguard.

The situation had been at the root of the Anglo-German dilemmas relative to Tsarist Russia. They have been resuscitated in kind in the American-Soviet quandary relative to Communist China. But two differences introduced a greater margin of time available for dealing with them into what has otherwise been an accelerating evolution of the international system. One difference is the considerable present disparity in capabilities between Soviet Russia and China; the other is the continuing American capacity to withstand Soviet Russia alone and unaided if necessary. There was, thus, room for delaying "final" options and waiting out developments affecting both the great and the lesser powers. Barring a dramatic deterioration in relations with its major allies, the United States had no pressing need to do more than was necessary to strengthen China materially and politically in her resolve to keep opposing the Soviets in Asia and elsewhere. Nor was there a visibly compelling need to accelerate partial accommodation with the Soviet Union into an alliance-like connection in the short run. Whereas the Sino-Soviet split made such an "alliance" unnecessary, a renewed Sino-Soviet fusion would make it unacceptable for the United States and unnecessary for the Soviet Union, even while making further independent rapprochement with the United States impossible for China. At the same time, however, to prolong delays and indecision indefinitely threatened to convert a present capacity to wait out events into future inability to manage long-feared contingencies with moderate means. Indefinite vacillation might compel the United States to engage eventually in diplomatic and other gambles infinitely more risky than the ones American policy had shunned previously in favor of a wager, postulating the coincidence of vital national interests with basically favorable and self-activating long-range evolutions.

It is peculiar to relatively flexible balance-of-power politics that any deficiency in resource, which compels adjustments and alignments with other states, can be compensated only by assuming commensurate risks; that the measure of specific concessions that can be safely made in the process to some states is a function of the added strength or advantage to be derived from constellations including other or more states; and that, to be safe, accommodation with a past major rival requires the concurrent dispersal of material capability to lesser states and secondary (or ulterior) rivals so that they, or the resulting configuration, may serve as partial reinsurance against the failure of such accommodation. Immediate tactical calculations and considerations will supply the incentives to the conspicuous interactions of the balance of power. But these will commonly only screen more basic, or organic, transformations in capabilities and energies and consequent stimuli to action. Next to perceived disparities in the rates of growth and decline, more or less latent structural cleavages are among the "basic" factors that tend to identify and polarize adversaries, before inducing efforts at accommodation.

In the post-Cold War/imperial phase, the cleavages comprised both the waning schism between land and sea powers and the waxing split between the industrial and the only industrializing (and wholly backward) countries. In terms of the maritime-continental dichotomy, China figured most conveniently as the land-based ally of an essentially defensive American sea power, contributing transfrontier pressures against the ascendant Soviet continental state with expanding maritime capabilities and overseas ambitions. Alternatively, China's active involvement, including an initial and potentially developing maritime capacity, could be viewed as stabilizing a three-power-plus global equilibrium, and a quadripartite interplay (including Japan) in Asia, wherein Soviet Russia and the United States were the alternately expansionist and assertive rivals combining major naval capability with massive continent-sized land base. By comparison, it was less likely that China would soon become the leading antagonist of the United States and the Soviet Union in their shared capacity as global maritime powers with a stake in unrestricted freedom of navigation on the high seas, on the basis of her identity as a coastal state with claims to far-flung offshore resources.

The second cleavage is between industrial and nonindustrial countries. In those terms a protracted "normalization" of China's relations with the United States would tend to disqualify her politically as leader of the remaining "revolutionary" third-world segment. It might also help make her increasingly irrelevant as a developmental model for the economically least privileged, even while the materially more favored sectors of the Third World became more prosperous economically and more pragmatic and pluralistic in politics. Such perspectives could not but condition China's commitment to the American connection. Conversely, it would be America's turn to be estranged from an economically stagnant (and politically disaffected) China, bidding for intensified active leadership of the least developing and most "revolutionary" elements in the Third World. Such a trend was apt to intensify American-Soviet rapprochement. The rapprochement would mean that an economically industrialized (and politically "liberalized"?) Soviet Union moved to become part of the "North" within a South-North cleavage that had received an operative politico-military significance from China's recommitment to radical "South." So motivated, Soviet-American rapprochement would differ in its conditions and potentialities from one due to the opposite trend in China's developments, making for a major developmental advance in China's military as well as economic capabilities along conventional or orthodox lines. At some point, such a development might be sufficient to attract or intimidate adjacent Asian powers (headed or not by Japan) and divert them from their Western economic and political attachments, while eliciting a defensive reflex in the Soviet Union sufficiently acute to push it westward and away from its "ideological" commitments. A Northern affiliation for the Soviet Union on essentially economic grounds would then be either replaced or catalyzed by a Western or European affiliation on grounds of security. If both reorientations might have moderating political consequences for the Soviet state internally, a recoil from China-led Asia was at least as likely to exacerbate the racial overtones of the Russian outlook externally.

In principle and in different time frames, then, America's strategy as leader in equilibrium entailed two possible choices. One was in favor of the closest obtainable alignment with China within a both relatively and increasingly flexible, nonpolarized and nonideological (and nonracial), international system. Such a system would replace the interstate relations once frozen by the Cold War and focused on the United States as the one paramount world power. The choice was indicated while the twin threat of Soviet assertiveness and Sino-Soviet recoalescence was in being. In the longer term, a far-reaching accommodation with the Soviet Union extending beyond accommodation to virtual or actual alliance was a possible and possibly imperative choice within a future international system at once expanding and repolarizing. In such a case the flexible postempire politics of the balance of power would prove to have been only an interlude, postponing the need for more fundamental adjustments, somewhat as the Bismarckian diplomacy had merely deferred the quandaries of the Wilhelminian phase for Britain and Germany in the past. The issues raised by the definition and implementation of all-round parity would then involve the United States with a Soviet Union near-equal in some respects and near-superior in others. Only in a still more remote future could the parity issue practically arise with respect to a China that had taken off into a growth faster than the Soviet Union's while the Soviet Union survived, or another power concentration arose, as a third-party threat precipitating the Sino-American parity quest. How to delimit meanwhile the scope and the rate of the U.S.-Soviet quest for parity was a function of the flexible balancing of power, so long as it was the dominant mode and concern of international politics. Not the least reason for such "dependency" was the necessary American regard for measuring concessions to the Soviet Union against the sensitivities and the counterweight potential of China.

Issues surrounding American-Soviet parity would become the dominating determinant within an international system that had evolved toward a new polarization, not least because concert on parity would become the precondition of a "constructive" superpower response to the new polarity. The success or failure of the parity quest and the kind and intensity of the new polarity would then be to a large extent interdependent; and the time margin available for making "final" choices would be foreshortened by the rising need of one or the other party for definite reassurances and definitive commitments. In a context tending to South-North polarization, the American disposition to offer inducements to the Soviet Union would be likely to grow with Soviet responsiveness and receptivity. Any Soviet effort to exploit the new schism, on the other hand, would tend to dislocate the foundations of the South-North cleavage itself by encouraging divisive American concessions to the South. The American dispositions vis-à-vis the Soviet Union would be less reliably forthcoming in a setting fraught with the new racial or cultural version of East-West polarity. A conclusive American denial of parity to the Soviet Union in such a setting would tend, in conformity with past precedents, to elicit a forcible or hegemonial Soviet bid for redress. Such a bid would respond to the foreshortening of the Soviet ascendancy phase, and be an alternative to Sino-Soviet recoalescence on China's terms, in conditions that threatened the Soviets with "encirclement" between a rigidly uncompromising (also because decadent?) United States (or West) and an unforgivingly revisionist China (or East).

Prior to any such new rigidities, a revival of more flexible balancing and a consequent resurgence of new alignment alternatives might well resurrect also the practical functions of alliances and alignments in the balance of power that had been dormant during the Cold War. The key, regulatory role of alliances with respect to the balance of power was only marginal in Cold War alliances, with the exception of the limited departures from alliance orthodoxy into independent initiatives and postures by France on the side of the Atlantic Alliance and Rumania on the side of the Warsaw Pact. The regulatory function was in the main subordinate to the role of alliances in maintaining the basic balance of military power by means of reciprocal deterrence, in moderating the scope and impact of organic transformations within and among (notably the Western) allies along the rise-decline curve, and in containing intraalliance conflicts of interests and attitudes now only including those that survived from the cleavage between mercantile-maritime and continental-military states.

The Soviet Union was able to contain coercively most of the intraalliance strains originating *inter alia* in the client states' reactions to its expanding global-naval excursions. And the Soviets could hope that the Sino-Soviet scission might be appeased in due course by a different kind of reaction, responding to the residually superior capacity of the United States as an insular-maritime power to play on the divisions among continental states. On the other side, it required the continuing need for the U.S. security function within the Atlantic Alliance to contain, and eventually convert into an incentive to closer union, a particular source of divisions. The critically divisive factor for the West in a period of détente was in the tendency for an alliance among purely or largely mercantile-maritime nations to give the lesser-power allies something of a veto over potentially costly or onerous strategic initiatives of the alliance leader, and his consequent conflictual involvements. In the emergent South-North context, this meant that, just as the British had to look over their shoulder to see whether their Dutch allies were following them into war in the eighteenth century, so the United States had a concrete reason to keep rallying the Europeans (and the Japanese) to firm, and even more to forceful, policies in and toward the South which might distribute costs and benefits unevenly if the lesser allies were allowed to stay aloof and make their own separate or private deals. Such a lesser-ally veto had an ambiguous effect on the global balance. It could either prevent strong American stands supportive of overall equilibrium or could help moderate American policies liable to overreact and shift the South into anti-Western postures of profit to either the Soviet Union or China.

Extension of interests and initiatives into the initially lower-pressure area of third-world South was partially a compensating response by the Europeans (and the Japanese) to their decline in the central balance of politico-military power. On the plane of the major military states, the extension reflected an American-Soviet stalemate resulting from the American failure to contain the Soviet Union effectively within the original regional compass; and it supplied an area and a mechanism for upstaging China as the weakest of the three "world powers" in her own right. If China and the third-world South continued to emerge to ever greater independence and importance in policy, even a less-than-thoroughgoing regulatory role of the consequent alignments was apt to supplement any prior weakening of the classic mechanisms relating to military force and conflict. The primary concerns of different parties were bound to differ, fluctuate, and check one another in a setting defined by military-strategic and economic issues on a more-than-usually equal basis by virtue of the parallel existence of at least two interacting axes along old or revised East-West and new South-North divisions. There was, consequently, apt to be both room and incentive for the principle of the "manageable ally" to assert itself, in the guise of concern with a roughly equitable division of benefits and allocation of costs from an alignment, and for the purpose of preventing any one's gains to be disproportionate to his effort or risk on any one particular issue. [2]

It was unlikely that any revised or new alignment would substantially exceed a size or scope just sufficient for success on the issues around which

2. See pp. 6–8.

it coalesced (i.e., exceed the "minimal-winning" coalition size). Just as no alignment could for long include both China and the Soviet Union with the United States, so China could not carry with her all or most of the South if she were aligned with either of the superpowers, for instance. And it was just as unlikely that the success for any one contestant would go beyond "minimum victory." Individually, any inclination of the most recently prominent actors, China and the more forward of the third-world countries, to exploit their different alignments with more conservative or traditional associates to the utmost were certain to run up against the desire of these, be it the United States or the Soviet Union, to maintain in relations with the more radical allies some kind of parity of advantage from the alignment and, incidentally, an opening to one another. It was wholly unlikely that the United States would "help" China to the point of significantly diminishing the Soviet Union, with the result of freeing China from Russian pressure for leadership in the Third World with possible or likely bias against American interest; it was only somewhat less unlikely that the Soviet Union would help third-world radicals, or that a third-world bloc would set out to help the Soviets, to decimate the West beyond a certain point within the area of distinctive interest to one of the partners, with results that would injure either the "value" or the "independence" of the too selflessly helpful other party in the future. Similarly, the tendency of effectively resisted or stalemated offensive alliances to dissolve into self-regarding "defensive" precautions by individual parties was liable to reduce the success of too-demanding third-world associations with economic goals, just as a too-enlarged "defensive" North or West (including the Soviet Union) was apt to loosen up or fall apart in revived old or new conflicts whenever it would move close to a too-crushing triumph over an "aggressive" opposition.

Even when only tentatively sketched out, the tendencies implying limitations on excessive gains of any one party or alignments are a reassuring supplement to American performance as leader in equilibrium politics. They improve the outlook against extreme imbalances in conditions that make deliberate management difficult. And, no less importantly, they reduce the portentousness of any one immediate alignment choice. Such advantages are likely to obtain as long as the process remained open-ended, because the key actors were untimately self-reliant or at least resilient. This meant, in particular, that neither of the principal powers, and mainly the United States and the Soviet Union, went into a decline of a kind and gravity that would make nonsense of any realistic quest for parity and incidentally transform the main function of the then-existing alignments. The results would be highly precarious or potentially explosive, depending on whether the alignments became again primarily either temporary covers for a drastic shift in power and influence between two or more states, or vehicles for imposing too-stringent constraints on the drive to convert rising power into dominant influence by one state.

Meanwhile, any American-Chinese alignment has been likewise subject to one or the other pitfall. It would be "precarious" so long as it was covering up for too-great Chinese material and military deficiencies, and it was susceptible to generating "explosive" reactions when imposing too great a constraint on China's local or regional ambitions. The immediate problem for constraint has been the part-symbolic and part-substantive issue of Taiwan, whose resolution to approximate Chinese satisfaction seemed necessary to consolidate the triangular balance-of-power interplay. Any first "formal" or "formalizing" act of American disengagement from the incumbent regime was, however, likely to be interpreted (and opposed) as a decision for a final surrender to one, and a betrayal of the other, party of the Chinese civil war; conversely, any half-way formal or formalized mainland-Chinese acknowledgment of such an initial step could be construed as acceptance of (unacceptable) dilution of the ultimate claim. Beyond Taiwan, similar tensions between the cover-up (or compensation) and the control (or constraint) functions of alignment underlay any Chinese tolerance or encouragement of a continuing American presence in Asia, as a counterpoise to the Soviets. That attitude recalled the earlier United States, when condoning the British presence in and adjacent to the "American seas" as a provisional placeholder pending the regional power's readiness to assert its superior entitlement. The prospect that Soviet Russia might be of use in regulating future Chinese expansionism imposed the effort to coordinate the triangular balancing mechanism and the longer-term movement toward American-Soviet parity. Concessions made to keep the superpower détente going might induce China to seek safety in re-accommodation with the Soviets; but, valid as it might be, that apprehension would give the Chinese an effective "veto" over the course of American-Soviet détente only if no other grounds could be imagined for a Sino-Soviet recoalescence outside China's capitulation to a Soviet ascendancy that American power failed to resist as much as American policy failed to regulate.

VIII
FROM SCHISM TO SYMMETRY. *Transformed Conditions and Continuing Conflict*

In the setting of the post-Cold War/imperial international politics, the parity issue concerned Soviet standing as a world power. The status bore on the technically difficult issue of nuclear parity for reciprocal stability and individual sufficiency. But, beyond and above the resulting quandaries loomed the politically yet more delicate issue of parity or equivalence in regard to readily usable capabilities and practically significant stakes. Foremost among the usable means were long-range naval capabilities, while at stake was the employment of such capabilities for asserting interests and diffusing influence or control far from the homelands. The United States and the Soviet Union approached the issue from historical backgrounds that were both different and similar, and did so in an environment wherein the relation of maritime to other forms of power displayed a blend of continuity and change relative to historical antecedents.

Until the Soviet Union broke out into the Eastern Mediterranean and the Middle East with qualitatively improved and potentially offensive naval capability (in the mid-1960s), the land vs. sea power issue had had only a latent role in the Soviet-American conflict. It was overlaid by the nuclear factor as well as kept in abeyance by Soviet naval inadequacy. The two together delayed the potential of the two universalist drives, ideological and sea-related, to reinforce one another in a way that had exacerbated the Moslem-Christian (or Byzantine) cleavage and the Anglo-Dutch conflicts with Spain even before confronting the "liberal" Anglo-Saxon powers with "autocratic" Germany and Japan. The conventional American Cold War theses emphasized Soviet continental expansionism. The expansionism could be viewed as typical of an aspiring land power and as one that reached, likewise typically, its inherent limitation in the abortive postwar Soviet bid to reach beyond Southeast Europe to the Turkish straits and to the Italian colonies in North Africa. The early land-based and land-directed Soviet expansionism may or may not have been genuinely defensive or only counterexpansive. In any event, the American response to it expressed the contrary urge of an islandlike sea power, seeking to replicate overseas the conditions of immunity first derived from its nature-given protective moat. The course of the Cold War was shaped by the initially one-sided operation of the balance of power. This happened as the United States benefited over against Soviet Russia and later Communist China from the traditionally privileged access to allies by a sea power that is economically attractive and politico-militarily not directly or overtly threatening; by a power that is geographically remote from the focuses of specific conflicts while being technologically within reach of them. Whereas the United States increased its land-based capabilities materially owing to alliances with powers on the mainlands of Europe and Asia, there were no "oceanic" allies to be had for the Soviet Union before Cuba and Egypt. If events surrounding Castroite Cuba successively requited and dashed the first wide-ranging Soviet bid for world-power status in the post-Stalin phase, the successors to Stalin's successor were seemingly as determined to move beyond the short-lived objectives of Stalin in the Mediterranean and in the North African-Middle Eastern area.

The Soviet strategic response to prevailing disparity in land- and sea-based power could be described in the terminology of either containment or encirclement. The inequality of access to allies rendered initially impossible, and subsequently insufficient, a strategy of countercontainment that would extrude American influence from Europe and the adjoining areas, and do so to such an extent as to reduce the bearing of American maritime superiority before the Soviets would set out at a later stage to match the bases of that superiority farther off. Soviet approaches and receptivity to France during de Gaulle's tenure and West Germany during the Brandt stewardship complemented the flirt with Egypt's Nasser as expressions of that strategy. The essentially only regional effort was not enough, however. Its insufficiency encouraged the Soviet leadership to add a global dimension to the quest for parity by way of geopolitical countercontainment and ideological counterencirclement. In theory at least, counterencirclement continued to mean in ideological terms matching if not outdoing the inherent accomplishments and the external attraction of the capitalist socioeconomic system. As the prospect of achieving this in a policy-relevant time period receded, the immediately more promising counterencirclement effort was directed to the maritime sphere. With the help of upgraded naval capabilities, the Soviets moved out into the Easterh Mediterranean, the present Middle (and former Near) East and Africa, the Indian Ocean and, marginally, the Western Hemisphere. In so doing, they reenacted the successive French and German attempts to find in roughly the same areas either a partial compensation for the superior positions of the then leading Anglo-Saxon power or a potential leverage on its policies within or outside the area of challenge. The object of the Soviet challenge was once again to move beyond merely token penetrations of the American sphere, such as Cuba, toward a more substantial reapportionment on a global basis. As had been the case for France and Germany previously, to challenge the dominant sea power in its element meant refusing a permanent qualitative inferiority, which could lead eventually to no better than an unequal alliance of the broadly speaking condominial type.

The issue of parity vs. preeminence in world-power status was continuously intertwined with contentions over the meaning and scope of American-Soviet accommodation. The troubled quest had been activated by evolutions originating in key setbacks for both of the two superpowers: the Cuban missile crisis for the Soviet Union and the Vietnam conflict for the United States. The crisis in the Caribbean demonstrated the continuing importance of naval capabilities and their worldwide and regional distribution and deployment, beyond and above their importance for seaborne nuclear deterrence. The crisis on the Asian mainland inclined the United States to meet the Soviets, themselves "mellowed" by the rise of a rival Asian power, in seriously reexamining the possibilities of the kind of special superpower relationship that had aborted in and immediately after World War II. The several crises transformed the issue of naval and related parity into a practical question of policy. But only the exact proportion of actual American-Soviet consensus and conflict in the second "postwar" era since 1945 would show whether it was possible to contain the contrary pulls, originating in the simultaneously heightened interest in seapower on the part of both superpowers.

Insofar as the Soviet thrust for sea-based global influence was potentially disruptive of the quest for accommodation with the paramount world power, the strain was the delayed consequence of past disparities in American and Soviet maritime status and experience. America's experience with the land-sea power schism within the European balance of power was that the schism brought profit to the United States as an expanding land and a rising sea power alike. By contrast, the schism's consequences were on balance unfortunate for Russia as both a commercial and strategic entity aspiring to unenclosed maritime outlets in Europe and Asia and a land mass directly or marginally involved in the European conflicts externalizing the schism. The divergence in experience helps explain why, *grosso modo*, the Soviet status as a naval power in the 1970s was closer to that of the United States in the 1890s than in the later decade, despite the two countries' common origin in overland expansion. In the early phase, both the United States and Tsarist Russia had been dedicated to building transcontinental railways more than they were concerned with controlling overseas shipping lanes. Their commitment to naval concerns was both secondary and intermittent. It coincided for America with the war of 1812 and the Civil War and for Russia with the conflicts in the North Sea and the Black Sea areas. Sustaining these basic predispositions was the fact that the capacity available to both countries at any time for coastal defense was undergirded by a high degree of immunity to hostile intrusions over the high seas. Physical nature did for Russia in this respect what friendly (first French and later British) fleets, or stalemates among foreign fleets, did for the United States. Moreover, both countries had a capacity for overland reprisals in more or less readily accessible adjoining areas—the Balkans and Persia or India in Russia's case and Canada in America's. The access supplemented defense with deterrence with respect to the dominant British naval power in particular.

The lines of evolution of Russia and America *qua* sea powers diverged substantially only in the period of fifteen years following 1890. In that time the United States built up a high-sea fleet for regional primacy over Britain (as the power sequestering the maritime commercial highways) and claimed parity in naval capability with Germany (as the state with the largest standing army). In the sharpest possible contrast, Tsarist Russia lost out in naval competition with Japan (as the offshore insular equivalent as well as ally of Britain in Asia). The Soviet naval build-up has been an attempt to narrow again the subsequently widening American-Russian gap. In her time, Tsarist Russia pressed clumsily overland on Persia and India rather than substantiating the British fears in relation to the Persian Gulf and the Indian Ocean. By contrast, the naval resource of the Soviet Union has become apparently sufficient to cause disquiet for a United States that was navally inferior to one-time imperial Britain in the Arabian and adjoining seas. The preceding Soviet effort bore on a type of military power that had become again most intimately related to economic and political stakes in situations short of major overt conflict. Apart from raising status, naval capability promised to help the Soviets circumvent nuclear and other stalemates and exploit the postcolonial vacuums that had not been filled to the full by either self-sufficient indigenous capabilities or a substitutive American presence.

Despite the changes, the scope of Soviet naval capability and ambition remained controversial, however.[1] And the Soviet Union did not become a primarily maritime power when compared with the United States. It was instead a navally aspiring continental, or unevenly amphibious, power so long as it lacked assured access to a wide range of remote shores and land-based facilities for either offensive or defensive naval activities, including submarine and antisubmarine warfare. It lacked, moreover, sufficient capability for seaborne resupply and carrier-based assaults, while being apparently disposed to depend mainly on territorial space for dispersing the strategic deterrent.

The differences in naval capabilities mattered. They helped assess both the likely future Soviet ambitions and the resulting conflicts and plausible parity adjustments between the two superpowers. But still more basically significant, and something of a prior question, was the current status of the traditional land-sea power schism received from the past. The relation of seapower to other forms of capability has fluctuated over time. Along with it have fluctuated the dispositions and interactions of states and empires differently endowed with military and economic capabilities. Just as sea-based power itself is ambiguously addressed to both military and economic purposes, so its characteristic relationship to land-based power will be a function of changes in dominant economic and military doctrines and practices. Mercantile seapower was typified by the merchant marines of declining Venice and Netherlands and of the early United States and Soviet Union; it differs from the military seapower of either paramount or ascendant naval states, typified by high-sea fleets and their changing extensions. The military dimension is expressed *par excellence* in the capacity to either inflict or interdict physical invasion by way of the sea in a climactic or catastrophic context. A qualitatively different capacity is to either inflict or prevent isolation from sea approaches in more moderate contexts as well. The specifically military and the broader, including economic, objectives and implications of seapower will overlap when the military navy is employed for economic purposes, even while an independent economic role for the merchant marine is diminished. One such possible

1. See Laurence W. Martin, *The Sea in Modern Strategy* (London: The Institute for Strategic Studies, 1967), and "Military Issues: Strategic Parity and Its Implications," in Robert E. Osgood et al., *Retreat from Empire?* (Baltimore: The Johns Hopkins University Press, 1973); Robert W. Herrik, *Soviet Naval Strategy* (Annapolis: U.S. Naval Institute, 1968); Hanson W. Baldwin, *Strategy for Tomorrow* (New York: Harper and Row, 1970); and Berry M. Blechman, *The Changing Soviet Navy* (Washington, D.C.: Brookings Institution, 1973). On sea-related issues see also Edward N. Luttwak, *The Political Uses of Modern Sea Power* (Baltimore: The Johns Hopkins University Press, 1974); Paul Cohen, "The Erosion of Surface Naval Power," *Foreign Affairs*, Vol. 49, No. 2 (January 1971); and Ann L. Hollick and Robert E. Osgood, *New Era of Ocean Politics* (Baltimore: The Johns Hopkins University Press, 1973).

purpose is then to impose or inhibit a blockade or another form of denial of vital economic needs; another, to secure politico-economic assets that would partially cover the costs of the naval build-up and deployment; and yet another, to distract the adversary or displace one's own assault or defense line to positions beyond the vital economic-industrial domestic foundation of military power and security.

Seapower is related to its counterpart, land-based power, in both the military and economic implications, if with different degrees of closeness. In the domain of economics, essentially mercantilist doctrines and practices render the relationship close to the point of virtual fusion, insofar as they favor navally secured and shielded access to the political control of territory for economic ends. The relation is correspondingly loosened in environments marked by freer trading across "free" seas. How close land- and sea-based capabilities are to one another in the military domain will vary with changing technology and tactics of warfare. The relation was very close during periods in which naval warfare was largely an extension of infantry-type land warfare to shipdecks. The two modes were disjoined, without nullifying their complementarity for ultimate effect, whenever naval warfare emphasized mobility and maneuver in "broken" lines over ranges exceeding either the practices or the possibilities of land warfare. The difference coincided with the high points of the infantry-oriented Roman and Spanish empires and of the British armadas under sail in the age of Nelson. The more recent tendency has been toward more fusion of seapower and land-based power. It was manifest in the economic domain (e.g., the neomercantilistic trends in claims to exclusive control over seabed resources); in the interdependence of political and economic access, as distinct from control; and in the military domain (e.g., coastal navies acting as advance land defenses; long-range mobility on both land and sea, although inferior to mobility by air; reciprocal substitutability of land- and sea-based deterrents, etc.).

The different possible relationships have a practical bearing on the land-sea power schism. It is arguable that the schism is most intense when land- and sea-based military capabilities and strategies diverge in critical respects (while the two spheres are interdependent or only unstably segregated in the domain of economics). By the same token, the obverse relationships will act as a solvent on the schism. Policy consequences can outlive supporting conditions in either case for a time by virtue of time-lags in strategic thought and doctrine.

The divergence in the range, mode, and consequent code of land- and sea-based warfare was sharpest, and the schism deepest, whenever seapower was uniquely fit to secure decisive military outcomes while land warfare abided by its bias to strategic stalemate. This tended to mean, furthermore, that a significant naval capability had to be at least equal with, and preferably markedly superior to, the one next in line, while constituting the currently ultimate weapon in relation to the operationally complementary land-based armory. A "significant" naval capability had to be equal or superior if it was to decide a particular encounter in favor of its possessor; and it could not be "ultimate" unless it was potentially and in principle decisive. The schism-maximizing actual divergence (between land-based and naval capabilities) and potential decisiveness (of the latter) were greater in the setting typified by the British fleet under Nelson than in that defined by the Spanish Armada under Medina Sidonia, in the phase of the dreadnought during the first German naval challenge under William II than in that of the early steam-propelled battleships during the last French naval challenge under Napoleon III. Correspondingly, the established maritime power intensified the schism when it viewed opposition to a matching naval build-up by the major land power as both necessary and possible: necessary, to forestall hostile military invasion with the help of favorable naval ratios; and possible, by means of deflecting or destroying the resources required for the matching naval build-up with the aid of the political balance of power. On its side, the preeminent land power maximized the schism when, being denied equivalence with the major sea power and the extension of equilibrium overseas, it embraced the aim of a significant naval capability as technically and politically possible for itself alone or in combination with the naval resources of allied continentals attracted by its substantial core-capability. A locally superior and globally matching capability by the continental state or states would neutralize the navy of the (previously) dominant maritime power and open thus the island state to military invasion or politico-economic isolation while thwarting its capacity to divide the mainland politically.

Such were the basic premises and policy objectives of both a Thiers for France and a Tirpitz for Germany. A lesser capability would be nonprovocative for Britain, but also unproductive of the decisive payoff for the continental challenger. Only when the latter's strategists would come to regard an outright invasion capability as being unattainable or unnecessary would they view a cheaper and inferior capability as sufficient, so long as it assured coastal self-defense and permitted forays against the dominant sea power's positions and interests at large. Such an essentially privateering capability can be internally homogeneous or combine a mix of men-of-war suited for isolation and invasion efforts. An insufficiently diversified capacity stressing the *guerre de course* tended to be insufficient for France before the advent of the submarine, while an insufficient concentration on underwater warfare may have been fatal to Germany in the period before the long-range nuclear-powered submarine came into being. More recently, the increased sufficiency of the submarine for politico-economic isolation and disruption through blockade has been conjoined with its uses for nuclear strikes. This reduced the natural physical immunity of the insular or quasi-insular sea power and, along with it, reduced also somewhat the incentive for blocking or impeding the build-up of the consequently less independently threatening surface capabilities of the continental power gone naval. The same factors caused an inferior naval capability to become sufficient, and a matching or superior high-sea fleet unnecessary, for significant action by the sea-worthy continental state against either the home base or the exposed allies or assets of the dominant maritime state.

There were other reasons for weakening the foundation of the land-sea power schism. The schism would fade even in technologically conventional conditions if the sea-protected insular state could anticipate falling back for self-defense upon a land-based military capability, and for self-sustenance on homebred economic resources, at least equal to those of the continental power that had either broken through the former's naval defenses or denied it critical access. That kind of capacity was beyond the means of Britain in the past, if not necessarily of America more recently. Moreover, developments antedating World War II somewhat weakened the schism when air power preceded nuclear power in introducing reciprocal insular-continental vulnerability. The addition of the third, aerial, dimension to land- and sea-based power depressed strictly naval missions to uses with more limited military effects in wartime and with more modest practicable politico-economic aims in peacetime. Even more than air power, finally, nuclear power replaced the naval weapon as one that is ultimate and potentially decisive in a brief encounter; either supremely deterrent or supremely final in ruling out ulterior fall-backs when deterrence failed; and contingent upon technological development while promoting technological change along with political policies for preserving weapons monopoly as long as possible.

If the decline of naval power as ultimate, and of superior naval capabilities as decisive, made opposition by the United States to the naval development of the Soviet Union less necessary than it had seemed to be for Britain facing France and Germany, other factors made it less possible. The necessity declined with the decline of the sea as a naturally insulating medium for security, and the virtual disappearance of a major or superior surface navy as the key threat associated with invasion; it declined also with the increase in the capacity of even inferior naval resources for isolating the United States (or its allies) economically or politically by action on the sea as a medium of communications. The scale of the sufficient "inferior" capacity could grow, moreover, as the possibility diminished to inhibit the build-up of such a capacity by other means than direct or forcible ones. Great Britain had been able to inhibit rival maritime build-up by employing the continental balance of power for two relevant efforts. One effort aimed to divert and drain the material resources of the critical continental state into either preparedness for land warfare or involvement in it. The purpose of the other effort was to isolate that state diplomatically from states that might become its allies in naval warfare, as a measure both preparatory and complementary to isolating it economically by blockade or colonial conquests in wartime. A strategy of this kind was not readily available to the United States vis-a-vis the Soviet Union in either the original or a revised form.

A revised approach would require eroding Soviet capacity for naval build-up by engaging the Soviet Union directly in an arms race covering the entire spectrum of weaponry. Its utility faded as the mobilizeable material resources of the Soviets expanded conjointly with the constriction of the scale of a "sufficient" naval capability relative to both the aggregate military capabilities of a superpower and the earlier prerequisites of respectable naval power. Nor was the existing balance of power among the major continental states of Eurasia so structured as to enable the United States to distract the Soviet Union more than marginally from the seas by mobilizing and augmenting overland West European and Chinese pressures upon it. It might be more productive to merely tie down a growing Soviet naval capability with the aid of a major naval build-up by the third powers including Japan, at the cost of shifting from inhibition to diffusion as an aspect of American "decline." All in all, the globe-girding belt of major powers had less inherent potential for aiding the United States to inhibit simultaneously a rival naval build-up and a wider diffusion of seapower than continental Europe alone had possessed in Britain's heyday. In addition, the outline of the overall balance of naval power was being reshaped within a global international system that displayed a growing number of relatively autonomous middle-sized actors with economic and political aspirations, and regional balance-of-power building blocks with corresponding implications. Both were related to seapower, and were either hostile or adverse to sea-command by any major maritime power or powers.

In the different circumstances, Great Britain had both a reason and the ability to impede the unification of the European continent by a major continental state with overseas aspirations, especially as long as extra-European powers such as the United States remained uninvolved. Conversely, the United States had neither an obvious ability nor the compelling need to mobilize the continental European and Asian states against the Soviet Union for reasons having to do specifically with seapower, not least while the overall global environment was resistant to preeminent sea-control by anyone. If the British context intensified the land-sea power schism and its disruptive consequences, the setting of American policy implied a moderating effect on both schism and related disturbance.

Nor did all the factors in the economic domain point in the opposite direction. The land-sea power schism was intensified whenever economic access overseas was seen as requiring integral political control, most markedly in an economic environment that was deteriorating or was expected to worsen. Accordingly, it became less necessary to oppose the navalization of a major land power when no one's naval capabilities were sufficient to assure full control in the face of adverse local attitudes, and efforts to secure full control were correspondingly unattractive in the absence of pressing economic need. In the contemporary context moreover, the pursuit of naval near-monopoly would be politically damaging so long as newly independent coastal states resented and resisted an (American or any other) interdict on diffusion of seapower among themselves and, by plausible extension, to the Soviet continental state. On the other hand, the possession and deployment of naval capabilities continued to facilitate political access while political access continued to make economic access easier, and might even engender informal economic control in a setting that tended toward neomercantilistic practices. As a result, seapower retained a greater, if controversial as well as contentious, role in issues identifiable with "isolation," also or mainly in peacetime, than in the central-security issue bearing on wartime "invasion." The trend was reinforced by the contemporary variety of fusion between continental and maritime spheres by way of political control, in relation to the material resources of the seabeds. As part of the fusion, some of the previously colonizeable peripheral areas became actors with offshore naval and colonizing ambitions of their own, anxious to minimize residual "neocolonial" dependence on the superior technological capacities of more or less remote major states and to hold off their politico-economic inducements.

The peculiar significance of naval power on political and economic grounds was thus continuing, albeit reduced. Along with the application of seapower to short-of-war politico-military crises in the global peripheries, this helped maintain in being some of the bases of the schism between land and sea powers. The remaining supports of the schism were, however, more than offset by second-ranking specific factors and developments that strengthened further the schism's primary solvents. Materially, the United States was not only a quasi-insular maritime state. It was also no less a continent-wide state than was the Soviet Union, endowed with large actual and potential resources within its confines. The dual character of the United States reduced the bearing of the differences in degree as between the sea-power and land-power status on the part of the two superpowers, when compared with past European states. Moreover, the Soviet Union had assured its regional base against forcible outside disruption on both land and sea before issuing the global-naval challenge to the United States. This made for more orderly sequence when compared with France and, even more, Germany; and, following the Cuban missile crisis, the both sustained and gradualist Soviet approach to expanding naval capabilities and acquiring world-power status offered no single climactic challenge to the dominant sea power. Furthermore, neither superpower could practically aspire to either continuing or becoming the single globally dominant sea power with assured sea-command in all major and minor oceanic areas. Any such claim, even before being opposed by the other superpower and the one-time major sea powers of Europe and Asia, was being challenged by the middling and still lesser states of the Third World. With respect to naval power alone, these states enjoyed or could acquire for action inshore and immediately offshore the technologically conditioned current advantage of land-based capabilities over seaborne offensive capabilities. They could thus act in principle as local policemen, or updated pirates, and collect forms of toll from both major maritime powers in the narrow seas just as Britain used to levy an indirect tax for policing the high seas. The ability of middle powers such as Iran, India, or Indonesia to practice peacetime gunboat diplomacy locally was enhanced by the reduction of a critical major-power capacity, to hold locally superior capabilities hostage to the ultimately greater overall naval resources of the global power. Britain possessed and wielded that capacity once with regard to France's local advantage in the Mediterranean for instance.

Side by side with middle-power naval activities, the claims of coastal states to offshore resources created likewise new occasions for maritime conflict between major and lesser powers. By sharing out the maritime "beds," the claims tended to territorialize vast stretches of the sea; so did the pretensions to full sovereignty for purposes of exploitation rather than communication. The resulting congruence of land- and sea-based capabilities and resources would revitalize one basis of the schism if it both encouraged and enabled a major sea power to reassert political control in the coastal states; short of such a trend, the "territorialization" of the sea did not significantly modify the worldwide trend to de-territorialize economic intercourse by disjoining it from full or exclusive political control by the principal trading powers over markets and raw-material resources. In the absence of a relapse, the offshore claims of the coastal states carried within them the potential for inhibiting the free movement of major-power naval craft and for stimulating coordinated resistance to such inhibitions. There might even be in such claims a theoretical basis for an alignment against the coastal states between major sea powers, with interests transcending their own offshore resources, and altogether landlocked states.

All considered, and despite qualifications in both technically peacetime and actually wartime context, the objectively given basis of land-sea power schism was substantially eroded in Soviet-American relations. It was eroded, one, by the convergence of land- and sea-based power on the plane of strategic deterrence, and the reduced decisiveness of superior naval capability per se in the entire military domain. And it was eroded, two, by the fact that, on balance, major seapower was effectively severed from political control over peripheral land areas in regard to the "old" or traditional economic issues, without engendering either a reliable incentive or self-sufficient capacity for controlling the distribution of political control over the "new" underseas or offshore material resources. This meant that the schism declined in importance on grounds of both strategy, related stakes, and status. Strategically, the ultimately decisive role passed to the nuclear factor. The stakes of seapower by and of itself were lowered from insuring an insular state against instant physical coercion by invasion of the homeland to promoting influence at large and isolating the adversary. Finally, as for status, the concern with unattainable global maritime paramountcy yielded to contentions over parity in world power, with important but no longer sole or necessarily primary seapower implications.

The new situation made it less useful as well as less feasible than before for the preeminent maritime state to inhibit the naval development and deployment of the preeminent continental state. There were undeniable specific and immediate disadvantages to the emergence of rival naval capability. Significant rival seapower was susceptible of inhibiting and even neutralizing the previously dominant navy in secondary missions and theaters, notably in peacetime; and it was apt to reduce or nullify the no longer dominant maritime power's privileged access to "lesser" oceanic allies, not least in wartime. But the disadvantages were paralleled by a potential advantage if the new qualitative symmetry created overseas or seaborne hostages for the still superior naval power in the short run, while inducing gradual convergence in more basic political interests and styles in the longer run.

In the main and in the meantime, however, the increase in symmetry and the decrease of schism did anything but rule out intense conflicts between the two major—American and Soviet—sea powers. Such conflicts could be expected to attend the parity quest in its broadest compass, as the rising Soviet capacity for peacetime naval diplomacy or suasion, consequent on the Cuban missile crisis, clashed with the rising American interest, following Vietnam, in an offshore security (or containment) strategy based on islands and archipelagoes in Asia and with intensified Western concern over secure sea lanes, highlighted by the OPEC-related oil crisis. The areas of possible conflict were thus not necessarily limited only to the requirements of either unilateral coastal defense or mutual nuclear deterrence. Nor would parallel developments necessarily mitigate the conflicts. Thus, the claims to extensive offshore seabeds and sea belts by lesser states reduced the expanse of the "free" high seas available to the major states for deterrence and other security uses while expanding the range of stakes of the material-economic kind. And the continuing imbalance in superpower naval capabilities was subject to volatile estimates and spells of competitive build-ups, while a movement toward naval parity and stalemate threatened to neutralize both parties tactically and cause one or both to attribute extreme and irreconcilable strategic goals to the other as a result. Equipping the Soviet Union with overseas naval capabilities was not, furthermore, a sure "liberalizing" antidote to the ideological undercurrents in the Soviet-American conflict. Seapower and the social ideology of Soviet Russia were alike in having direct and potentially reinforcing economic implications, while Soviet navalization injected into the American-Soviet conflict individual mind-sets and reciprocal attributions and misperceptions that had been associated with the land-sea power schism in its heyday.

Even an intense competition or conflict over partially sea-related stakes will differ from the structurally conditioned land-sea power schism. Conflicts revolve around specific stakes in a multifaceted balance of military and economic power; the schism revolves around the very right of the land power to overall equivalence with the insular sea power, implying more than a marginal naval capability as one singularly critical for globalizing equilibrium. Conflicts disturb the international system and help fill out its lacunae in the process; the inherently unbridgeable schism tends to disrupt the system, ultimately beyond repair within its original confines.

In principle, therefore, the change from schism to conflicts represented a gain for the international system, and might engender a derivative gain for all of its major constituent actors. In practice, however, the fact that the land-sea power schism faded, and was replaced by the issue of parity in status as a navally equipped world power, did not mean that old-type conflicts over overseas assets might not be kept alive or even intensified by association with new long-term issues. Among these figured the balance of nuclear terror and the balance of economic trends in development and performance, supplementing and updating the traditional balances of power and trade. Nor was it certain, or even likely, that the tension between parity and preeminence would be significantly moderated if the primary touchstone or index of parity in world-power status was displaced. As a matter of fact, a shift has been occurring from the traditional issue to a new issue. Traditionally at issue used to be the right to possess a naval capability having automatic and automatically assumed consequences in "legitimate" employment; the new issue revolves around the right to actually employ and utilize for politically significant commensurate ends a naval capability that the leading continental state has acquired and the leading maritime power has implicitly conceded. The new issue may prove to be still more problematic than was the traditional one. If so, the one but critical gain would be that the contentions surrounding the issue are inherently limitable and the issue itself is an essentially negotiable one.

IX
FROM PREEMINENCE
TO PARITY. *Recurrent*
Problems and Long-term
Process

Parity connotes equal right or opportunity of access to different sources of power and forms in which power is manifest and employed. Preeminence connotes acknowledged superiority, based on privileged possession of critical assets and a related role. Parity is as different from equality in only material resource as preeminence is from preponderant weight. Both parity and preeminence concern also role and functions, and are contingent on outside acknowledgment of their utility for their consolidation.

The peculiar attributes of parity do not make it easier to agree on either its meaning or the means of achieving it. In considering parity, it is first of all necessary to decompose the time-frame into the more clearly perceived present and the only prospective or hypothetical future. This creates problems, not the least of which is that the same concession may promote the challenger toward parity or propel him beyond parity to preeminence, depending on the relative rise and decline of the parties to the parity quest in the long run. The time-and-trend problem is compounded when the parity-preeminence dynamic comprises, as it usually does, different inter-penetrating or interacting spheres of activities and interests. Thus the parity-preeminence issue between the Papacy and the Empire was exacer-bated by the interpenetration of the spiritual and temporal spheres and stakes (which had largely contributed to the issue arising in the first place); and the more modern parity-preeminence issues have been aggravated for secularized political powers by the interpenetration of the maritime and the terrestrial spheres with both military and economic facets, and subject to either universalist tendencies (the maritime sphere) or to expansionist ones (the territorial sphere). Whereas the medieval contest had been focused in the dual role of the clergy as stewards of both immortal souls and incipient states, the more modern secular contest revolved somewhat comparably around the dual role of war in regard to territorial conquest and overseas commerce. Perpetuating the changeover, the most recent focuses of the parity quest were the several substitutes for open warfare promoting or impeding diluted forms of conquest and multifaceted extensions of commerce.

The harder it is to define and to concert parity at any one time between only two parties, the more attractive it is to visualize and try to implement the quest for parity as a process, and one that is contingent on a plural setting. Only a contention unfolding over a period of time might attenuate the dilemmas of evaluation and judgment going beyond sheer measurements. And only the impingement of other parties is apt to stimulate a genuine pursuit of parity and to reduce the anxieties inherent in the fluidity of the dividing line between parity and the preeminence of one of only two antagonistic powers. A plural setting will heighten the incapacity of the two principal parties to conclusively subdue one another, which incapacity has impelled the parity quest to begin with; and it will introduce third parties as targets of shared ambivalence offsetting reciprocal antagonism, and as either objects of joint action or subjects to fall back upon for protection against violation of the parity agreement. Thus the American-Soviet parity quest has taken place in relation to evolving conditions and attitudes in the Third World comprising China. Without reproducing them, it was reminiscent in this respect of the relationships of the Byzantian and the Carolingian empires relative to the Moslem powers; of the Empire and the Papacy relative to the emergent territorial realms; of the Catholic and Protestant forces in the Holy Roman Empire relative to the centralizing emperorship; and of Britain and Germany relative to the United States as well as of Britain and the United States relative to Germany.

Even when stimulated by a plural setting, to be serious a dynamic politics of parity must be sustained by an at least tentative commitment of the parties to a gradual and managed evolution toward a currently meaningful equivalence, including equal access to rights and opportunities. As a present condition, consequently, parity will tend to mean in the early stage of the process no more than a set of dovetailing disparities that have been discounted in the evaluation of comparative status, and minimized in the practical effect on policies, by the shared commitment to the process and the consequent anticipation of future "equality." So unfolding, the protracted process itself and the momentary problems of evaluating the minimum conditions and requirements of parity will be subject to various tensions and superficial contradictions. In addition to being two-dimensional in time as between actual present and anticipated future conditions, the process will occur on two levels or tracks and involve two-pronged quandaries.

The levels or tracks correspond to symbolic and substantive issues or stakes, the first conditioning primarily status and the second involving concrete assets and strategies more directly. It will matter whether first to be adjusted are the symbolic-status issues as either a preliminary to tackling parity in the substantive-strategic concerns or as self-sufficient and terminal to the detriment or exclusion of corresponding substantive adjustments. Capabilities that are practically hard to use at all or "offensively," such as nuclear and certain forms of naval capabilities, can be treated as primarily symbolic and status-conferring. When this is the case, it will be both plausible and tempting to treat the military capability and the employment of the capability for geopolitically significant ends as distinct and separate tracks or levels. If they are thus segregated, it will be possible to raise the issue of parity either in only one of them (capability *or* employment) or in a preferred sequence. Either sequence is possible if the political dividends that normally accrue from a capability can be meaningfully conceded prior to its possession, if only to dissuade the favored party from an early or maximum development of the capability.

As for the two prongs of the quandary, they stand for the technical and the political complexities that beset even a bona fide commitment to the parity quest. The complexities grow with efforts to reach explicit agreements on parity, in formal instruments or formulated doctrines. Technical difficulties bear mainly on identifying what constitutes equivalence between different capability-mixes, with the aid of supposedly objective standards. More specifically, political difficulties arise when parity in capabilities and parity in their employment are to be combined in one comprehensive parity-mix, agreeable to both parties from their subjective viewpoints. The technical difficulties are aggravated by technological change, and the need to subject its projection to estimates of long-range political trends. Simultaneously, competition over proximate political stakes is apt to thwart even a serious commitment by both sides to broadly identical end-results of the parity quest. Finally, contentions over the interprepation of both the technical and the political aspects will occur in the context of particular interests, both domestic and external and institutional and individual, whose proponents are committed to the parity-evolving process only secondarily if at all.

The technical obstacles are implicit in the relativity of equivalence in regard to the capabilities of parties that are differently situated and insecure. The political obstacles tend to overlap with the technical, and will involve proportionality between agreed-upon or one-sidedly acquired and conceded military and other material capabilities and their authorized, or unopposed, employment for political and economic ends. It is possible to attenuate the impediments to calculations of parity and consensus about parity by all kinds of tradeoffs and linkages, involving potentially complementary interests and assets. But the party starting from a superior position can also inhibit the parity quest by efforts to rigidly segregate and discriminate between theaters (continental and overseas); objects (capabilities and their employment); or stakes (national power or influence and role in world stability or order) which are involved in the quest for overall parity. Whereas ordered sequences may be necessary, rigid separations are apt to be impossible; and whereas disparities constitute the starting stimulus to the parity-evolving process, insistence on perpetuating inequality in the area or areas that the initially inferior party regards as ultimately critical will deal the process its terminal death blow. Thus, the question arose in the United States relative to the Soviet Union, as it had arisen previously in Britain relative to Germany: what was the proper sequence to observe between the challenger's demonstration of commitment and contribution to a certain kind of world order, and his being conceded an unresisted widening of national influence? The unavoidably related question was: how unequal could be one side's contribution and the other side's concessions at any one time, without prejudicing the appearance of good faith of the "superior" power and justifying the worst suspicions of the "ascendant" one?

An agreement about sequences and sufficiencies will not be easily forthcoming in the best of circumstances. It will be foiled when the superior insular and the rising continental parties misperceive one another. Thus, the relatively receding insular power will confirm its image as intransigent if it projects upon the other its own habituation to "total" security. In so doing it will attribute to the challenger an insatiable ambition for total domination, to be checked only by denials of even relatively marginal geopolitical gains overseas. The resulting crisis will not be dispelled by representing the opposition to reapportionment of access and influence as being only provisional, to disappear with the evolutionary growth of moderation or maturation inside the ascendant power and within the expanding international system. Nor will it help much if the initially superior party confuses the multilaterial approach with multipolarity. The first may inhibit the quest for two-power parity by an inordinate stress on the immediate negative effects of adjustments on third parties, while to promote the second may be both stabilizing for the wider system and stimulating to the bilateral quest. Alternatively, difficulties will arise if the ascendant party thwarts the trend to multipolarity by a too aggressive unilateral response to what it perceives as a conclusive denial of parity.

How the principal parties react to what they see as premature demands or too persistent denials of parity in capability or its employment can be thus to a large extent a function of short-term multilateral inhibitions and longer-term multipolar preconditions of adjustments tolerable for both. The result will depend on ways in which preconditions are orchestrated with stages in what is typically a prolonged and tortuous process. This means practically that, while the parity process is two-dimensional in time, spans two tracks or levels in operative emphasis, and is two-pronged in dilemmas, it will also encompass two overlapping and possibly recurring phases in regard to grand strategy. The balance-of-power approach will have to be applied in the first phase to the ascendant party, with the aid of third powers and with sufficient effect, to make it receptive to the full-scale parity process; in the second, the concurrently evolving structures will have to be part-managed and part-depended upon to sustain and contain two-power parity as an accomplished condition. But it will not do to apply balancing so as to suggest an indefinite denial of full-scale parity, and thus propel the ascendant power into trying to sidestep both balance of power and parity by recourse to one-power bid for hegemony.

As they unfolded, explicit American-Soviet transactions bearing on parity in military capabilities comprised primarily nuclear-strategic power (SALT) and land-based force-reductions mainly in Europe (MBFR). They bore on naval capabilities only as involved in the nuclear-deterrent balance. Situated in only the third rank of the weapons hierarchy, the conventional Soviet naval build-up was nonetheless a major element in the overall issue of military parity and the related strategic concepts. It was such with respect to both equivalence in arms and equality in effective security of the two differently situated superpowers. So long as the Sino-Soviet rift continued and made the Soviet perceive themselves as being exposed to either a nuclear or an overland assault from two sides, the Soviet Union would pretend to equivalence in the form of superiority in nuclear and land-based military power. By the same token, the United States, as a nation enclosed by two oceans and dependent on several other seas for its lifelines and interallied communications, would interpret equal security as entailing superior American capability in surface and antisubmarine naval capabilities. Being exposed to a two-front situation, the Soviet Union was also, like Germany before, a two-faced power subject about evenly to anxiety and to ambition, fearing for its physical security mainly from the East and for its economic standing mainly in relation to the West. By contrast, the United States was a typical quasi-insular power, unable to match the Soviet Union's self-sufficiency in mineral resource and even less in its overland access to actual or potential clients along internal lines. It was, consequently, vulnerable to different forms of isolation by increasing Soviet seapower, either in a prolonged and nonnuclear military conflict or, especially, in peacetime competition. A Soviet naval capability that would stay within the limits of overall arms equivalence and equal security was unlikely to constitute, led alone outdo, a "risk-fleet" capable of attracting naval allies or supporters to a major core-capability in the form of long-range task forces around attack carriers, these being the contemporary equivalents of the dreadnoughts of yesteryear. Barring such an expansion, the Soviet would remain an inferior navy with the inferior navy's compensating capacity to take considerable risks in relation to the superior one and create new risks for it.

An equivalent mix of the various military capabilities constitutes formal parity. A more comprehensive, material parity comprises also the political ends or assets to be sought by employing (or foregoing) such capabilities. Phrased differently, the "parity-mix" encompasses and transcends the mere "capability-mix." The relationship of capability to its employment can be the straightforward one of propensity, when capability engenders the tendency to employ it for more or less proportionate political or other ends (while employment stimulates the drive for more capability, and so on). A species of perversity can replace "straightforward" propensities. This will happen when the denial of the right to equivalent capability by the superior party makes the inferior party overestimate the ready and profitable usability of such capability, or, alternatively, when a conceded or "authorized" access to what would be the normal political or other returns on capability has made its acquisition in full redundant for the ascendant party. Moreover, if the dilution of the structural land-sea power schism can intensify overt conflicts because it shifts the key issue from apportioning capabilities to their use, the real difficulty to calculate equivalence or parity in naval capabilities or in a weapons-mix comprising them will have a matching result. It will render all the more critical the possibility to agree on the permissible scope of political or other objectives and gains, to be pursued by the ascendant party by employing or adjusting its capabilities.

The employment of a capability such as naval has a tactical or military dimension and a strategic or geopolitical dimension. In conditions short of a major war, which minimize missions in coastal defense and nuclear exchange or deterrence, even an inferior Soviet navy could interfere with communications and inhibit or deny seaborne American access or interventions. A physical naval interposition might partially isolate the United States politically from its clients in an extreme case. It would depend on American will and capacity for counteraction to what extent a risk-*creating* Soviet fleet could or would inhibit America's initiatives; interfere with her material needs; and isolate her from facilities and allies. Similarly, the rapport between diplomatic or still more active United States opposition and tacit or explicit concessions would affect the extent to which the Soviet fleet either could or would act as a risk-*taking* one. Taking risks would mean going beyond making an impression on lesser parties (by "showing the flag") to their intimidation (e.g., in connection with fishing); and it would mean compounding efforts to insulate congenial political changes in small countries from unfriendly seaborne reactions with acts intended to encourage or initiate political change or altered policies, including the grant of naval facilities to the Soviet Union. In order to acquire a presumptive (though not necessarily effective) capacity to interfere with American or allied communications, or to promote other desired outcomes, the Soviet Union distributed economic and military aid; and it deployed naval and diplomatic resources in ways designed to promote Soviet access to areas and countries close to narrow maritime passages or shipping bottlenecks as well as to "vital" sea lanes, thus in the Eastern Mediterranean, the Persian Gulf, the Indian Ocean, and in South Atlantic. This embarrassed the United States potentially, while reducing its capacity to respond to Soviet interference with overland United States access routes (e.g., to Berlin) by interdicting Soviet maritime transits.

Soviet naval capability became critical when its actual or possible uses changed the geopolitical status quo by expanding Soviet access to sea-adjoining areas or to influence in them. In military uses, the Soviet range is from passive inhibition of American action to active interference with American initiatives and on to effective isolation of the United States. The possible objects of extended geopolitical access range, in turn, from protection of Soviet national security to a role in shaping world order as one of the world powers and on to seeking unilateral influence or even control as part of a new imperial ascendancy. Some surface similarities could be discerned in the direction and method of Soviet efforts and the earlier ones of Imperial Germany. If the direction was to the Persian Gulf and Southwest Africa, the shared tendency of the two ascendant powers was to compensate by military-political means for the admittedly unequal and differently conditioned difficulty to project productive capacity into commensurate economic tools of policy abroad. Both powers proceeded by way of either only symbolic or also substantial support for remote and seemingly congenial challengers to the dominant sea power (Germany's for South African Boers and the Soviet Union's for Castroite Cuba); intermittent bids to participate in the shaping of order in contested areas ("collective security" in China for Germany and in Southeast Asia for the Soviet Union); and more sustained efforts to achieve, with the help of military "aid," the politico-economic penetration of avenues toward the Indian Ocean—Germany via the Berlin-Baghdad railway and a generally pro-Ottoman and pro-Moslem policy, the Soviet Union via the Suez canal and a pro-Moslem and pro-India policy.

The key question continued to be to what extent the initially but token penetrations would become individually or cumulatively significant world-wide, or could be allowed to become such for lack of opposition. A reciprocal American-Soviet recognition of the "right to security" for each could mean no more than conceding to the Soviet Union a regional *glacis* as the continental power's equivalent of the sea power's oceanic moat. Or, the United States could go so far as to acknowledge the claim of the Soviets to world-power status on par with America's. Once the United States had recognized Soviet right to security in Eastern Europe as part of the passing of the Cold War (formalized in the Helsinki agreements of 1975), the issue of world power was bound to surface as the main source of deepening accommodation or reintensified contest.

The interplay between regional and global theaters was likewise certain to raise questions of tactics and involve criteria for strategy. The Soviets could use penetrations in areas either adjoining or remote from their regional domain in Eastern Europe as tactical leverage or bargaining counter for securing actually preferred acquisitions, either elsewhere or of a different kind. And the United States could concede Soviet control in Eastern Europe unconditionally, or even foster its implantation in politico-economic depth by cooperative functional transactions, in attempted exchange for Soviet self-limitation worldwide. The diametrically opposed approach would be to view and even value a global dispersion of Soviet power and presence as the prerequisite to gradual relaxation or coercive controls in the regional domain by natural evolution; or else, newly acquired remote Soviet positions might be used and usable not only as Soviet leverages for securing other prizes but also, and more effectively, as hostages to the superior American sea power, facilitating pressure on the more vital interests of the ascendant Soviet state. The overseas possessions of France had long been hostage to a Britain anxious to immunize continental approaches to the narrow channel. Similarly, just as Western Europe was long hostage to the Soviet Union, so a Cuba or an Angola could become hostage to the United States in peace almost as much as in war. Any de facto exchanges and other transactions between adjacent possessions and vaster but more remote and less secure positions and possibilities would follow the pattern of the prolonged, and finally abortive, bargaining over the succession to the Spanish world empire in Europe and overseas in the late seventeenth century. And the related criteria for strategy would involve subtle distinctions similar to those between "spheres of (mere) interests" and "spheres of (outright) in-fluence" in China in the 1890s and would differ, by the same token, from the crass division between largely impermeable "blocs" in Europe in the 1950s and 1960s. Accordingly, to reapportion was access rather than control; and, anchored in a few strong *points d'appui*, access was to be either shared or competitively divided between the superpowers in a fluid manner rather than partitioned along rigid and mutually recognized lines. The issues of the comparative scope of the "spheres," and of their internal structures of control and influence were not the only ones, however. No less important was the question of the rate of Soviet expansion and the modalities by which the Soviet Union would pursue its overseas objectives. Some rates and modalities would be more and others less compatible with American-Soviet "détente," and engender different degrees of mutually competitive or hostile involvement. The related question was how far it was necessary, and to what extent possible, to rewrite for the détente/reapportionment phase the tacitly evolved rules of the game and the criteria of permissible action that had been tacitly evolved for the Cold War/containment phase. The various options in tactics and strategy for immediate objectives could not, moreover, be separated from more fundamental purposes. These bore on the question whether the Soviet Union sought gains to enhance its influence as a means to "equal security" or also in order to be able to perform a role in the management of world "order" (or "peace") as an attribute of equal world-power, if not superior imperial, status. Supposing furthermore that it was possible to reach an American-Soviet consensus on the nature of the world order to uphold, and that the United States desired the Soviet Union to participate in upholding it as a coequal party, the related question was how much the United States was prepared to "pay" for the Soviet performance or how far it could either "legitimately" or practically deny such payment in the coin of access and influence in particular regional areas.

Both kinds of questions were latent in the declaratory American-Soviet commitments to joint peace maintenance (e.g., the Moscow Declaration of 1972) in regional disorders, such as that in the Middle East. It had been a simple matter, in connection with the Suez crisis of 1956, for the United States to reject the Soviet bid to participate in maintaining order in the Middle East while simultaneously conceding the reimposition of Soviet control in Eastern Europe. The situation was to become more complex and ambiguous by the time of the Arab-Israeli war in 1973. It was then possible to argue that the Soviets broke the just-concluded agreement (of 1972) by failing to alert the United States to the impending assault by their Egyptian and Syrian clients. But the later United States so-called strategic alert, too, could be seen as constituting such a breach. Insofar as the alert barred the Soviet bid to support the United States in restraining *its* Israeli client in the final phase of the conflict, it undermined the Soviet ability to participate effectively in stabilizing or pacifying the Middle East in the period following the conflict. There were related uncertainties. If the United States tolerated Soviet intervention or cointervention then or at any other stage, would this reflect the recognition of Soviet status as a world power or merely acknowledge the capacity of the Soviet Union to disrupt a particular region and its entitlement, as still only a regional power, to be concerned with events in an area abutting on Eastern Europe? And finally, if the partition of Europe had been both consummated and relieved on the basis of conditional mutual recognition of juxtaposed predominance, was the actually conducted American policy in the Middle East pointing to the goal of a jointly performed superpower role in the maintenance of regional order and peace, to a system of mutually tolerated privileged access by each superpower to different local parties, or to the pursuit of an American monopoly of influence exclusive of Soviet access and involvement as far as feasible?

The transition at issue was from ratifying Soviet gains in Europe to deciding whether and how extensively, and on which side of the equation, to rectify a growing disproportion: between the steady rise in Soviet military capabilities, tolerated by the United States, and the lagging American sanction for the employment of these capabilities for worldwide influence. In the quandary whether to condone and how to control movement beyond formal toward material parity, the United States confronted basic policy choices and interacted with the Soviets within certain basic constraints not peculiar to either party.

One basic constraint was inherent in "subjective" attitudes. An insular or quasi-insular sea power will tend to arrogate unto itself the right to confer or deny "legitimacy" to overseas gains by the originally continental state, and to claim automatic legitimacy for its own resistance to such a state's ambitions. It will tend in this direction on the strength of reciprocally reinforcing moral and material pretensions. One pretension is to superior political virtue, going back to the period of voluntary self-isolation; the other is to the superior need for resisting even an incipient outside capacity for imposing material isolation on the sea-enclosed state. As before the British, so the American attitude in this regard partook of a certain sanctimony. It was met by Soviet ambiguity, carrying on the German, insofar as the ascendant continental state will typically seek world power as a matter of both antagonistic competition with the privileged insular power and admiring imitation of it, being equally anxious for technologico-economic convergence with that power and apprehensive of internal-political assimilation to it. In such a subjective setting, hyperbole will continue to be normal for reciprocal imputations, parallel exaggerations, and matching denials bearing on the two differently constituted parties' goals and related perceptions of needs and threats.

The other, "objective" constraint resided in the limitations besetting both principal strategies of accommodation open to the superpowers. One method was that of complementary imbalance, the other of parallel equilibration. The approach via complementary imbalances means that the party that is quantitatively or qualitatively stronger in one theater is allowed to develop or consolidate that advantage to compensate for its continuing inferiority in others, also because it is not able to automatically extend or project that superiority outside the theater in which it is favored. The approach via parallel equilibration means by contrast that the party that has a quantitative or qualitative advantage in one theater is free to use, but is also compelled to use up or yield, that advantage in bargains and barters over access to the theater or theaters in which it was previously inferior or absent. In relations with France, the British resisted systematically the first mode (French superiority on the European continent). And they applied the second mode (equilibrium in Europe and overseas) only intermittently and partially. The principal instance was in eighteenth-century peacemaking, when French conquests on the Continent were bartered against British conquests overseas, the two theaters deriving still some autonomy from physical distance under existing technological conditions. In the Anglo-German relationship, essays in the first mode in the Bismarckian phase were followed by the inapplication of either mode, with consequences including American expansion.

Bringing the United States actively into the international system followed from its support for Britain's refusal to tolerate German preponderance on the Continent as a match for the British empire in India and the American hegemony in the Western Hemisphere. And it ensued from encouraging British reluctance to condone the expansion of German maritime-mercantile power in the Atlantic and the Pacific toward an approximation of parity in exchange for restraint in Europe. The same strategy and attitude were applied to Japan, beginning with the Philippines, by virtue of the denial of complementary imbalance on the mainland of Asia and of parallel equilibration in the offshore insular realm. The response to the ambitions of the Asian power was still an Anglo-American strategy, but it was more clearly under American leadership than had been the approach to the European state. The rising curve of American initiative reached the peak in strictly American responsibility when the issue reemerged between the United States and the Soviet Union on a global scale as a stake in the Cold War.

A straightforward kind of complementary imbalance in the contemporary setting would consist of Soviet preeminence in a "unified" Europe, moderating the Soviet sway in Eastern Europe by its extension westward, and a correspondingly expanding American involvement and influence in the Third World. If the first "imbalance" remained possible, the second appeared to be decreasingly so. A more preverse and less stable form of complementary imbalance than any geographically differentiated variety would be the functionally defined disparity between growing Soviet arms superiority and Soviet self-restraint or abstinence in employing that superiority for geopolitical ends. Such a standoff could be only fragile and temporary inasmuch as it is as awkward to rest passively for long on cone-shaped missiles as it used to be to sit on bayonets. The process of elimination reduces plausibility to very particular imbalances within and between geographic and functional areas, so circumscribed in scope as to merge the kind with parallel equilibration. As part of such a near-merger of the two prototypes, the movement toward material parity between the United States and the Soviet Union would or could comprise both the several military capabilities and worldwide access in a number of regions, while allowing for moderate inequalities in favor of one of the superpowers in particular areas and for growing third-power constraints on both superpowers and their efforts at accommodation in most. The implied far-reaching American concessions would be ideally offset, apart from coincident changes in the configuration of forces and interests, by reductions in the scope and method of Soviet dominance in Europe. But they would tend nonetheless to erode American leadership in global equilibrium to the extent that the leadership was based primarily on superior geopolitical access rather than resting, as it might increasingly, on an excess of the American over the Soviet range of diplomatic and alignment options in relation to the third parties rising coincidentally with the redistribution of geopolitical access and diplomatic advantage between the superpowers. Any consequent repolarization of the international system might foster further American-Soviet rapprochement. If, conversely, the trend was toward an increasingly mutlipolar balance of power and concert of powers, the two superpowers would more likely compete over which would act as the conductor-power in the concert over a particular issue. Reproducing one of the Theodore Rooseveltian variants of postempire equilibrium foreign policy for the United States, the balance of power-cum-concert dispensation would be the most beneficial possible consequence of the concession of material parity to the Soviet Union, and would compare favorably with the worst possible consequence of its denial.

Subject to both the subjective and the objective constraints, concessions that are premature or excessive will be as damaging as are too-prolonged or rigid denials. Imbalance in capabilities, or disproportion between capability and its unopposed employment, resulting from deranged concession-rationing will tend to overstimulate the ascending power and impede orderly progress toward greater symmetry between parties to the parity quest.

Greater symmetry between powers such as the United States and the Soviet Union comes into being when the maritime empire is involved in the central, Eurasian balance of power and the continental power becomes capable of actively pursuing the *équilibre* (if not *partage*) *des mers*; when, that is, the first power is "continentalized" and the second "navalized." Ideally, as this kind of symmetry increases, the divergence of socioeconomic and political doctrines affecting internal structures is liable to decrease. So will differences of foreign-policy doctrines arising out of an ingrained land-sea power schism. Changes toward convergence are apt to affect the rising continental state more than they do the so-far superior maritime state, as evidenced by the widely shared anticipation to that effect inside Imperial Germany. To the extent that this is so, the maritime state has an interest in diffusing the external frustrations and internal "liberalization" following unevenly and with uneven certainty from an active part in far-flung world politics and economics, even while it acquires additional leverages and hostages from the worldwide expansion of the continental state's interests.

The denial of material parity complicates deterrence and defense with respect to compensatory or retaliatory drives, whereas concessions toward parity may cause deterioration of another kind. Concessions may bear on capabilities or their employment, on status or substantive-strategic assets; and it will make a difference whether they are made from strength or weakness, implement a strategy for parity or express a disparity in capacity or will. Similarly, denials will have a different political and psychological effect if they are expressed in the form of mere diplomatic vetoes or are buttressed by counterinvolvement; and, relatedly, if gains for the so far inferior power are opposed merely to shield local vacuums for their own sake or, instead, in order to meet the positive strategic or other needs of the superior party. Most importantly, finally, the grand strategy will hinge on the actual rapport between either concessions or denials and consequently changing constellations and configurations over time. Assessed by such criteria, American policies were defective insofar as they were attuned mainly to the tactical and short-term perspectives; widened the gap between the "track" of capability and the "track" of its legitimized employment by conceding the Soviets' increasing military capabilities while seeking to block their employment for geopolitically significant commensurate ends; presumed to interdict Soviet efforts to bring capabilities and employment into balance by threats of diplomatic reprisals in the area of détente rather than opposing them by means of direct American involvement in the field; and failed to determine conclusively whether geopolitical concessions to the Soviet Union were more likely to affect constellations favorably (i.e., by making the Soviets too "big" for accommodation with the Chinese or too "expansionist" for finding favor with the third-world countries) or unfavorably (by making the Soviet Union appear irresistibly overwhelming and the United States irreversibly decadent).

The dominant American purpose seemed to be to deny the Soviets all access to assets and areas that might be damaging, rather than maintain or enhance an American access that might still be useful; and the policy seemed to be to apply the only negative and narrowly preventive outlook even within areas, including Southeast Asia and the Persian Gulf-Indian Ocean complex, that had been deemed vital for the West at the height of the American imperial engagement. In a serious quest for parity, however, the initially superior power will have to determine the momentary balances of concessions and denials, and the rates for each, by more positive assessments of both likely and desired specific conditions, diplomatic constellations, and structural configurations conditioning and conditioned by the parity-evolving process. Whether they are political or technical, bear on the short or the long run, the assessments will be no less hypothetical for being positive so long as they concern the supposedly irreducible or minimum security needs of the superior power and the presumed maximum political goals of the inferior state. The fact that security needs are relative to the different geostrategic situations of contending powers raises the issue of equal security. That in itself ambiguous criterion, obscuring the tension between capabilities and intentions and the relationship of intentions to evolutionary change, is matched, and may be outdone in elusiveness, by the issue of proportionality. Just as geopolitical and other ambitions may or may not be (with different consequences for their denial) proportional to the relative capability of an ascendant power aiming overtly at equal security and status with the previously superior power, so the concessions of the latter may or may not be with equal safety proportional to the capability-supported pretensions of an acquisitive power that is more or less satiable this side of equal security and status in the long run.

Technologically wrought increases in mobility hampered parity agreements in the past by increasing the value of space and the importance of deployments and defenses in depth. The difficulty may have become self-liquidating, as no amount of protective space could guard either kind of power against the expanded radius and speed of air- and seaborne vehicles of destruction. A meaningful global reach on sea required either long-range and readily resuppliable, carrier-based and other, high-sea forces or widely scattered in-land facilities. At the same time, the number of required facilities may have decreased since the era of coal-supplied steamships that had attended America's first flirt with world power and conditioned the era's serious world politics. The American combination of technological capacity and in-land facilities in regard to the Indian as well as the Atlantic and

Pacific oceans continued to be superior to that of the Soviet Union. It offset whatever relative disadvantages the United States had because of exterior lines and less complete self-sufficiency in key raw materials. In terms of the naval-and-geopolitical complex, parity was thus definable by the extent to which the Soviet Union could be allowed to narrow the gap in naval capabilities *and* inland facilities without becoming able to exploit America's limitations in lines of communications and in mineral and other resources, and this regardless of any offsetting overland pressures that the United States might or might not be able to mobilize against the Soviet Union at will.

Quite apart from technical calculations and technological projections, the American assessment of a tolerable latitude for Soviet advances was colored also by perspectives on self as well as others, and on the historically evidenced and presumably continuing relationships between capabilities and intentions, intentions and competition, and competition and coordination of effort for a joint object. The first critical question bore on the relation between a regional naval capability and a global one and, specifically, on the rate, modalities, and purpose of the transition from one to the other. Early America had inclined to depend for defense tacitly on the bigger and longer-range navies of other powers. Her coastal and regional naval capability was neither a sustained nor a mainly defensive force as a result. This meant two things for the regional-to-global transition. One was that the United States foreshortened the sum-total of active spells during which it possessed a coastal-regional capability to the point of virtually overleaping the regional phase. The other was that, when it had been attained, superior regional capability was for dominance more than for defense, while global capability was evolved soon thereafter in World War I for defense more than for dominance. By contrast, the coastal-regional navies of Britain, Germany, Japan, and Russia were a serious and relatively continuous business; and they grew out of manifest and pressing self-defense functions while their reach beyond narrowly regional defense could be plausibly attributed a predatory purpose (as compared with the merely "preclusive" one of the United States global navy at worst).

The earlier American experience favored certain biases. One was to depreciate the coastal-regional defense role as a sufficient warrant for substantial naval capability; to see a direct relation between a naval build-up and acute conflict (e.g., in the war of 1812, the Civil War, the Spanish-American war, and the two world wars); and to postulate the possibility of a rapid transition from regional inferiority to global superiority. Furthermore, the record of other powers suggested a close relationship between global naval capability and aggressive or acquisitive intent. Moreover, if the relationship between coastal-regional defense and global

deployment was thus conditioned historically, it was also currently complicated by any possibility for an aggressive power with global maritime reach
to convert seaborne nuclear-deterrence capacity into a first nuclear strike,
and nuclear-powered capacity to isolate into one to harass if not invade the
rival's homeland. Superimposed upon diminished and malcoordinated naval
capabilities of essential United States allies, such scenarios perpetuated the
American bias in favor of clear U.S. naval superiority. They also consigned
Soviet naval equality to the status of a nightmare in worst-case planning,
such as had been a hypothetical Germano-Japanese coalescence of land-
and sea-based capabilities before World War I.

When the parity issue is extended to comprise, next to naval capability,
also geopolitical positions, the dynamic of the situation will tend to confront
the claim of the satiated "insular" power to total security with the limitless
ambition of a presumably insatiable continental state. If one side comes to
suspect the other of being insatiable, it will become intolerant of even minor
concessions translatable into rival gains. The sea power will perceive all
movement by the land power beyond a narrowly defined regional security
orbit as encroaching upon its own regional security, defined broadly. For the
primarily continental state, such as the Soviet Union, to claim regional
security on land and in adjacent waters *and* parity in the overseas global
arena will appear as conclusively demonstrating an ambition that is both
unlimited and incompatible with the need of the maritime-insular state for
naval superiority globally as a condition of regional security equivalent with
that of the continental state. The real or apparent "insatiability" of one will
evoke the real or apparent "intransigence" of the other when a superior sea
power such as the United States denies or disputes to its rival both of
partially interchangeable assets, such as land-based facilities in third
coastal states and long-range carrier-centered naval capability, and dis-
counts to naught the difference between transient and stable geopolitical
gains.

In most or all peripheral areas, access could no longer be readily
buttressed by control. Any attempt to impose control nonetheless in one
place threatened to jeopardize progress toward mere access in a wider range
of other areas for the ascendant even more than for the preestablished
power. There was a tendency in the United States to project on the Soviet
Union the British perception of Imperial Germany as an insatiable power.
The projection took place in political and technological conditions that had
substantially slackened the link between intentions and their realization.
This should modify the projection and moderate the resulting conflict, even
in conditions that reactivated the interest of both major contenders in
maritime stakes.

In the American-Soviet as in the Anglo-German context, moreover, the quandaries of technical and political assessments were compounded by those of accounting. Such accounting bears on the estimation of gains and losses to ensue for the initially superior power from the global extension of the inferior one. The critical relationship is between conflict over access, for national influence or security, and a possible coordination of roles in upholding world order. How much a superior or satiated power might be prepared to "pay" in concessions for contributions to upholding a world order it can live with will depend on its need for the supporting performance in the existing configuration of forces. How much of a concession the inferior power can reasonably demand, as a step toward its satiation, will depend also on the supply of assets, including lesser-power alignment and allegiance, that are available for allocation or reallocation among major states without profoundly unbalancing an international system at large or in a particular region. Ideally, therefore, the propensity to concessions of the superior power ought also to be a function of the system's capacity to absorb the concessions in the existing ranges of assets and actors, and the prevailing elasticity in alignments.

As long as the international system is seen as essentially static, it will be difficult or impossible to either redistribute assets concertedly toward parity or effect any other basic alteration in the allocation of roles in it.

The question of what the Soviet Union could do *for* the United States, in the efforts for regional peace and order in Southeast Asia or the Middle East, fades then before the more immediately urgent question as to what an accretion in Soviet capability that would be "optimum" for joint order-maintenance might do *to* the security and interests of the United States or of its local clients or protégés with yet greater certainty if "misused." The resulting quandary is readily reminiscent of the earlier one of British statecraft concerning Imperial Germany's capacity for an ordering performance in China, stabilizing influence in Europe, or assured security vis-à-vis Russia and the Franco-Russian alliance, as compared with the German threat. Consenting no or merely minor concessions, or concessions confined to one sector, will stimulate an ascendant "revisionist" power to revolutionize the world order overall or by regional installments rather than uphold it. A Soviet support for a world order, and for regional ones in either Southeast Asia or the Middle East, that would be congenial to the United States was unlikely until the Soviet Union became "equal" in status and coresponsible in function on the basis of a comparable national capability and access, within a setting of increasingly autonomous and plural third powers. Nor were agreements on nuclear parity likely to be stable unless they were extended to revisions of the existing global or regional entrenchments of the two superpowers, away from a deteriorating complementarity in imbalances and toward parallel reequilibration.

The struggle over succession to the failing Europe-centered world order, initiated in the Second World War, reproduced on an enlarged scale the earlier struggle for succession to the Spain-centered world order climaxing in the world wars of the eighteenth century. Britain in the first critical period and the United States in the second were involved simultaneously in two or more balance-of-power theaters. These were interrelated, without being necessarily equal in the magnitude of power deployed in each. For Great Britain, one set of balances of power was in North America in the period of the first empire and, thereafter, in the Indian subcontinent and, following its unification under the British raj, in the ever-widening circles around it. In high-tension periods, the peripheral balances were subordinate to the central, European balance of power with its more direct bearing on British insular security. That same central balance was to become primary over the more limited intraregional Pacific and Atlantic equilibria also for the United States, although at first as a matter of vicarious identification with the security and survival of Britain. The question whether the Atlantic and Pacific regional balances of power or the central, or Eurocentric global, balance ranked as primary faded in the Second World War also for the United States. It did so as American statecraft adopted the earlier-developing perceptions of the European great powers, and as the regional balances became ever less autonomous (i.e., separable from one another and meaningfully distinguishable from the central or global one).

After World War II, nuclear and ideological instruments resegregated regions or subregions to an extent. This allowed for the resumption of complementary imbalances in force. Just as Soviet preponderance in Eastern Europe was shielded from effective roll-back with outside support, so Soviet influence was kept from extending at all westward in Europe and substantially southward in the Third World. The alternative mode of parallel equilibration could get tentatively underway only when Soviet capabilities were being extended and dispersed, also via the naval arm, into areas hitherto monopolized by the Western powers. But the mode would be internally balanced, and the Soviet advance toward world-power status could become more widely accepted as legitimate, only when a relaxation of the Soviet monopoly in Eastern Europe matched Soviet capacity to increase or decrease pressures and maneuvers elsewhere in Europe and in the world at large.

X

FROM PAST TO
PRESENT. *Risks,*
Rules, and
Recourses

As the American public mood began to shed the disillusion induced by
the war in Asia, which wrote an apparent finis to the latest spell of empire,
two interdependent issues emerged as critical for the lowered sights of
equilibrium politics in the future. The very general one concerned the risks
to run in support of any new concept, outside those of overspending on
military hardware; the more specific one, included in the first but not
exhausting it, concerned the management of American-Soviet relations in
conditions of controversial equality in strategic weaponry. The intercon-
nected political issues linked the future of American foreign policy to the
future of the international system. They exceeded in long-term significance
the attention-absorbing economic issues, whether related to the so-called
energy crisis or to the so-called South-North dialogue (or confrontation) over
a new economic order. These latter issues were essentially secondary in the
nature of the stakes, which, like all purely material ones, could not be
conclusively adjusted in isolation from the matrix of high policy; and they
were derivative in their status, because their transient preeminence was but
a function of the temporarily becalmed course of greater affairs.

Most critical in international relations are not the routine risks of
diplomatic or military confrontation. The critical risks inhere instead in the
configuration of power that either is being fostered or must be endured.
Risk-entailing configurations result commonly from the concession of en-

hanced role and responsibility in foreign affairs to both rival and ostensibly friendly (if, eventually or even immediately, also competing) states. In the contemporary setting the risks to incur or refuse to endure have included those associated with the "new" China and the "new" Europe. They paralleled, and could enhance or mute, the yet greater risks of either confrontation or concessions involving the Soviet Union.

There were unquestionable risks in building up China's role in the international system. The reconstructed Asian power was currently too weak and withdrawing for genuine concert, and might become too strong, dangerous, and pushing for comfort in the far-off future. The immediately critical time-span is, however, the intermediate one. Moreover, the diplomatic leverage that can be derived at any time from a state is not only a matter of its present physical weight and active thrust, but is also a matter of the state's place in the wider constellations and of its long-term prospects. And finally, the presumed ideological, ethnic, and other immaterial strengths of China, which might make her dangerous one day, were likely to fade in political potency as she grew in physical power and lost as a result her earlier assets and appeals, just as the Soviet Union (and, in a way, also the United States) had done before her. It was, therefore, not necessary to overestimate China's current potential or relapse into romantic Sinophilia in favor of the "good" Chinese against the "bad" Soviets (as, previously, the "bad" Japanese), for the makers of American foreign policy to do more than sip tea with the Chinese dragon each time they had supped with the Soviet devil. Nor was it necessary, even if it were possible, for a foreign policy that set out to be creative, to juggle the China ball and the Soviet ball as if this were still the eighteenth or the nineteenth century. Among the superficial risks of an either even-handed or balancing policy has been to incur Chinese rebuffs and recoils while enjoying insufficient reciprocity and having to cope with excessively pressing revisionism. They paled in comparison with the latent danger of precipitating Sino-Soviet recoalescence. American foreign policy could promote such reunion by failing to live up to the barest implications of "normalization," such as assisting the development of China's countervailing power and striving for more than accidental concordance of American and Chinese policies on issues not confined to either Taiwan in particular or Asia in general.

The risks of either bringing or failing to bring China in have been a match for the risks of pressing or failing to press Europe to move outward. Devolution in that respect entailed American resolution to have Western Europe stand on her feet more than she felt inclined to. This could not be done by occasional rhetorical exhortation; it required risk-taking exposure of the Europeans to the political and global implications of both the opportunities and the vulnerabilities of their regional economic power. Such exposure was not consistent with the United States' resisting, as it intermittently did in effect, both the enlargement of the Europeans' narrowly regional basis (thus lately toward the Middle East, in connection with the energy crisis) and the expansion or consolidation of their domestic political systems (thus lately in the direction of the Left). Injunctions against the drift toward an increased role for Communism in domestic affairs reechoed an earlier American opposition to Europe's developing toward Gaullism in foreign affairs. Nor was the domestic trend in key parts of Western Europe without a causal link with the U.S.-promoted frustration of that earlier, outward-directed, striving. Since Europe was not to be a real *power* in foreign affairs between the American and Soviet "hegemonies," more and more Western Europeans felt free to flirt with the compensating pursuit of an ideal *polity* between U.S.-style "capitalism" and Soviet-style "socialism" domestically.

Seeking to bar the social developments was also like the earlier obstruction of the status aspiration in that it threatened again to place the United States in a "special relationship" with West Germany, only superficially legitimized by the British annex to it. Yet, to isolate West Germany from the rest of Europe in the West would mark the defeat of America's European policy since World War II. It would also give an ironic twist to an earlier hope to isolate Communist East Germany by peacefully engaging with the other Eastern European countries outside Russia. Moreover, to consolidate American-German dualism for good would invert too radically a still remoter past and do more than lay to rest, within a genuinely multilateral alliance, the consequences of American opposition to German foreign-policy aspirations since before the First World War. An outright Washington-Bonn axis would tend instead to resurrect resistance to German ascendancy in Europe under unpredictable auspices. The kind of auspices—American or Soviet, or joint Soviet-American, or just "European"—under which all of Europe was to be reunited one day has continued to be, however, the principal latent stake of world politics. There were risks in relaxing American constraints on the process of that very special kind of unification. But they were no greater than were the risks of appearing to block a historically necessary—or, better still, likely—eventual consummation. It was not automatically exculpating to invoke hypothetical trans-Atlantic possibilities alongside immediate necessities. The former had been either missed or frustrated in the past and had to remain in abeyance while Western Europe strove to sort out internal social and political ferments, and to put her economic house in order, largely even if not wholly on her own.

In any event, it was possible to limit the risks from relaxing American protection of Western Europe, against both self-inflicted internal political dangers and externally generated economic threats. To do this it sufficed to lower only gradually the American shield against strategic-military dangers from the East and to raise again the American sword to a posture from which it might credibly strike in last-resort recourse against politically inspired economic dangers from the South. As long as the Europeans continued to perceive the need for American protection against military adventures, and could recover confidence (while disclaiming interest) in American safeguard against ruinous economic exactions, the United States would retain a tacit and, as long as it was conveyed silently, effective veto against any and all "adventurism" by the West Europeans themselves. Moreover, even if an enhanced affinity of a socially reformist Western (or Southern) Europe with "socialist" Eastern Europe failed to develop along lines that both superpowers could live with, even if not condone, her affinity with the parts of the Third World groping for a socialism of its own, along roads entailing bankruptcy for no one else, might forge a new coalition against the Soviet version of a southern global strategy. If nothing else worked, the Atlantic system could be more effectively reintegrated eventually on a basis that had been restored by reconfirming the absence of viable alternatives; it might even be strengthened into a genuine Atlantic confederacy between a Western Europe that had found her way out of a multi-faceted depression and a United States that had successfully negotiated a no less testing descent from solitary summit.

There have been thus two major sides to the issue of risks: the Asian-Chinese and the European. The Soviet Union mediated the two sides as the power situated in the middle geographically. And Japan did the same, as a nation linked to China by cultural affinity and political geography, and to Europe by the similarity of both economic and political or security problems. Connecting all major parties were the two strands of American policy for "managing" the abidingly central U.S.-Soviet relationship in the age of strategic equality. One strand has consisted of military-political counterpoise to Soviet power and aggressiveness; the other of the essentially economic or functional entanglement of the Soviets with the United States.

Counterpoise will work best when the dispersal of military power (and related roles and responsibilities) among both major and regional powers for support or fall-back is combined with upholding American military parity and, in some areas, superiority with respect to the Soviet Union. The psychological damage from failing to implement either of the approaches would become a disaster of policy if public calls for Soviet self-restraint were to continue being all the more intense in tone for being devoid of a follow-up in action. The acquisition of strategic parity (or better?) was unlikely to be an end in itself for the Soviet Union, as a matter of either symbolic status or even the security of the national habitat. Just as political penalties continue to automatically attach to military weakness, so political gains are still expected to flow from military strength. A nuclear Armageddon was no more the sole alternative to a spell of detente than its remote prospect would nullify immemorial political dynamics.

By entering upon the process of accommodation with the Soviet Union, the United States admitted tacitly that parity or equivalence overall, including political and economic positions next to military hardware, was the minimum final goal of Soviet policy. How could the American signer of the Nixon-Brezhnev Declaration of 1972 otherwise seriously expect the Soviet Union, in terms of either will or capacity, to participate in the maintenance of peace in the world's regions? And how could the Soviets not gradually gain a measure of access to the areas of crisis as a consequence of such a role, even if they did not as a precondition to it? The United States has kept the undoubted right, as the initially superior power, to have at least as great a role as the Soviet Union in determining the rate of the Soviet progress to "world power." But the United States also undertook, if only implicitly, to accept that the rules governing the quest for all-round parity would be somewhat different from the rules that had constrained the all-out contest of the Cold War. Not all Soviet efforts to expand influence would be held henceforth to invest a local crisis with the quality of rule violation just because they represented a Soviet encroachment on the very recently established American "vital" or "historical" interests; nor could all attempts of the Soviets to compensate for their U.S.-induced setbacks in one area (e.g., the Middle East) by gains in another area (e.g., Africa) be thus regarded and automatically condemned.

The narrower the definition of what constituted violation of the new rules, the broader the support that could be expected for American actions to enforce their definition and penalize their infringement. And, to conform to that requirement, the new rules would have to define more clearly than has been the case so far what mode or method, rate and location, of attempted Soviet penetration the United States was to tolerate as "legitimate," in return for what manner of American counterinvolvement in the area of "historic" Soviet control in Eastern Europe and as an alternative to what manner of opposition, ranging from commensurate counterintervention to merely verbal interdictions. Was just any Soviet attempt, or only successful Soviet attempt, to extend presence and influence geographically to be regarded as constituting a violation of détente? Or only if it was implemented by military means indirectly or directly? Or only if such penetrations occurred too quickly one after another, or occurred without the excuse of compensating for a Soviet setback in another area; or when occurring in a place particularly sensitive in its inherent makeup or in its bearing on American interests? If the definition of what violated détente was to be so sweeping as to be no definition, a gross imbalance was apt to develop between an effective shrinking of American will and capability to intervene and the broad scope of the occasions on which American force ought to be employed to thwart infractions by America's partner in inter-superpower accommodation.

At issue was American lucidity when entering upon the accommodation process. It was the immediately more serious issue to face than was Soviet good faith in implementing their (clearly avowed, if ideologically phrased) understanding of the scope and limits of "détente." Immediately behind the issue of lucidity was the question of American consistency: Why has the United States made concessions toward strategic parity (or better?) for the Soviet Union, in either the SALT agreements or in the American defense build-up, if it aimed at keeping the Soviet Union bottled up in Eastern Europe? A proper critique of U.S. concessions under SALT was not that they were "preemptive," in the sense of anticipating Soviet demands or entitlements. It was that the concessions were not seen from the beginning as being only preliminary. They introduced unavoidably a protracted contention over the meaning and shape of a parity process that would ramify into geopolitical stakes and require not only restraint on both sides but also the investment by each party of comparable deployment of resource and acceptance of risk.

The second strand of the total American foreign policy (during the Nixon-Kissinger-Ford era) was to entangle the Soviet Union in economic (trade) and other functional (including technological) cooperation and interdependence. The contradiction lurking in that particular strand was not only the simple one between explicitly or implicitly *conceding* (military) capability or positively *conferring* (economic) strength, and then either denying or not anticipating the employment of such assets for geopolitically significant ends. Another possible or even likely contradiction was one between the "tactical" or short-term and the "structural" or long-term dimensions of the entanglement strategy.

Before it could manipulate interdependence with the Soviet Union, the United States had to allow interpenetration to develop by granting credits, liberalizing trade, selling food, and the like. What was, thereafter, the supposed or intended structural consequence of entanglement? The conservative or prudent version envisioned an increased complexity and modified priorities of Soviet decision-making, first at the commanding heights. A more far-reaching version would relate the pluralism underlying enhanced complexity and changeable priorities to long-term "liberalization" in both the values and the substance of policy, on the part of both the regime and the society as a whole. However different on the surface, both formulations imply that containment-related "mellowing" of Soviet power, without which entanglement could not have been added to counterpoise, could be carried on into some kind of progressive "maturing" of the Soviet system internally and in its manifestations also externally. The pressing issue was thus less how to describe the precise nature of maturing structures in theory and more how to promote the maturation by the tactics of conferring and withholding American economic "aid" in practice. The anticipated trends had to be fairly reliable if they were to offset the risks inherent in the diffusion of American economic assets in the Soviet direction. But the efficacy of the withdrawal threat was apt to be questionable. It would be reduced by prolonged political divisions in the United States and by the reluctance of special interests to forego the profit of an established Soviet connection even temporarily. Moreover, a persistent American effort to employ the economic leverage tactically was apt to jeopardize the structural potential of the economic entanglement. It would make the entanglement hard to accept for a Soviet Union that was a sovereign government and saw itself as a world power. The Soviets had rejected once already a trade agreement bound up with Congress-promoted strings. It would take more subtle manipulation of the economic leverage and greater congruence between economic means and policy objectives to overcome Soviet obduracy. In the best of cases, the risk was considerable that the tactical and the structural features of entanglement would be not so much complementary as frustrating for one or both, unless the American strategists were either superlatively adroit in tactics or settled for being supremely fatalistic about trends.

The case of Angola (in 1976) was an example of the impossibility to orchestrate the two policy strands. If confidence was lacking between the Executive and the Legislative, no shared understanding of the practical meaning of either détente or parity existed between the United States and the Soviet Union. The Congress denied finally the means for effective military counterpoise in Africa, and the Executive forfeited the capacity to orchestrate its remaining weapons by allowing itself to assign an absolute priority to SALT and concluding rigid economic agreements on sales of grain to the Soviet Union. A contractually committed Executive was unable to threaten the Soviets with a delay or suspension of sales; nor could it face Congress with having to compensate irate farmers if Congressional refusal to extend moderate military aid to West-leaning Angolans left no alternative to a massive denial of economic "aid" to the Soviet patrons of their opponents. All considered, it seemed hazardous to depend on a theory about economic means to a long-term transformation in the Soviet Union, so long as U.S. foreign-policy making deranged the domestic bases for tactical management of the strategy while contributing to the confusion about the ultimate meaning of inter-superpower accommodation on the basis of parity.

The American-Soviet relationship was too new despite the more than three decades of its duration, its technological setting too untested and dynamic, and its larger politico-economic environment too volatile, to permit either affirmative (hard or soft) policy blueprints or authoritative analyses of alternative courses and their outcomes. Instead, the relationship could be approached only from a variety of partial perspectives highlighting the variety of its facets and blending analogy with analysis, as a means of circumscribing its character (and the challenge to statecraft it presents) rather than firmly concluding as to desirable specific strategies and probable evolutions. There are no readily applicable mathematical or scientific formulas for either formal or material parity any more than for the proper capability-mix or parity-mix. Nor could a graph do more than visually represent hypothetical intersection points between equal security for two differently situated powers and parity-constituting equivalence of, and proportionality between, capabilities and claims and unopposed gains of two unequally evolving powers. The matter remains one of judgment in concrete instances as they arise, refined by technical expertise, historical experience, and hypothetical speculation about future implications and possibilities in about equal measure. What the so enlarged approach lacks in rigor of both method and conclusions is made up for if it guards against rigidities of outlook and criteria rooted in one or both powers' location on global topography and evolutionary trajectory.

The abstract boundaries of the American-Soviet parity quest circumscribe the possible results of alternative American responses to expansive Soviet thrusts. The boundaries define the American-Soviet interplay as intermediate between the earlier Anglo-German and the earlier Anglo-American interactions over parity in regard to basic structures of power and ostensible stakes and results of policy. Several specific comparisons illustrate the point and suggest its significance for policy choices and emphases.

The Soviet Union has become the navally ambitious preeminent continental state of the day. In this basic feature of structure it resembled ascendant Germany before World War I. In more dynamic terms, the Soviet drive into the Middle East as the fragmented strategic underbelly or southern entrance gate to Eurasia invited an analogy even closer than Germany's southward drive: America's penetration into the Central American-Caribbean complex undergirding the continental Western Hemisphere. Moreover, in respect of the organic side of structure, the Soviet Union was less effortlessly ascending than had been the United States, but was moving up from a material basis which, despite weaknesses, appeared to be more solid than had been Imperial Germany's (or France's, notably in public finance). At the same time, the United States was less patently declining than had been Britain. As a stake for policy, the accommodation process had been of more immediate and exclusive concern for the United States in 1900 than it was for the Soviet Union in the 1970's in regard to the respective land-bridges and passageways (Central American and the Middle East; the Isthmian and the Suez canals) and the immediately adjoining waters (the Atlantic-Pacific and the Mediterranean-Indian Ocean). But the geographically limited stakes were no less, and may have been more, critical or central for the Soviets than the corresponding stakes (Berlin-Baghdad railway, etc.) had been for the Germans relative to the British. Somewhat in keeping with this graduation of regional concerns, the Soviets were less vocal in aspiring to global positions beyond the critical geopolitical segment than had been the Germans. But they supported their wider aspirations more substantially than the United States had backed its own before World War I.

American readiness for concessions to the Soviet Union was likewise intermediate. It hovered somewhere between the very high earlier British disposition vis-à-vis the United States and the very low Anglo-American disposition vis-a-vis Imperial Germany generally, as modified by the higher-than-usual British disposition to concede positions in the "Near East." So graduated, the basic readiness to concessions corresponded to the degree of accommodation that actually materialized. At the same time, the differences between past and present, including the relative capabilities of the principal parties and their structural makeups (as well as the constraints from the environment or from third parties), intimated the measure of possible American-Soviet accommodation. Yet another indication could be derived from comparing the objectives of parties to the parity quests. A plausible American objective has become a revised or revitalized equilibrium system under the leadership of the power guardedly retreating from empire. That objective was, again, intermediate between the British strategy of integral retention of empire vis-a-vis Germany and the actual piecemeal transfer of supremacy to the United States. Consequently, an effort at American-Soviet accommodation was not as certain to succeed, and be definitive, as had been the Anglo-American one. But neither was it as foredoomed to failure as had been the Anglo-German dialectic.

When contending with Britain, the early United States had possessed a hostage in continental Canada. Both Germany and the Soviet Union had one in continental Europe when facing up to the insular Anglo-Saxon adversary. Conversely, Germany's overseas possessions were vulnerable (as had been France's) to Britain in major conflict. They were exposed to acts of force just as had been America's coastal cities in the more lackadaisical Anglo-American warlike contentions. And they were subject to more direct expropriation than the Soviet overseas gains and targets were likely to be, provided the assets remained limited and American-Soviet competition remained moderate. It would depend on both capabilities and dispositions of the parties whether and how much a further expansion of Soviet overseas positions would correspondingly increase the Soviet interest in keeping the competition moderated. Geopolitically defined hostages were especially significant and potentially useful for America's relations with a Soviet Union that was not ready for a broadly based economic involvement in the world markets, and entanglement with the United States, as a basis for restraint. The fact that they were not ready for either exposure or expansion in the economic sphere dispensed the Soviets from having to cope with the (German) dilemma regarding the correct sequence between military-political and economic strategies for world power. It depressed in the same time-span also the chances of American foreign policy to substitute politico-economic "synthesis" for geopolitical-military "symmetry" in the relations with the Soviet Union. The limitations left to meaningful controversy only the issue of Soviet (as before German) "satiability."

As a factor in accommodation, leverage between adversaries via hostages is one thing. Another and closely related thing is the influence flowing between differently unequal and exposed allies. The white dominions opposed Britain's accommodation with Imperial Germany, but came to favor on balance the appeasement of the National-Socialist Reich while opposing that of Japan before the Second World War. The dispositions of America's essential European allies were comparably uneven when the allies extended guarded support for an American-Soviet détente while opposing an American-Soviet entente that would amount to a condominium in Europe and, over European heads, globally. Nor was the Japanese attitude fundamentally different. Uneven attitudes of key associates of an imperial state will point to a tension between the policies of empire and those of equilibrium in periods of indecision and transition between the two. They may also encourage the dominant partner to finally prefer equilibrium on a rebound from empire.

Of more limited use as precedents and indices in the American-Soviet relationship are past parity quests involving only regional stakes and status, both immediately and in the last resort. Such were the parity issues engaging Great Britain and the United States with Imperial Japan, as well as those between Britain and the France reemerging from the wreckages of the *ancien régime* and the Napoleonic empire. At stake in the case of Japan was essentially the Pacific theater, territorially focused on Manchuria-in-China and, later, insular and continental Southeast Asia. The late French stake was in the Mediterranean, territorially focused on Spain, North Africa, and Egypt. The issue between the United States and Japan resembled in some respects the Anglo-Japanese efforts at accommodation, while interfering with these efforts and finally thwarting them in all other respects.

The controversy bore on rough material parity comprising ratios in naval capabilities, access to continental or insular geopolitical realms, and access to both trade and raw materials. The actual or only attempted American-Japanese parity agreements took place between parties, both of which were regional, Pacific, powers of comparable standing in mobilized or readily mobilizeable military capabilities. The United States was bidding for a superior navy as a means to "equal security" encompassing the distant and vulnerable Philippines. The Japanese in turn were bidding for unimpeded economic access to the Western Hemisphere and a preferential standing in China (Manchuria), as a means to "equal opportunity" replacing America's protective stance in the former and open-door pretension in the latter.

In all or most past instances, the direct clash between the superior and the inferior powers was in large part the result of physical intersection and policy imitation. It so happened that the clashes occurred at the point of intersection between two broad movements: the accomplished east- and westward globe-girding movement of the superior power, and the south-ward-directed initial thrust of the inferior one. This placed the particular points of intersection in Central America, in the Middle East-Mediterranean area, and in Southeast Asia. The underlying imitation of the superior power by the inferior one was manifest on the part of the Soviets as much as it had inspired the Japanese and the Germans. It also influenced the liberal-bourgeois Orleanist Monarchy in its narrowed concern to enable the French to enrich themselves abroad as well as at home, as a departure from the more varied French motives as well as endowments in the earlier (Bourbon-Bonapartist) period of the Anglo-French contest. The geographic locus of the intersection conditioned the implementation of the claims to parity by its military-strategic implications. More significantly still, the imitation in policy motivation and purpose conditioned the very temper of the ensuing contention. Imitation did so by imparting to the claim for material parity the intangible element of right and righteousness and by converting the claim to national power into an issue of international fair play if not justice.

The superior powers differed in their responses to the partially similar claims and claimants. So did the effects that the various responses had within the major parties and on the international system. On the spectrum of concession and denial of regional positions with more or less of global ramifications, the concessions by Great Britain to the United States consti-tuted one extreme, while the other extreme consisted of the American denials to Japan and the British ones to Orleanist France. Imperial Germany was denied more than she was conceded, and occupies correspondingly an intermediate position on the range of responses. The British conceded regional primacy to the United States without restraint, reciprocity, or even reinsurance (in consequent configuration) against the shift in local ascendancy being extended worldwide. Nearly equally unqualified were the American denials to Japan, of primacy in Manchuria and of naval parity regionally. With superficial fluctuations, the American attitude opposing regional "monopoly" by a foreign power extended from William Howard Taft to Cordell Hull. It resembled the British denials to France from the 1830s to the 1880s over a period witnessing such markedly different styles as those of Palmerston and Gladstone in England and of the Bourgeois King and the Republic of Buddies in France. And the American attitude thwarted, finally, whatever inclination or incentive the British may have harbored to accommodate Imperial Japan in matters of both status and substance with the aid of alliance from 1902 to the 1920s and without it in the 1930s.

Unsafeguarded concessions produced the integral takeover of the conceding (British) by the ascendant (American) empire. The more or less unqualified denials intensified aspirations to relative parity into a total bid for "hegemony." The aggravation was manifest in the case of Japan and of Germany, and applied by way of their unequally powerful but comparably assertive Bonapartist successors also to both late-Bourbon and Orleanist France. Concurrently with "total" bids abroad, the regimes that were denied the wherewithals of prestige and prosperity (or the immediate successors of such regimes) exhibited also sooner or later greater radicalism in internal orders with something like "totalitarian" overtones. The radical-totalitarian sequel to frustration is antithetical to the potential that a policy for maritime-mercantile parity has to liberalize the domestic and foreign policies of the initially inferior power; it differs less, but still significantly, from the conservative-reactionary domestic reinsurance that an inferior autocratic power will be inclined to attach to a transient or limited détente with its major "liberal" rival. On the other hand, conceding assets without safeguards or compensations will have no less deleterious effects. Such concessions will tend to demoralize the declining polity and will space inadequately the internal maturation and role-assimilation of the rising one. The precipitate concessions by Britain to America had these effects on both sides; and they also distorted the evolution of the Europe-centered international system within its classic compass, by rendering apparently unnecessary the otherwise imperative (Anglo-German and related) adjustments. The collapse of the European system was near when, instead of graduating both concessions and denials to fit evolving configurations, near-total concessions to the United States were attended by near-total denials to Imperial Germany overseas in the first phase. It was imminent, to the provisional advantage of powers from outside the traditional system and inherently hostile to (even if subsequently imitative of) its traditional concepts, when far-reaching concessions to Nazi Germany in Europe were not counterbalanced in their consequences by those of matching concessions to Imperial Japan overseas.

The domestic and the foreign consequences are most closely intertwined when an externally thwarted ambitious regime seeks to protect its internal tenure by staging increasingly assertive actions abroad. The crisis flowing from a regime's endangered life expectancy will intensify if the regime depends for redress on an unreliable ally. Bourbon Spain was such an ally for France and Austria-Hungary and Italy were such allies for Germany. The Soviet bid for material parity has been relatively open-ended in terms of domestic tolerance for delays. But the bid was under possible time pressure in the broadly speaking alliance sphere. The pressure derived from the uncertainty about continuing attraction of the Soviet system for third-world countries and unchangingly effective control over Eastern European clients.

The American-Soviet parity quest displayed a blend of similarities with the earlier quests of the same kind and differences from them. Even partial similarities could be instructive for the contemporary interplay of a primarily continental and initially inferior state with the initially superior and more markedly maritime power. And partial differences sufficed to reduce the probability that past scenarios would be fully and literally reenacted in the future. The nature of the differences, moreover, along with the practical lessons that could be drawn from the similarities, were on balance favorable to effecting an American-Soviet accommodation over both ups and downs in the basic trend and a prolonged period in the available time.

With the waning of the land-sea power schism,[1] the focus of the parity quest shifted from the right to substantial naval capability to the more elastic issue of the scale and rate at which an existing capability would be utilized. Also changed was the link between a contentious quest for parity and an acute conflict over predominance. Most of the earlier contentions over parity preceded a hegemonial conflict that then followed upon the quest's failure. A partial exception (next to the Anglo-American pseudo-contest) was the late and relatively moderate phase of the Anglo-French contest after 1815. Conversely, the American-Soviet effort followed on a hegemonial contest that ended in a draw at its European center, differing thus from the two world wars more than the two trials by fire differed from one another. Since the outcome of the Cold War was not conclusive, however, an increasingly contentious interaction over parity on a global scale could easily reintensify conflict. There is no dearth of precedents. Thus the compromise peace of 1748, which failed to resolve the parity vs. predominance issue for either Germany or Europe or the overseas realm, led to a bigger war in 1756; the failure of the continuing Austro-Prussian parity quest within the Germanic Confederation in the 1850s and 1860s engendered the wars of 1866 and 1870; and the Anglo-German transactions just preceding World War I, while going farther than anything before

---

1. See ch. viii.

toward accommodation overseas, were "too little and too late" to reverse the momentum of the previous departures from the initial, Disraeli-Bismarckian, compromise.

To be sure, the two superpowers were more fearful of ultimate conflict than had been the earlier parties. And they did not have a single, absolute alternative to agreement on parity while such an accord was seemingly still possible any more than either of them disposed, when the possibility would have seemingly disappeared, of a last-resort remedy against an accelerating relative weakening. Britain had had such an alternative in the American connection, while Imperial Germany and Japan had had such a remedy in all-out war. The modern superpowers also feared crippling economic injury at each other's hands less than had the earlier actors. This meant that they had both the incentive to explore, and the time for exploring, different methods and conditions of progressive accommodation as well as various provisional alternatives to a "final" one. Moreover, the United States had less apparent reason to deny Soviet global expansion, and more residual capacity to regulate and confine such expansion, than had almost any previous superior power. In conditions short of major war, the United States was less dependent on the navy militarily, and on its indirect economic payoffs materially, than had been Great Britain. Similarly, the American situation was also far from desperate in a major war. America's land-based capacity relative to the Soviet Union was larger than had been Britain's relative to Germany. And the Soviet navy's potential for invading the American continent from remote land bases was less than had been either Germany's relative to Britain or, for all that, Imperial Japan's relative to the Philippines, Hawaii, and even America's own west coast. Finally, if less certainly, the United States had less to fear from Soviet naval capacity to isolate the continental domain than the British isles had to apprehend from the German surface and underwater fleets. It would take an altogether major Soviet expansion worldwide to radically alter these givens. On the other hand, the capabilities and the drive of the Soviet Union made its parity bids more urgent for the United States than had been true for Britain facing late French pretensions in the Mediterranean and Africa.

The United States retained so far the ability to slow down Soviet expansion sufficiently to fit it into a concurrently expanding active international system and adjust it to that system's potential for offsetting realignments. It had, however, no self-evidently peaceable and reliably constructive capacity to prevent such expansion indefinitely if the Soviet drive continued unabated. The optimum was for moderate adjustments to set the stage for no less safe and more substantial ones at a later date. The obverse was for the American-Soviet parity quest to grow in acerbity and forfeit some of the favorable contrast with the earlier efforts. This was apt to come to pass if a relatively declining United States and a relatively ascending Soviet Union were to converge not only in capabilities but also in mutually incompatible pursuits of wider leadership from geographically distant heartlands. The worst possible outcome of an inconclusively festering or finally aborted parity-evolving process would find the United States (cum Western Europe) regressing into a position that would be analogous in kind, if not necessarily in degree, with the earlier position of Britain (cum Belgium-and-Holland). In that most dismal of scenarios, a complex with predominantly mercantile orientation, consisting of an offshore "island" and marginal-continental entities, would again face from behind a diminishing naval and other protection a navally ascendant state of continent-wide scope. A thus situated Atlantic West would gradually and irreversibly fall behind a Soviet Union that (still *ex hypothesi*) had ceased being restrained by adequately compensating pressures from the continent of Asia and had not been compelled to capitalize on a possibly only ephemeral advantage by seeking either definitive composition or decisive conflict.

Parity equations are always ambiguous and concessions are always costly. So are surrenders of claims. The more this is so, the more the outcome of a parity quest will depend on whether viable alternatives exist to accommodation. Such alternatives are at all times a function of diplomatic constellations that are momentarily possible; they depend in the longer run on structural configurations. If the "constellations" involve alignment of power in function of policies, the "configurations" involve changing distribution of assets inspiring ambitions among both established and emerging principal actors. Intractable rigidities in the parity equations can delay or distort constellations that would be otherwise possible. More importantly still, rigidities between parties to a parity quest can be relaxed by changes in constellations that have revalued either the bearing or the gravity of concessions in the eyes of imaginative policy-makers. And, most significantly, changes in the configuration of capabilities are apt to relieve, replace, or resolve the dilemmas and the quandaries attendant on both concessions and denials by recasting their structural or institutional settings.

Both Britain and Imperial Germany disposed of well-defined alternatives to an immediate parity agreement. Britain could either move toward an alignment with the United States or make a different kind of sacrifices for a far-reaching reconsolidation of the empire. Imperial Germany could either renounce parity with the Anglo-Saxon powers or wage war. The American and Soviet alternatives were more fluid and the choices less pressing. Any kind of difficulties encountered in attempts to define and implement United States-Soviet parity in the immediate future was unlikely to affect decisively the structural convergence of the two superpowers or inflect materially the diplomatic reconstellations involving also third parties. It was more likely that such difficulties would be themselves reduced somewhat by the significance of claims and concessions being revalued in the light of the degree of reconstellation that was already underway. A rapid and complete overcoming of the difficulties would, however, be possible only at the cost of surrender by one of the parties. The United States would have to give up the remaining elements of its superiority, or the Soviet Union relinquish overall parity as the irreducible long-term goal and object of "détente." Either surrender would influence seriously the position of China (among others) in the triangular balance of power, while the American surrender would by itself suffice to severely destabilize the situation created as a result between the two abruptly "equalized" superpowers.

Thus, the dilemmas surrounding parity could be attenuated only progressively, and be resolved "finally" and usefully, only within three potentially interlocking developments. One development would consist of continuing changes in the capabilities and dispositions of other states, dispersing the two-power contest conclusively into one or several three-or-more-cornered contests. This would help relieve the parity dilemmas between the two original contenders, if only by reducing the attractions and anxieties fostered by the possibility or prospect of one-power superiority. Another development would witness a new dominant conflict, emerging from the prior dispersion or more directly superseding the prior dominant conflict, with the result of repolarizing the system while restructuring the equilibrium if any. This would in large part replace the inter-superpower parity dilemmas with like problems besetting the new contestants. And in yet another development, occurring as the concomitant or consequence of the two prior changes, the old conflict would be transcended in an institutionalized association or political alliance between the formerly rival superpowers. This would resolve the dilemmas of parity and preeminence into the easier (if not automatically self-solving) dimensions of a more or less "equal" partnership.

A tripartite dispersal of the American-Soviet conflict has already begun. In keeping with the several antecedents, it has already moved the conflict over predominance in the direction of one over the conditions and meaning of parity, if perhaps only provisionally. It remained to be seen whether the dispersal would make it easier to evolve the parity formula by moving the international system toward either a rigid repolarization or a complex equilibrium. Either one or the other could narrow the psychopolitical distance between the two superpowers by giving rise to common interests against principal new disturbers of the established positions, even if a rapprochement would not automatically culminate in something akin to alliance between the senior and the ascendant junior maritime power.

XI

FROM DÉTENTE TO ENTENTE. *Polarities and Pluralisms*

The future of American-Soviet relations was bounded by a conceptual near-certainty and an evolutionary uncertainty. The near-certainty was that resolving the issue of parity between two parties, within or without an integral repolarization and alliance, was different from either an integral condominium over the world's sea and land spaces, or their partition, which would reduce third parties to subordinate or subject positions. On the contrary, a contentious parity quest was more likely to depend for success on the continuance and growth of third parties as active participants in the international system. The evolutionary uncertainty was due to the parity-evolving process being unlike a conflict such as the Cold War. It has neither relatively self-evident rules of the game nor, relatedly, an inherent dynamic, which would make its course broadly predictable.

A conflict short of war tends to intensify until it has reached a climax, and it will thereafter move toward either open war or a kind of routinization and erosion or deceleration that will reflect the inconclusive prior outcomes and the concurrent removals of the initiating asymmetries and revisions of the initial stakes. The Cold War was an example of such conflict. Its predictability was increased, moreover, by the identity of the United States and the Soviet Union as both rising powers and founding members of a largely inchoate and, but for their reciprocal interactions, permissive international system. By contrast, the later American-Soviet quest for parity was occurring within a more crystallized international system with an indeterminate mix of (multilateral) obstacles and (multipolar) stimulants to agreement between the two principal powers. And the two powers were uncertainly diverging in some of the organic traits and trends, even while converging in others. In the absence of a built-in momentum either way, the parity-evolving process, which was coterminous with spells of "détente," depended for velocity and direction on a largely contrived network of changeable stimuli and sanctions; and it was as much subject to influences originating outside the two major parties as it was contingent on their own internal calculations of comparative momentary benefits and liabilities. Moreover, the questions as to who gained or lost more from accommodation at different stages of progress and various levels of intensity were answerable even less readily and reliably than are similar questions addressed to conflict. This was the case especially so long as such questions were raised in isolation from conjointly changing constellations and configurations and outside any mutually agreeable vision of the terminal parity state.

The result was an indeterminacy that could be only partially relieved by factors that improve the awareness of the parties and enhance their motivation. Regarding the awareness, the process of accommodation will typically dispose of one or (more likely) several salient points of transition, between parity in specific material capabilities and parity in their actual or "authorized" (i.e., unopposed) employment for geopolitically significant ends. One such instance was the dénouement of the Venezuelan crisis in Central America between the United States and Britain; another may well prove to have been the East-West agreement at Helsinki for Central-Eastern Europe. Such transitions will be often manifest only in retrospect, while the conferral of status (or "legitimacy") which consummates shifts in relative material positions will be retroactive as it were; but the transition points will nonetheless reduce somewhat the parties' lack of bearings in a protracted undertaking. Regarding the motivation, the accommodation process is lacking in the built-in inducement to moderation that conflict possesses in the prospect of mutual destruction. A potential alternative inducement will be the existence of a third party or parties equally hostile or threatening to both contenders over parity. The ascent toward accommodation over several plateaus or resting places will thus be punctuated by a succession of both inhibitions and incentives without effacing the distinction between two basic phases. One is marked by inconclusive contestation, the other by finally compelling configuration. As it moves into the second phase, the accommodation process will actualize its fundamental similarity with a conflict such as the Cold War. In both, the causal impact of evolving structures is ultimately greater than is that of episodic events or immediately perceived "facts." The more superficial aspects merely prompt questions that will be incapable of reliable answer, such as who was sacrificing to the accommodation process first or more and who violated foremost its controversial rules.

At the beginning of their relations as independent powers, the young United States and mature Britain were the overtly antagonistic tacit allies against the Holy Alliance of the continental-European powers. Following a midperiod of futile British efforts to contain the expanding United States on the North American continent, Britain attempted to involve America on her side in world order, at first in the Far East. In an only partial contrast and derangement of sequences, the United States and the Soviet Union commenced a meaningful and sustained relationship by being tacit adversaries overtly allied against the Axis powers. Following a midperiod of first American and later reciprocal containment efforts, they moved hesitantly in the direction of the early Anglo-American posture. Its contemporary analogue was for the superpowers to act as competitive antagonists who are also tacit allies, not only against "nuclear Armageddon," but also against some forms of radical-revolutionary alignments in the Third World opposing real or imagined "holy alliances." Thus the United States tried, if only fitfully and halfheartedly, to involve the Soviet Union on its side of the world order in Southeast Asia and the Middle East. The American initiatives met with a response that was no more consistently negative or positive than they were themselves. To the limited extent that it began to make itself felt, the sense of American-Soviet affinities, as advanced industrial societies deriving from Europe and having a joint stake in elementary stability, was analogous in kind and function to the opportune discovery of familial Anglo-American affinities at the earlier juncture. So far, however, the tension between American-Soviet conflict and concordance remained essentially sterile. It produced no one major event in areas adjacent either to the United States (Cuba) or to the Soviet Union (Middle East) that would match the resolution of Anglo-American contention in the Isthmian and Venezuelan crises. Only in Eastern Europe were the Soviets able to match the earlier American claim to suzerain (or "practically sovereign") status in the Western Hemisphere, which had been substantiated by the British surrender over Venezuela. The so-called Brezhnev doctrine echoed the Olney dictum of the bygone era, while ultimately resting on an American surrender. In comparison, the United States handled with ambiguity Soviet pretensions to a role in Middle Eastern peacemaking. Being also status claims, the pretensions were designed to move the Soviet Union closer to material parity with the United States, globally as well as regionally, rather than to ratify effective superiority of power or monopoly of influence within an enlarged Soviet orbit.

If the American-Soviet parity quest was to succeed in due course, the old East-West conflict had to be finally superseded. It had to give way to either the simplicity of a recast confrontation, replacing the earlier conflict and predominance issue with a new kind of polarity, or by an enhanced degree of complexity, confusing and confounding the ongoing superpower competition and relieving in the process the ongoing parity quest. In either case, if to different extents, the American-Soviet relationships would (have to) be shifted from the issue of predominance and parity to one of more or less guarded and equal partnership. The course and outcome of any such transition depended on the interaction of developments in several functional-geographic areas. One comprised the conflicting requirements, in the Third World, of a unifying solidarity of the "South" against the "North" in relation to land- and sea-centered economic issues on the one hand and, on the other, of the divisive-conflictual formation of regional balance-of-power systems more directly related to political issues within the South itself. Another had to do with the material and, in consequence, political and ideological evolution of China. The two developments were bound to be broadly simultaneous with the unfolding American-Soviet parity quest with respect to Europe and, increasingly, beyond.

The several areas and arenas were partially independent from each other and partially interdependent. And specific events within each would be molded by interlocking strategies of the two principals. One strategy would have the superpowers stress reciprocal restraints and accommodation; the other would emphasize the build-up of third powers by diffusing resources and devolving responsibilities. The Soviet Union was increasingly able to play the double-strategy game. It was also constrained to do so when attempting to give weight to its parity claims by attracting and strengthening overseas clients. Its problem was mainly tactical: how to incrementally patronize lesser forces without irreversibly disrupting the central parity-evolving process at one blow. The demands on United States foreign policy were of the higher order associated with any long-range design firm in conception and flexible in implementation. The Soviet Union could press for maximum obtainable concessions and let effective gains be defined by contentious interactions. On its part, the United States had to calculate what precise scope and kind of concessions would keep the American-Soviet parity quest on course while keeping in existence the constraints from third powers that both fueled and bounded that quest; and it had to delay far-reaching concessions until they had been made safe by constellations and configurations that had projected into being either equalizing counter-weights to Soviet enlargements or unequally greater threats to Soviet interests.

To assign a fixed priority to accommodation with another power would be a delinquent policy in the absence of dispersion and devolution in favor of third parties. Equally self-defeating is the obverse of such a policy, however. The British made near-simultaneous concessions to the United States, France, and Russia (next to Japan) before World War I. The cumulative impact of these concessions on Britain's standing was only obscured for a time, optically, by common opposition to Germany; and it was deferred, fortuitously, by the weakening or regression into passivity of the non-British parties (other than Japan) as a consequence of war. The British erred also by allowing themselves to assume (in the post-Theodore Rooseveltian period) a posture of more intense and fixed hostility with Germany than was that of the United States, even as the French did the same in comparison with Britain. In a "correct" strategy, consequently, the initially superior United States would soft-pedal the parity quest in the first phase while it managed devolution in favor of China, the third-world middle powers, and perhaps also America's major allies. A key object is to equalize at the very least the threat, and the perception of the threat, that the critical third party or parties represented for the United States and for the Soviet Union. Anything that the United States would concede in order to diffuse resources to third parties for managing local balances of power and structures of order would be self-compensating, moreover, if it reduced the need for concessions to the Soviet Union in either the immediate or the "terminal" stage of the parity quest. Suitable concessions for diffusion will, finally, either trigger or consolidate changes in both diplomatic constellations and the more basic configurations of national assets and ambitions. Such transformations will either devalue the conceded assets from the American viewpoint or make their transfer to third parties preferable to their retention.

One hypothetical example is conceding a leeway to Iran as the regional power in the Persian Gulf and to China in the Taiwan strait. Soviet diplomatic position would be weakened insofar as a strengthened Iran lessened India's need for Soviet support against China; this would automatically lessen Soviet leverage on the United States. Moreover, it would take fewer United States concessions over time to satisfy Soviet parity with an American access and involvement that had been lowered *pari passu* with Iran's ascension. The original concession to the Iranians would be devalued if U.S.-Soviet competition declined in the region commensurately with Iran's filling the local vacuum, and American interests might even be served if Saudi or other opposition to Iranian hegemony increased the need and occasion for a locally favored, moderating American reinvolvement. Similarly, the first-degree American concessions to China on Taiwan, as part of initial "normalization" and consequent reconstellation, intensified the Soviet interest in détente with the United States. Second-degree concessions might alter also the structural configuration, insofar as a changed Sino-Taiwanese régime increased China's material strength. An increase in Chinese strength would enhance pressure on the Soviet Union to accelerate accommodation with the United States after having faced the choice between the rising costs of a contentiously pursued "equal security" and the enhanced benefits of a consensually defined "essential equivalence." A new factor would enter also Sino-Japanese relations, facing Japan with the choice of refurbishing or basically revising relations with the United States. The first-degree American concession on Taiwan was devalued within the constellation it had helped along. A reconfiguration to China's material advantage, due to second-degree concessions, could well further reduce the value of an anti-Peking orientation by Taiwan and might even serve the long-term American interest in a fundamental recasting of the global equilibrium.

General principles, guidelines, and caveats do not intimate specific policy acts. They do so least in regard to the balance of concessions and restraints intended to make third parties equally "antagonistic" to the principal parties to the parity quest, or even relatively less so to the United States. But they do suggest that diffusion of power at large is the necessary complement to the "equalization" of power at the center. It is the best reinsurance against the quest for parity failing or derailing in the shorter run, and the most steady stimulant to its succeeding in the longer time-span. They further suggest the importance of timing and phasing in the foreign politics of concession-mongering, keyed to manipulating momentary interactions (crystallized in constellations) and to managing evolutionary directions (crystallized in configurations). Timing and phasing of sequences are as important for the course of the parity quest as the stability of its outcome is contingent on the configurations that the concessionary politics had seconded if not wholly secreted into being.

A favorable configuration will recast the international system into an either complex and dynamic or comparatively rigid and static equilibrium drawing the two principals closer to one another. Thus the Soviet Union might move toward closer association with the United States and Western Europe (and Japan?) against China and much of the Third World (and Japan?) headed or spearheaded by China. Or a more complex-dynamic pattern might evolve. One possibility would be a moderate tripartite equilibrium among the United States, a "united" Western Europe, and the Soviet Union, while a matching equilibrium theater would comprise China, Japan, and an association centered on India or Indonesia. The two equilibrium theaters would be interrelated by the agency of the United States and the Soviet Union as world powers facing both ways and extending themselves into subordinate regional balance-of-power systems adjoining Europe and Asia. The more or less rigid patterns of repolarization would reflect the emergence of new dominant conflicts and consequent solidarities. One cleavage would be between the South and the North, if conflicts and

solidarities were principally functional and "socioeconomic"; another between Europe and Asia (or a "new" West and East) if they were principally
regional and "racial." A rigid polarity could reflect either of the two axes of
conflict and solidarity; the more complex one would be biased toward the
regional-racial axis. Albeit to different extents, the Soviet Union would be
closer to the United States and Western Europe than before on both of the
two axes, in function of a newly determining Soviet identity as either an
industrial-Northern or regionally European power. But Japan would lean in
different directions under the two scenarios, and each of the scenarios
would also differently subdivide the lesser third-world countries as either
more or less capable of development, or more or less Asian and susceptible
to attraction or coercion by the principal Asian and "European" powers.

As a potential precipitant of repolarization, the developing "South" was
subject to internal divisions and contrary pulls from the outside. As a result,
whereas repolarization along the lines of South-North cleavage was the
more immediately possible of the two, it was even less likely in the long run
than one along the revised East-West lines. The two axes would overlap
meanwhile if a "revolutionary" Chinese leadership took over in the poorest
South by initially stressing the socioeconomic ideological theme over the
Asian-racial theme as a means of exploiting Southern disappointments with
the results of indigenous (i.e., OPEC) leadership. Short of such great-power
leadership, however, the issues introduced by the South were apt to act
more effectively as the gradual solvent of the American-Soviet polarity and
conflict than as the crystallizer of a new, neat cleavage. They were apt to
give rise to a race between the possibly growing "solidarity" of the developed industrial-maritime powers and the possibly decreasing solidarity of the
unevenly resource-rich, industrialized, and maritimized lesser powers,
rather than spark a head-on collision over specific stakes that would transform vague and partial solidarities into solid bloc cohesion on either side.

A Chinese leadership unifying a large segment of the Third World was,
again, possible but not very likely. The reasons were both general and particular. In terms of the land-sea power dimension, it had proved impossible
historically for a major continental state, such as Bourbon France or Imperial Germany, to have the right amount of strength for freely accepted leadership. To be such a leader, the aspirant would have to be just sufficiently
strong to make "united" resistance to the dominant maritime-mercantile
power assuredly successful, and thus attractive, while not being so strong as
to assuredly convert successful leadership against one dominion into a supremacy yet more irksome for lesser-power allies at some later stage.
China's contemporary situation as a predominantly continental state was
broadly comparable. Her seapower was of only regional scope, related to

coastal defense and protection or promotion of offshore oil exploitation. But the growth of China's maritime potential and reach was liable to bring her into conflicts, including economic, with a widening range of third-world countries and concretize any existing rivalry over political leadership in several regions with local middle powers. It was, moreover, not at all certain that the China model of a largely self-supporting political and economic revolution-cum-development was widely relevant for third-world countries with different indigenous mores and both human and material endowments. The model was, instead, apt to become increasingly irrelevant. Relevance would decline if and when the model became successful, and then moved China outside the underdeveloped ranks; and it would wane also if the Chinese experiment in self-reliance proved abortive and required outside, Western (or Soviet), support for a second breath. Nor was it likely that China could effectively project the revolutionary development model while conducting conventional intergovernmental relations. These were so far devoted to maximizing relatively orthodox influence, by inserting one form of official Chinese assistance into interstate politico-military conflicts (e.g., between India and Pakistan) and another form of aid into interstate economic needs (e.g., the railroad linking Tanganyika and Zambia in Africa.)

The less assured it was that the Third World could be led and unified by a great power acting as one-half fellow-member and one-half outside federator, the more the South was liable to inner divisions.

One line of division was essentially political. It marked the third stage in the evolution of fragmented and undeveloped areas such as Central-Eastern and Southeastern Europe were in the past and the third-world regions more recently. An initial phase comprises competitive bids by two rival sources of orthodoxy for a monopoly in activities aiming at conversion. Such competing orthodoxies were the Western-Roman and the Eastern-Greek churches proselytizing in the pagan parts of Europe, and the liberal-capitalist American and socialist Soviet creeds in backward Afro-Asia. The intermediate stage, combining aspects of the first and the third phase, will be typically ideologico-pragmatic. It will display two rival authorities with global or universal pretensions (e.g., the popes and the emperors and, lately, the United States and the Soviet Union as "world powers") contending over the capacity to invest the key local actors (formerly the clergy and, more recently, the newly independent elites) with material (or "temporal") and ideological-doctrinal (or "spiritual") attributes, expected to condition the performance of the local actors in state-or-nation building. The third (and, in the Third World, current) phase is essentially pragmatic. It is characterized by contests among intraregional middle powers and more or less remote great powers over concrete stakes ranging from a mere access to local small states to an outright hegemony over them. Such contests will be affected only superficially by either ideological rationalizations on the part of the major parties or by relapses into a parochially radicalized ideological mode on the part of the minor ones.

Another line of cleavage had a more markedly economic character. In that respect the nominal solidarities of the South found expression in the call for a new economic order and (secondarily) for the withdrawal of outside, nonriparian naval-nuclear forces from waters abutting on third-world coasts and coastal shelves. Nuclear-free seas and a largely cost-free economic development were to be secured by assorting consultations and confrontations when dealing with the North. The new solidarity found ample room for the participation, and even leadership, of politically moderate-to-conservative regimes of economically well-endowed countries such as Saudi Arabia and Iran. But it was no more solid than had been the unity under radical-neutralist auspices of the earlier ideological era, for political decolonization and moral third-world ascendancy. As far as it went, the common front was based on the facts and fictions of reciprocally useful assistance: from the newly rich (OPEC) countries to the poor ones by way of economic aid for immediate survival and (more importantly) economico-political leverage for a better long-term "deal" from the North; and from the poor and poorest to the newly rich countries by way of legitimizing morally the immediate triumphs of the new over the old rich and, perhaps, their eventual transition into "northern" ranks. A third Southern sub-group, of countries (such as Brazil, but also Taiwan and South Korea) deficient in energy-sources but developing none the less, was biding its time before exchanging a largely formal identification with the South for the capacity to become part of an enlarged "North" in terms of material identity, even if not immediately of institutionalized membership.

The tactically motivated reciprocity papered over the substantial disparities between countries with underground or undersea mineral resources and the resource-poor or landlocked states, between countries capable and incapable of sustained development and more or less dependent on continuing outside aid. It was unlikely, however, that so precarious a coalition could long withstand either the widening economic gaps within the South itself or the intensifying of inevitable political tensions among countries only beginning to face the issue of intra-South regional "hegemonies" as a condition of liberation from worldwide northern "exploitation." Crystallization of regional balance-of-power systems within the South and a global confrontation of the South with the North had almost certainly clashing long-term implications. Only in the short run were hegemonial aspirations by indigenous middle powers apt to be more acute than feasible. They were still vulnerable to insufficient coincidence between economic and politico-military weights on the part of potential regional leaders, such as (only) militarily strong

Egypt or India and (mainly) economically strong Saudi Arabia as compared with an Iran disposing of both kinds of assets but at least equally prone to internal upheavals as the others.

All in all, there was a considerable distance between agitation for a new economic and oceanic (including offshore) regime and the actualities. If the agitation involved dogmatic demands and "paper reservations," the realities were those of divisions in both the support for claims and the opposition to them. Divisions in northern responses reflected serious divergencies in economic and politico-military needs and resources. A far from single-minded Western Europe and Japan had greater economic needs and less usable politico-military assets vis-à-vis the Third World than had the United States. And the Soviet Union had a greater need for additional politico-military outside facilities and, in some respects, more readily usable resources for military and arms aid abroad than had the United States, while its needs for foreign raw materials and resources for foreign economic aid were less. Consequently, most of the European governments and the Japanese were more steadily disposed to conciliate the Third World than was the United States. And competition continued to prevail over solidarity in relation to the Third World between the two superpowers as they pursued their respective requirements in the South deriving from reciprocal containment and including nuclear deterrence and strike capacity. In addition, the Soviet Union was increasingly concerned with encircling China. Nor would either superpower forego the capacity to intervene in the affairs of the lesser states. Within the bounds of conflicts around "shared" stakes, the balance between superpower solidarity and inter-superpower discord was thus uneven and was bound to be a shifting one for a long time to come.

Since the Soviets only began to be involved in world economics, the significance of the maritime dimension was correspondingly enhanced. The competitive naval-military globalisms of the two superpowers aimed at consolidating reciprocal deterrence and at securing a hold on vital sea lanes for each. The stakes were augmented by either one or both leaning toward "offshore" strategies; and they were at variance with third-world claims to extended off-coast sovereignty, potentially supported by improved local capacity to interfere with superpower navies. The definition of stakes was also subject to the temptation to graft specific and short-term superpower interests onto the small-state claims. Notably the United States and the American-controlled multinational corporations would seek to secure a "neocolonial" hold over the new form of offshore colonization by the coastal countries. And notably the Soviet Union could prefer to support even extreme claims in exchange for needed naval facilities as a new variant of spheres-of-interest formation. Meanwhile, the United States sought spasmodically to enhance safe and secure access to underground and underwater oil and other minerals by reverting to the food-without-force strategy reminiscent of other eras following politico-military exertions (in World Wars I and II). On its side, the Soviet Union was seemingly the more willing of the two to use a force-for-fishing approach against third-world countries impeding the relatively greater Soviet stake in continuing free access to high-sea fisheries.

The third-world countries had both more to fear and more to expect from the American (or Western-cum-Japanese) near-monopoly of capacity for high-technology exploitation of the offshore resources, either alongside or in substitution for underground mineral wealth. On the other hand, the "western" part of the industrial North had more to fear from the third-world countries if they set out to exploit near-monopolies in key mineral resources in a coordinated manner for purposes of political and economic leverage. It was possible to view the parallel near-monopolies and capacities for exploitation of the "Northwest" and the "South" optimistically, and to manage them constructively, as constituents of interdependence. But the relationship was apt to remain for long a problematic one. While this was so, a Soviet commitment to solidarity around the "northern" pole was unlikely to develop, and the Soviet preference for exploiting North-South pitfalls without a major economic cost for political advantage to diminish. Only when Soviet maturity as an industrial power had made the Soviet economy more vulnerable to the Third World (via enhanced needs for raw materials and, consequently, the insufficiency of indigenous ones), was the Soviet state likely to become more receptive to identification with the West on economic grounds, notably if a measure of convergence between the two economic systems had evolved from their respective inadequacies in the meantime. Before the Soviet Union developed a mature industrial capacity and a worldwide trading potential, its military interest in the freedom of substantial maritime stretches was unlikely to be matched by an equivalent economic interest. Nor was the strategic interest alone likely to either overcome or substantially alter in the near future the countervailing Soviet political interest in countries that, because they adjoin narrow seas and shipping bottlenecks, could harass the superior Western needs for free passage. These countries—such as Egypt, Algeria, South Yemen, Somalia, Indonesia, adjoining such narrows as Suez, Gibraltar, the Straits of Hormuz and Malacca —were at one time or another the preferred and receptive, if not always reliable, recipients of preferential Soviet military and economic aid.

Any basic changes in Soviet policies were contingent on structures developing over a fairly long term. By contrast, American postures were more a matter of changing tactics and strategies. Thus, in the climactic phase of summitry during the Nixon administration, inter-superpower accommodation was attended by absence of the kind of interest and involvement in the

Third World that would test the nominal U.S.-Soviet agreements on co-operation in peace maintenance. When specific occasions to implement the agreements arose, they were aborted by concurrently revived American interest in the Third World and reactivated American-Soviet competition over the Middle East and Western and Southern Africa among others. By that time, the change in politico-military dynamic originating with the two super-powers was compounded by emanations from the (Euro-Japanese)-U.S.-Southern triangle, making the United States more sensitive to third-world stakes on economic grounds. Yet, for the two superpowers to woo the Third World again with increased gusto was unlikely to foster inter-superpower solidarity, including the "negative" kind of community of interests. More solidarity of any kind was least likely if competition was revived by each superpower for different reasons, and was conducted by different tech-niques, in a departure from the comparative uniformities in both motive and method during the Cold War era.

A different kind of conflict could be introduced into America's own de-volutionary policy if it were to promote China and third-world middle powers simultaneously. A U.S.-supported material growth of China would alienate, and might drive toward the Soviets, the more developed middle powers if their bidding for leadership in Asian and other regional subsystems pro-voked a countervailing Chinese involvement in support of the weakest states. The "systemic" grounds and the "national interest" motives of the small powers behind such an involvement might counteract the fact that America's material aid to China had previously disqualified the latter as a revolutionary leader of the least-developed third-world poor; and the Chinese involvement would be for that reason no less frustrating for the local candidates for hegemony even while reinforcing China's position in a setting that might well combine the formation of regional balance-of-power systems with global or system-wide repolarization. A new set of both op-portunities and constraints would confront then also the Soviet Union within a modified South-North or East-West (Europe-Asia) polarity, which has been loosened up by complex balance-of-power interplays around both political and economic issues while being essentially simplified by the con-tinuing atrophy of ideological and revolutionary features.

Taken by themselves, the South-North issues were not sufficient to en-courage accommodation between the two superpowers in anything like a sustained and cumulative manner. The issues were far too diffuse and hard-to-manage in complex-to-chaotic situations, and did not represent therefore a sufficiently specific and unifying threat or challenge besetting both super-powers more or less evenly. To be "unifying," a particular threat or chal-lenge would have either to impede the separate self-assertions of the two superpowers beyond any opportunity it offered for competitive self-aggrandizement, or it would have to contravene their concerted definition and joint affirmation of basic rules of the game. As things were likely to stand for some time to come, the South-North equation was not likely to be soon such as to recommend far-reaching accommodation to the Soviet Union in its capacity as the currently more assertive or expansive party. It would take the injection of an extraneous element into the economic-maritime complex to supply an additional, decisive impetus. One such element might be the regional-racial, or modified East-West, factor. The resulting threat for the Soviet Union as China's foremost target might then exceed Soviet opportunities in the South-North context. Concurrently, it would be necessary for the "old" West to abstain from exploiting to the full the anti-Soviet opportunities arising out of the new East-West cleavage, if only in view of the costs and dangers of denying a Soviet bid for "Europeanization." The alternative would be to opt, instead, for the lasting encirclement and reduction of the Soviet Union, even while a radical uncertainty surrounded the ultimate scope and, consequently, target of the new Asian solidarity.

Since it was proving impossible to dispose of the land vs. sea power schism in the narrow setting of Britain and Germany alone, the German emperor dreamt of transcending it within an expanded and reconfigured balance of power. Such a balance, to achieve the objective, would have had to shift a Europeanized Great Britain to the side of Germany in joint opposition to the non-European, American and Japanese, political and economic ensembles. Charles de Gaulle of France attempted more recently in a similar vein to Europeanize Soviet Russia in her policy by mobilizing China diplomatically as a complement to her ongoing internal mobilization by ideology and organization. He would simultaneously reorient a French-led Western Europe to a more flexible middle position between the American and the Soviet "hegemonies." Whereas the Wilhelminian conception might have freed France from British tutelage as late as 1912 (by placing her in a subordinate but marginally regulatory position between Britain and Germany), the later Gaullian conception aimed no more successfully to free Western Europe in the enlarged, but analogous, setting.

The key problem before and following the two world wars had been the Russo-German relationship. That relationship became subordinate to one between Russia-in-Europe and China-in-Asia. Just as a Sino-Soviet coalescence would exert an overwhelming weight on Germany, divisions between the two major Communist powers produced additional leverage or inducement operative on Russia to the possible advantage for West Germany and her allies. In the past, a shared antagonism to a narrowly conceived exclusivist West might have made Germany into the technologico-organizational brain of the Russian brawn. The alternative was for Germany to be a forward anti-Russian barrier in defense of a West that was expanded to include

Germany either as a mere auxiliary (in periods immediately following German defeats in war) or as a full partner (in subsequent periods of peace and reconstruction). In the Sino-Soviet relationship, it was China's Maoist regime that viewed itself as the ideological brain for a Russian body politic that had enhanced meanwhile its brute power by modern technology and military organization of its own. The leaders of Soviet Russia refused to play the role assigned to them in a division of labor that would resemble the one the British had previously designed for the United States in the Anglo-American relationship. They sought instead to represent the Soviet Union from time to time as the advance bastion of either Europe or the West against China, to serve as such on the basis of a ratified Soviet security position in Europe and of selective accommodation with the West outside Europe.

In the East-West polarity underlying the Cold War, the American objective of confining Soviet expansion adjoined various alignments and constellations to mobilized American capability and will. That strategy culminated in the "normalization" of relations with dissident China. Were the resurgence of China to crystallize and intensify a new kind of East-West cleavage, it might well become the American interest to limit the exposure of the Eurasian Soviet state to the external pressures from its two-front situation and to the internal tensions of its multiethnic structure. A major displacement of politico-military power in Eurasia would in itself constitute a significant reconfiguration globally. An actual disintegration of the innermost Soviet core-empire would be a yet more dramatic event, with yet greater impact on world equilibrium than had followed from the disruption of the multiethnic empires in Europe just before and following World War I. Any developments that would open up such perspectives even remotely would test the American commitment to the post-empire role of moderator and equilibrium leader, if not a continuously engaged material balancer, among comparably cohesive major powers contending more intensely with one another than with the United States.

To practice a policy for congenial world order on the cheap would seek to economize on American capabilities, commitments, and (hopefully) risks. So much is legitimate. It would be a different matter if the American policy for equilibrium sought merely to offset deficient military counterpoising of the Soviet Union by displaying marked partisanship in favor of China as part of a revised "open-door" tradition. Comparably romantic motives and biases might encourage also, and more probably, a self-consciously liberal-humanitarian policy for the Third World on commodity prices, credits, and commercial outlets. Such a policy would favor generalized conciliation along with selective cooptation of third-world claimants to the exclusion of both a persistent containment of disruptive forces or exactions in the South and a systematic promotion of crystallizing regional balance-of-power systems in the Third World. If carried out one-sidedly and single-mindedly, the combination of illusively liberal and romantic biases in U.S. foreign policy would carry within it risks and consequences not unlike those dogging the earlier British choice for "free trade" over reordered empire and for the United States against Imperial Germany. It might also reflect, under the cover of reverting to the habitual postempire pattern of equilibrium- or economics-centered foreign policy, manifest before World War I, the more or less conscious drift back to conditions prevailing after that war at the then (European) center of the international system.

The postwar and interwar conditions combined social upheavals within countries with fundamental asymmetries in power, will, and perceived evolutionary trends between "victorious" Britain and France and "defeated" Germany and Soviet Russia. A drift backward would be characterized by the deepening of similar asymmetries between the United States and the major Communist powers individually or in re-formed combination. It would display, furthermore, socioeconomic upheavals in the West aggravated if not caused by the exactions of the present era's incarnation of revisionist "have-nots." Political and social instability would replace the post-World War II vacuums of power which the United States was able to manage by virtue of both constructive national policies and competitive interactions with the Soviets generating new "third" powers before stalemating the main rivals. Despite an inferior Soviet material endowment and, initially, also entitlement to equivalent political role, the open contest between the two ascendant powers with open-ended, long-term prospectives produced a but middling level of fluctuating hostility. The contest differed thus favorably from the post-World War I situation. Then, the rivalry and hostility among powers with multiple asymmetries had been for long but latent, only to be released eventually in a violent conflict which brought to a head both the social malaise within countries and the politico-economic maladjustments among them.

The United States could not continue to merely moderate interactions from an essentially uncommitted liberal-economizing posture if the situation was rapidly crystallizing and, in the process, deteriorating on the South-North axis, a new East-West axis, or the old East-West axis exacerbated by the mismanagement of the other axes or any possible intertwining of these. Relations with the Soviet Union, and the course and outcome of the contention over parity, could then evolve in basically different directions. On the revised East-West axis one possibility was to receive a receptive (because "Europeanized") Soviet Union fully into the West, for improved balance in immediate deterrence or defense against China-led "Asia" and for accommodation with the latter in due course. Both the initial defense and the eventual accommodation would be fostered if the strengthened new West softened the "racial" aspect of the cleavage. To that end it was imperative to eschew and offset any politico-economic incentives for Japan, and any politico-military pressures on her, to side with a resurgent China against former associates in the industrial-Atlantic West. Another possibility was to reject a receptive Soviet Russia, by a West strong or rigid enough to quarantine her between West and East, and direct the Russian weight and thrust once again toward Asia. A major hegemonial drive (to forestall a rising China while still possible) would then be the Soviet alternative to a major effort at Sino-Soviet recoalescence (on terms that would be consistent with expanding and expansive Chinese power in the first phase of reconciliation at the very least). On the South-North axis, be it straightforwardly economic or modified by Chinese leadership, a receptive because more fully industrialized Soviet Union could again be either coopted or repelled. It could be coopted into the North for the purpose of securing better terms from the South in a confrontation leading to accommodation. Or the "Northwest" could repel more or less cryptic and conditional Soviet bids for solidarity. It might do so if the prime interest was to tighten its hold on residual geopolitical assets and possessions at large, or to diffuse the South-North cleavage by means of continuing politico-military contests within and over the Third World involving local and remote powers of all categories.

A movement from American-Soviet détente to an entente resembling alliance might be the sole alternative to intensified conflict. An entente would formalize a converging superpower response to growing, and increasingly shared, threats from either a revived or revised East-West cleavage or from a neorevolutionary South-North polarity masterminded by politically either radical or reactionary regimes. In such a case, the United States would embrace the Soviet Union as the only available substitute for a nonexistent major "liberal" ally, such as the early United States had been for Britain. It would do so in the hope, moreover, that the American "alliance" might cumulatively liberalize the Soviet regime itself. Such internal liberalization pertains to the potentially moderating role of interallied relations, as distinct from the regulatory one in the balance of power.[1] It is also conceptually distinct from any equalizing effect that alliance can have on powers that, having been compelled by events to initiate the parity quest, proved unable to overcome the obstacles to its success outside of a closer association. But "liberalization" and "equalization" will tend to interplay positively in practice none the less.

When looking for final "conflict resolution" in their structurally conditioned rivalry, maritime and continental powers faced traditionally the

---

1. See ch. i and pp. 130–32 for "regulatory" and other functions of alliances.

extreme choice between total or integral alliance and total and in some respects disintegrating conflict. So did often mercantile-maritime powers, as distinct from land-focused states, contending among themselves. In the case of imperial Britain, this meant total conflict with Bourbon and Napoleonic France and with both Germany and Japan, and close alliance with defeated United Provinces and a more unevenly close one with depressed France. Since naval power had ceased being ultimate, and the land-sea power schism unbridgeable, the extreme choice was giving way to more partial and gradual modes for resolving conflicts. At the same time, the shift from naval to nuclear power as the ultimate capability displaced crude balancing of military and economic resources to more subtle and elusive forms of multifaceted stabilization. There was thus a better chance for a gradual and curcuitous approach to an American-Soviet "alliance." It was possible for such an association to be initially only limited and partial, as it had been for short-lived alliances also in the past. The association could be in addition, as past alliances had not been, also equal or equalizing externally and liberalizing of the more coercive ally internally.

A partial or limited alliance between the dominant sea power and the navalized preeminent continental state was historically possible only if the military (or militaristic) state imitated the maritime one likewise no more than partially. That is, the continental state had to confine its overseas goals and accept both considerable and unequal costs of the association. The obverse of a limited alliance based on conditionally tolerated, partial imitation is an integral or total alliance. It habitually implements unqualified reciprocity by raising the so far "junior" ally (or "inferior" party) from imitation to identity with the "senior" ally (or "superior" party). The identity may be one of character as an amphibious land-sea power; or it may be also one of role and status as a world power.

Imperial Germany would not consider a limited and unequal alliance with Britain. In this she acted unlike France in the several postwar or peacetime ententes that punctuated the protracted Anglo-French conflict from the post-Utrecht period in the second decade of the eighteenth century on. The type informed also the Anglo-Japanese association. For such an alliance to be cohesive, the junior ally had to accept restraint by the senior partner in return for de facto neutrality while making gains, mostly on land (e.g., France's in Lorraine just as Japan's in Manchuria). With equal regularity, the alliance would be inhibited and finally disrupted by the lesser ally's revolting against the degree of imposed resignation. French revolts against the British alliance were periodic and only culminated in the Gaullist rebellion against the Anglo-American one, just as Pearl Harbor merely climaxed Japan's revolt against the American pretension to apply more rigorously the restraining function slipping from the hands of the enfeebled

British. Concurrently, the senior ally would come to fear lest his "neutrality" reverse inequality within the alliance to his disadvantage. British fears of a reversal behind the alliance screen helped disrupt the first Anglo-French entente in the Walpole-Fleury era after a worldwide conflict over succession to the Spanish empire. Similar British concerns helped preclude altogether an Anglo-German accommodation prior to the global conflict that initiated the demise of the successor British empire. And, at a still later date, similar American apprehensions conjoined with the resistance of the "junior" Soviet party to constraints in inhibiting a détente that was not related to an eventual entente in either concept or conduct.

If the Soviet Union lined up with the United States under severe external pressures, an initially limited American-Soviet "alliance" would tend to perpetuate the respective senior and junior status of the associates. In any other situation, the classic modalities of a limited alliance were hard to apply to the American-Soviet relationship. Thus, apparent failure attended the American attempt to exchange, under the name of détente, a both belated and retroactive U.S. neutrality in regard to prior Soviet gains on the European continent for future Soviet self-limitation overseas. But the failure did not mean that a limited alliance could never be aimed at restraining Soviet foreign policy behavior, and that some initial inequality of status between the associates might not even be helpful in promoting restraint. The possible scope of effective restraint would, however, be circumscribed not only by the ratios of usable American and Soviet capabilities, but also by the purpose of such an alliance. The most likely such purpose would be to routinize progression toward a common front in policy and overall parity in standing as the interdependent terminal states. In the process, the extent to which the alliance itself restrained Soviet conduct would be only superadded to other constraints and be greatly contingent on its potential for combining interallied equalization with liberalizing the Soviet political system. An American-Soviet association for parity and counterpoise was unlikely to be a condominial alliance in either intention or practical external effect, but it could be antidictatorial in both American intention and internal Soviet results.

The alliance could not be globally condominial if parity realized the defensive concern of both superpowers with outside factors and forces. These may incite a belated try at condominium. But their very potency will in such a case remove automatically the prerequisites for the attempt's success. The alliance might be antidictatorial, however. Restraints on foreign policy among allies can be linked with revisions of domestic order if the senior ally fosters the internal liberalization of a major autocratic association while conceding both the forms and the practices of interallied equality. Only imminent equality will make restraint subtle, domestic revisions ostensibly spontaneous, and the combination or interplay of restraint and revision acceptable to the affected party. Since the Anglo-French alliance was typically unequal, its liberalizing effect in France was only sporadic; and since the Anglo-Japanese alliance did not evolve manifestly toward equality of status and rewards for Japan, and may have evolved inversely under American influence, its initial liberalizing impact was precarious and the final reaction to frustration catastrophic. The alliance of Republican France with Tsarist Russia failed to translate the liberal doses of financial aid to the autocracy by the French rentier class into political liberties for the Russian middle classes. But largely to blame was the inverse inequality of politico-military and economic needs and dependences, which gave the upper hand to the financially weaker ally. And, despite the hopes entertained along liberal lines among proponents of an Anglo-German connection inside the political system of Imperial Germany, the latter was not to be tested by such an alignment. Britain would not risk an equal alliance any more than she would countenance a total one, for fear of forfeiting restraint over German foreign policy before reforming German domestic politics. Moreover, a liberalized Germany might have been a threat to Britain yet harder to meet head-on in world trade than an autocratic empire was in the scales of world power.

So long as the United States did not have to fear similar derangements, it could hope to restrain Soviet foreign policy and promote revisions in the domestic Soviet practices simultaneously. If the ends and means of foreign policy have been moderated within an equal, if limited, alliance of sorts by tolerable methods, and moderation abroad is not the result of internal decay, interallied restraint will tend to "liberalize" the domestic order of an autocratic major power. Restraint itself will do so by reducing the organizational pressures and social strains that are commonly associated with a foreign policy that, being ambitious, requires the backing of vast resources. And the actual effects of restraint on foreign policy will dampen the kind of irrational mass support for an autocratic regime that assertive foreign policy commonly engenders when it is successful without being materially ruinous. Conversely, when gradual liberalization has enhanced a regime's security of tenure, its need for the domestic byproducts of an adventurous foreign policy will wane and "irrational" supports will become actually embarrassing. The moderating tendencies will not operate, however, when the foreign policy has been restrained from the outside too massively and has become manifestly inapt as a result to satisfy basic needs and widely held aspirations. Nor would moderation occur when, after it was "liberalized," a regime was forced to let its foreign policy be overstimulated by the need to compensate for the ineptitudes of a pluralistic politics that had been internally assimilated only insufficiently if at all.

It is, therefore, important that an equal alliance of an ascendant continental (and thus somehow radical) state with an established (and thus internationally conservative even if internally liberal) maritime power act as a sword as well as a shield. Alliance will act as a sword when it opens up not only new kinds of access abroad but also avenues for diffusion and exchange of values that extend the imitation of the "senior" by the "junior" ally beyond foreign policy to domestic mores and practices. Alliance acts as a shield when it reinforces regime defense against an inassimilable rate of change, even while inhibiting retrogressive regime reprisals against moderate pressure for change. An alliance will do both when it conditionally legitimizes the internally autocratic regime to a point at which the regime can afford to be increasingly lenient while the "liberal" opposition becomes sufficiently confident of the outcome to be patient as to the rate of change and restrained as to the means of promoting change. Any such beneficent revision is much more likely to flow between near-equal major powers than from a major to a minor state. No power is likely to be "major" under modern conditions unless its sociopolitical structures are fundamentally ready for a relatively "liberal" order. Moreover, an equal alliance is possible only between comparable powers, and only an equal alliance will permit a hitherto autocratic regime to relax internal controls because it ratifies, as the institutional expression of parity, the regime's past foreign-policy achievements as a basis from which to manage domestic pressures for change.

In promoting revisions of domestic power equations in depth, reassurance of the less secure or stable regime by alliance will vitally supplement any strains and pressures that simultaneously operate among powers. Acting alone, externally originated pressures and strains will suffice only to superficially redistribute power by way of reversible changes in alignments. However, the same strains and pressures will be helpful, and may be necessary, if significant internal pressures on a regime are to be properly phased and graduated, and if outside reassurance for internal reform is to have significant chance of success. The external strains and pressures can originate in an earlier alliance of the continental-autocratic state, or in its prior antagonism with the liberal-maritime power. Prior distortions in interallied equity, no less than derangements in interadversary equilibrium, will tend to increase receptivity to a combination of restraint and reform within an alternative alliance as the price to pay for essential equality in both status and payoffs. Thus even if an American-Soviet entente were to be more critically tested by its success in restraining Soviet foreign policy and revising domestic Soviet structures than in countervailing third parties and stabilizing general international relations, the origin of such an entente would still be found in the regulatory function of alliances in the conventional balance of power. That is, the Soviet Union would have moved toward the United States in recoil from previously unmanageable allies, first and foremost Maoist China and subsequently and secondarily third-world allies such as Egypt or India and their likely or possible successors. If the accommodation process with the United States were to prove likewise abortive, however, the Soviet Union would be bound to explore alternatives. It might seek to renew the connection with China or radicalize the links with the South, merely revert to a totalitarian polity and unqualifiedly aggressive policy, or evolve an unprecedented response to the failure to achieve the minimum goal of parity. And the Soviets might then face a United States incapable of reversing its own evolution from empire to equilibrium and beyond to nonstrategic economism, and of reasserting in full either the Cold War/imperial ethos and energy or classic balance-of-power skill and resilience.

In a general way, regulation of the conventional balance of power by sufficiently "flexible" alliances will interplay with the moderating, restraint-and-revision, role of relatively "equal" alliances in any strategy and structure susceptible of fitting an ascendant autocratic power into a stable framework. Such a power will typically, if not necessarily, be also a continental or land-focused state. Failures and ineptitudes in implementing either of the moderating, restraint or revision, functions will tend to activate the regulatory function of an alliance, and may misdirect it into realigning interstate associations or national policies in ways contrary to equilibrium, just as the effective working of the regulatory function for equilibrium in one alliance may give another association the chance for moderating the era's critical aspirant to parity or preeminence.

A movement toward a limited American-Soviet alliance or entente was not the only possible consequence of either rigid or complex repolarization in the international system. Changes in U.S. alliances with Western Europe and Japan might be more readily forthcoming if increased Soviet power were to lead to either reintensified antagonism or to relatively indeterminate or transitional, three-or-more-cornered, interplays for equilibrium implicit in the more complex variety of repolarization. Such adaptations might see Western Europe tilt toward the Soviet Union, but they were unlikely to see soon the Western Europeans join Japan in alliance with China against an American-Soviet effort to go beyond conciliation, on the basis of parity, to condominium for joint predominance. Conversely, a failure for U.S.-Soviet accommodation might engender strong pressures to reconsolidate the residual American empire for the long pull in the aftermath of the post-Vietnam lull; or, a revival for empire-centered policies in the original or a modified form might itself cause an American-Soviet accommodation effort to fail. Whether a cause or an effect, imperial reconsolidation was apt to entail a basic revision of both "hierarchy" and "integration" within the major Western alliance in the direction of more or less interallied equality and role-sharing, to be followed by the recovery of some of the positions that had been lost in the twilight of America's latest, essentially still national or unilateral, empire phase. Pending any of the possible new departures, however, it was tempting to mark time before facing in earnest the choice between the rigors of reascent and revision of empire and the risks of descent onto the more restful plateau of equilibrium.

Nor did past precedents guarantee anything. The state system of the 1830s was partially repolarized along the liberal vs. conservative, or East vs. West, axis, away from the traditional land-sea power axis. This helped relieve the conflicts attendant on the parity issue between France and Britain. But the ideological issue was not sufficiently operative in the realm of practical politics to either redeem the French ambitions or reduce British denials of parity to France as part of joint opposition to the Eastern or "autocratic" powers. Even less fruitful were Emperor William II's ambitions to repolarize the international system between a European combine (preferably including Britain) and the ascendant extra-European powers of America and Japan. They did not come anywhere near influencing the Anglo-German parity quandaries. And in regard to alliances, finally, the wartime associations between the United States and Great Britain resolved the issue of parity between the two kindred empires peacefully, but only in favor of conclusive disparity also globally. Britain's alliance with her insular analogue in Asia, Japan, lacked both time and autonomy to prove itself. And whereas the lopsided British ententes with France relieved regime-differences and repressed rivalries only temporarily, no close liaison promoted liberalization or consummated accommodation in relations with Germany. As an atypical "third party," the United States had a part in some of the past failures. Following a first impact on the Old World as a revolutionary example for freedom from internally concentrated power, America's mere existence (even before any interference) became a constraint on evolutionary adjustments in that same world's balance of power. Existence has since done its work on the example; but experience with both concentrated and countervailing power ought to have been sufficient to permit consulting the past without idealizing the beginnings.

XII

CONCLUSION. *The Conceptual Environment of American Foreign Policy*

Any attempt to draw upon a historical inquiry for guidance invites questions rather than produces predictions. But presumptions about tendencies, which are rooted in an analytic effort, ought to be useful in informing the consideration of basic alternatives. They ought also to justify the analogico-historical approach as a complement to both intuitive political sense and imaginative anticipation of unprecedented transformations. Fundamental questions dominate other queries. Can the United States escape the constraint of historical antecedents and recurrences, be they those connected with earlier (Roman and British) empires, earlier (European and Eurocentric) international system, and earlier (American) foreign policy experience and aspiration? Will American statecraft, in other words, inspired by antecedent frustrations and impelled by onrushing future challenges, be able to weave separate strands in the fabric of the past into a wholly new texture of polity or policy? Or will it be confined to less dramatic adjustments?

In neither case is a viable outcome likely to move outside the scope of either equilibrium or empire, much as it might vary in implementing the two broad and elastic modes. A major power can opt for equilibrium as the prime objective or priority; or, if empire is the preferred or reluctant choice, equilibrium interplays with other concentrations of power and among political forces internally are of interest mainly as supportive or subversive of the empire. The first kind of equilibration involves powers in an international system which itself evolves as an incident to cross-pressures within it; the second kind of policy places higher demands on purposively inflecting evolution as it reaches the critical crossroads separating a plural from a hegemonial international system. Although both policy priorities entail alignments and alliances, each impresses upon them a different form and prime function.

If the United States rules out self-isolation in both the national or continental and the regional or west-hemispheric compasses, its historically indicated options will be limited to revising the approach to world empire or resuming in full the tradition of rebounding from empire to an equilibrium or balance-of-power policy. A revision of world empire would have to incorporate the experiences accruing with its growth and the misjudgments attendant on its late shrinkage. The prime objects of revision would include the relationships with major allies and between the essential industrial core and the developing peripheral segments abroad, and between changing foreign-policy elites and the changeable general public at home. A steadied reversion to postempire equilibrium statecraft would occur in a setting at once larger and more complex than had confronted America in the comparable earlier instance, in the days of Theodore Roosevelt. Statecraft would have, therefore, to incorporate more efficiently than ever before both of the interdependent requirements of effective action. It is one, and an easier, thing to manipulate constellations in variable conformity with the disparate diplomatic options and policy objectives of the principal parties. A different and more exacting task is to manage evolving configurations in the structures of power and conflict over the longer term. Only when it has interlocked the distinct operations in a coherent strategy will statecraft know how to mold to national and, perhaps, also larger advantage the two-faced issue of parity and preeminence in material capabilities and in their geopolitical consequences and counterparts.

Moving beyond two centuries of trial and error, American statecraft faced a combined, empirical and conceptual, environment of current givens, alternative basic formats of minimum order, and critical policy dilemmas and related choices. If the alternative formats have been, so far, the historically tested immutable ones of empire and equilibrium, and the futilely tried economism in one form or another,[1] the givens were time-bound. They consist of such (previously reviewed) matters as, in the military domain, the American-Soviet arms balance; in the economic domain, the South-North relationship in general and oil-power vs. industrial power (and vulnerability) in particular; and, in the political domain, the lopsided

---

1. See the Introduction, pp. xi–xiii.

character of American power (reascendant in its economic base more rapidly than in its politico-strategic application or applicability) and the inversely unbalanced Soviet power, as well as such policy-relevant features as the ambiguities of China, the fragilities of unevenly economically and militarily strong (or weak) third-world middle powers, and the vulnerabilities of Western Europe and Japan. Combining in one way or another all of the military, political, and economic functional traits were, moreover, the territorially bounded crises in the Middle East, Southern Africa, and Eastern Mediterranean in particular and, seemingly or ultimately all-transcending, the quintessentially "environmental" problems of food, energy, climate, and the like. Intermediate in degree of specificity between the basic concepts of order and the territorially confined crises were the policy quandaries and the alternative, more or less practicable and perfect, responses to them. Whereas the quandaries comprised the issue of balance within policies, the policy responses entailed also such questions as the timing of risks, the assigning of priorities, and the synchronizing of (policy and trend) maturities, as aspects of more or less desired or desirable outcomes.

Whether and how to evolve a "balance" between strategic-military and geopolitical parity with the Soviet Union, between approaches to SALT and access to the Southern Hemisphere, was not the only policy quandary for the United States. Similar choices between balance and discrepancy within issue pairs bore on relationships between détente with the Soviet Union and the development of links with China; between the cultivation, in the South-North setting, of a usable military-strategic framework and of economic-financial formulas, checking or not any future unilateral Southern forcing of issues by revived American capacity for forcefulness; between stressing great powers as objects of concern and emphasizing the middle powers and, among the latter, between promoting third-world middle powers as geopolitical surrogates for the United States and containing them when they act as actual or would-be economic subversives in relation to American-favored order; between approaching Europe as a whole by a policy that is global in long-term implication and sharply compartmentalizing approaches to Western and to Eastern Europe within an approach narrowly Atlanticist in its implication; and finally, within the United States itself, balance between policies appealing to humanistic "softheads" and policies more attuned to nationalistic "hard-hats" within a regalvanized social structure and elite-mass interaction.

In themselves static and structural, such dichotomies and issues pairs will be brought to dynamic life by decisions about priorities in policy emphases and by attitudes on risks and maturities, which incorporate together the dimension of time.

Conceptual priority ought to be assigned in function of both the inherent importance of an issue or actor and one's own ability to directly or indirectly influence its course. Even though operative priority might shift from case to case, it was still misguided, though always attractive, to strive first and foremost at solving specific, territorially bounded issues and conflicts over the short term. Even as a new U.S. administration sought to wrest diplomatic triumphs from questionably solid prior transactions, there continued to be little prospect for quick solutions to either the still conflict-saturated Middle Eastern and Eastern Mediterranean (Cyprus and related) issues or in preconflict Southern Africa. If intrinsic reasons were apt to prevent negotiated settlements, intolerable domestic or external costs impeded one-sided or imposed ones, leaving only postconflict Indochina and Cuba open to productive diplomacy in the short run. In the middle term, the issue of American-Soviet material parity continued to rightfully possess conceptual priority for U.S. foreign policy. It was the ultimately most important stake and one at least as apt to affect as to be circuitously conditioned by either less critical or less directly influenceable lower-priority issues or actors. The latter included, in a descending scale of priorities, second-level third-world middle powers eligible as geopolitical surrogates in local balances of power without being economic subversives (or satellites, either); potential "third" great powers (China, Western Europe, Japan); and the South as a geo-economic and ideological aggregate (excepting the independently important key third-world middle powers).

If it avoided equating immediate priority with longer-term importance, American foreign policy could reduce its primary concern to no more than keeping Western Europe from collapse (as she strove for an ideal polity following de Gaulle's quest for real power); to helping China directly or indirectly to steer her course away from internal convulsions or consequent external coalescence with either the Soviet Union or the South (as she moved to acquire real power following the Maoist quest for an ideal polity); and to helping Japan maintain a viable polity and environment for economic prosperity (at a time when Japan was past attempts to find ideal polity in either dictatorship or democracy and was not yet ready to reassert real power). By the same token, the ranking of the aggregate South in the scale of priorities depended on wholly indirect concerns and related criteria, having to do with its capacity or inclination, under the impetus of different American policies, to threaten Western European (and Japanese) economic survival (cum political democracy); to alienate Japan from the United States or activate her prematurely; to present China with an opportunity for revolutionary leadership (in the South), and the Soviets with a potential for exploiting South-North tensions (as a pseudosouthern rather than para-northern party).

Being both important and directly subject to American action, the relations with the Soviets had priority; they also linked other issues with the question—and, ideally, American choices—of more or less immediate or delayed risks. In the narrow superpower context, to deny geopolitical concessions (promoting material parity) to the Soviets entailed the early risk of precipitating a second cold war; making substantial concessions delayed the risk to second-order containment having to cope with the consequences of material parity and its potential for degenerating into Soviet paramountcy. A properly controlled or managed Soviet progress to material parity in the world at large was a way of promoting a positive all-European evolution; it entailed also prior risks in regard to both China and the South. In Europe, relatively early risks would attend any determined American action against the spread of Communst-tinged socialism in Western Europe (e.g., by intervening in the Middle East to relieve a politically debilitating Western European economic crisis or by decidedly pushing for an enhanced Western European political role at large as an offset to civic apathy and demoralization). Conversely, American inaction on the issue of "Euro-Communism" was apt to delay risks to the later point of localized or worldwide confrontation with the Soviet Union, due to either offensive Soviet efforts to exploit NATO's disintegration or defensive Soviet reactions to the actual or threatening effects of a chain reaction from a socialist Western Europe on Eastern Europe. In regard to China, the conferral or denial of geopolitical concessions to the Soviet Union ranked *mutatis mutandis* with the denial or conferral of economic and military aid to China herself as creating either the early risks of China's revolutionary coalescence with residual (or development-incapable) South or a conventional rapproachement with the Soviet Union, or else engendering the later risk of China's bid for regional supremacy or global parity with the United States alone (in possible coalescence with the Soviets on China's terms).

Similarly, complacent concessions to the South verging on appeasement engendered an early risk for trilateralism (by way of causing economic hardships in Western Europe and Japan of a kind highlighting the difference between the support of the essential allies for the accommodation process with the South and their vulnerability to its consequences). Conversely, a radical denial of concessions to the South entailed a possibly later risk for triangularism, as China was tempted by the chance for revolutionary leadership of the economically weakest Southern elements or the Soviet Union responded to the possibility to exploit the resentments of the economically stronger Southern powers. And finally, imposing settlements on the Middle Eastern or South African issues to the detriment of local minorities culturally and otherwise cognate with the West, leading up to their protracted decay or dramatic collapse, entailed early risks for both the local balances of power and the domestic foreign-policy consensus in the United States; whereas allowing a gradual erosion and supersession of these conflicts by more pressing or up-to-date contentions and concerns to take its course augmented the longer-term risk of eventual American-Soviet confrontation at some stage of the protracted conflict-terminating process.[2]

The more delicate the balances (vs. discrepancies) in the issue pairs, and the more troublesome the choice between early and delayed risks, the more imperative it will be to reach for the highest art in statecraft, in the effort to coordinate and synchronize the maturities of policy strategies and of the trends the strategies are designed to foster.

Just as (to repeat once more and for the last time) geopolitical concessions to the Soviet Union must be timed to coincide with evolving configurations in the Third World and conditions in Europe (so that they are devalued by the devolution of American responsibilities to local third parties even as they are compensated for by the dispersion of Soviet outlets diminishing Soviet inducements to coercive control in Eastern Europe) so the globalization of Soviet policy or navalization of Soviet power ought to climax concurrently with China's capacity either to bid for hegemonial self-assertion on racial or revolutionary grounds in Asia or, alternatively, to claim parity worldwide with the two major powers. And the key China-abutting regional middle powers ought to be ready by that time for effective leadership in local balances of power or, alternatively, for countervailing regional imperialism. Likewise, a climactic confrontation with the South, if ever necessary, ought to be delayed until concurrent developments have detraumatized Americans in regard to order-maintaining (or imperial) military missions, or else shifted their trauma to economically conditioned frustrations; until such developments have projected the Soviet Union into a postindustrial and China into an economically developed and postrevolutionary condition; and until they have immunized Europe and Japan substantially to temporary disruptions of key supplies. As an alternative to confrontation with the South in the aggregate, the full cooptation of development-capable (or middle-income) third-world countries into the "northern" industrial system ought to be timed so as to be in place for the onset of a second cold war with the Soviet Union or, more likely, second-order containment of the consequences of Soviet globalization; so as to offset the possible reversion by China to self-isolation (or possible necessity to reconsign her to isolation); and so as to complement the integration of Western Europe and Japan into a U.S.-centered new world equilibrium or empire. And finally, the reintegration of the essential industrial allies would be most fruitful if it matured along with their enhanced readiness for a more active participant role in the aftermath of successfully overcome internal political and economic crisis.

---

2. See Postscript, pp. 218–46, for discussion of related points.

Promoted along these or comparable lines, the synchronization of maturities was liable to require some delaying of critical policy choices at the always possible partings of the ways for alternative trends or courses (e.g., toward resumed containment or deepened cooperation with the Soviet Union and, inversely, cooperation with China as against containment of China). Synchronization of maturities entailed also, in part as a result, the subordination of facile morality in foreign policy to sophisticated manipulation, transferring the moral warrant for the long-term strategy to the quality of an effectively sought and partially achieved outcome.

The adjustment of the critical balances within issue pairs and the timing of risks, setting of priorities, settling of specific territorially bounded crises, and, most critically, the coordinating of maturities were liable to either maximize pressures for a new American empire as an alternative to American decay or world chaos if the operations were neglected or mismanaged, or foster progress toward equilibrium if they were attended to with skill and success. An integral reversion to empire would be to one more confined spatially but also tighter structurally than had been the supremacy spawned, initially unnoticed, by the Cold War. The "next" empire would be different because based domestically on a new blend of American nationalism and imperialism, fed by the just-incurred historical experience, and sustained (as the post-World War II empire had not been) by a conscious awareness of its true character, by concrete economic compulsions (next to abstract security equations) and, consequently, by a sociologically well-defined constituency in the form of ethnically more variegated elites and politically upgraded blue-collar mass. Conversely, the new equilibrium would be larger and looser (i.e., functionally more inclusive) than the classic balance of power. It would encompass autonomous (Western) Europe and Japan in one way, horizontally, and third-world middle powers in another way, vertically, as buffers or insulators between the two or three main military powers. Alternatively, a synthesis was possible of the two prototypical, empire and equilibrium, formats and outcomes. It would have two to three centers in a liberal-cooperative if U.S.-centered Atlantic Confederacy, linked to Japan and to select third-world middle powers (such as Brazil, Iran, or Indonesia); in a loosened Soviet preeminence in Eastern Europe, liberalized by a combination of more "organic" regional foundations and worldwide overseas outlets (in occasional order-maintaining association with the United States); and possibly also in a China-centered Asian sphere evolving from revolutionary to conventional patterns in both doctrine and control mechanisms. Having two or three centers, such an equilibrium-empire synthesis would have two geopolitical levels, an interregional one ultimately controlled by the major powers and an intraregional one centered on local middle powers. And it would have two key functional sides, a geostrategic one, constituting the framework of individual and reciprocal security, and an economic one, ministering to individual and collective welfare.

The key difference between an unadulterated enlarged equilibrium and the equilibrium-empire mix was apt to be found in the political domain. The role and position of (Western or also Eastern) Europe and Japan, and on the more distinctly vertical or hierarchical axis also of the third-world middle powers, would be one of autonomous insulators among the superpowers in the first scenario and one of ultimately dependent associates within the relaxed imperial frameworks in the second. Conversely, the key overt difference between a tightened American empire or endemic chaos on one side and the both pure and empire-modified equilibrium on the other was apt to lie in the economic dimension. On one side were two varieties of economism, one characterizing a declining or otherwise beset empire reduced to using residual politico-strategic leverage to repair seasonal or structural economic weaknesses (illustrated or only intimated by the "Nixon shocks" of the early 1970s) and the other characterized by a politico-strategically unsupported reliance (from actual or assumed economic strength) on ultimate mutualities of material interests as inherently tractable in isolation from noneconomic constraints and leverages, even if not inherently harmonious (as propounded by the more extreme of the world-order advocates in the immediately succeeding era). On the other side was an appropriate harmonization of economics and politics, economic and politico-military power, in a complete approach to a normatively satisfying world order empirically based on an equilibrium that either incorporated or was largely free of elements of empire.

Both a pure and an empire-qualified equilibrium were positively tied up to the successful unfolding of the American-Soviet quest for parity. A contrary evolution threatened to transmute America's post-World War II imperial role into intensified American imperialism (in self-defense against the alternative of chaos), whereas a wholesale degeneration of economic instrumentalism (previously employing "foreign aid" in the service of imperial order-maintenance) into institutionalized economism was liable to open up avenues to such chaos. If "imperialism" would attend, as either cause or effect, the collapse of the parity quest, the variety of "economism" divorced from empire would remove the bases from under the quest by shifting the requirement of American self-assertion (as the necessary counterpart to concessions) wholly from the employment of power at the peripheries to an unrestrained military build-up at the strategic center.

The mapping of the pathway toward America-Soviet parity (and away from alternatives to it) will continue to depend on a viable conception of the meaning of parity.[3] The implied mix of capabilities constituting formal

3. See ch. ix.

parity (e.g., Soviet military superiority on land in Europe, American superiority on the world's seas, and parity approximating equality in strategic nuclear deterrents) stands for reciprocal vulnerabilities or, at the extreme point, reciprocal indefensibility of the superpowers (and their allies) in the central relationship. It may come to stand also for the military capacity of both for reciprocal denial of marginal gains and peripheral access in secondarily important theaters or situations in conditions of nominal peace. Material parity, as the necessary corollary to formal parity, stands on the other hand for the principle of qualitative status equality, *in posse* if not immediately *in esse*, for the initially inferior party. It correspondingly involves the acceptance by the initially superior party of the implications of such prospective status equality for balanced or balancing geopolitical gains in peripheral theaters (eventuating in parallel equilibration). The combination of one party's accepting revisions and, consequently, the other's spacing the satisfaction of ambitions, would minimize the political pressures on the central-strategic theater and reduce also the propensity actually to employ the military denial capability for reciprocal frustration at the peripheries. So conceived, the parity-evolving process is keyed to the reduction of incentives to military conflict between the major power over time. It addresses thus, with the aid of dialectically emerging supportive global configuration, the initiation of conflict rather than being thwarted by a continuous linking to hypothetical conflict outcomes, estimated in terms of worst-case calculations and linear projections.

The relationship between military capabilities and political contexts can be illustrated, and the underlying issue posed, in the form of a question. In the missile crisis over Cuba in 1962, and in the mining of the Haiphong harbor ten years later, was the American success over Soviet initiative in the first case, and the immunity of American action to Soviet military reaction in the second, due only to local naval American superiority (endangered by the intervening, and apt to be nullified or reversed by a future, Soviet naval build-up)? Or else, were likewise critical the political facts, of Cuba being in the American sphere and the sphere being illegitimately invaded by the Soviet Union and the mining of Haiphong being part of a face-saving American retreat from an advanced position, tolerable as a result by the Soviet Union without significant damage to its prestige? Assigning a substantial role to the political factors would be in conformity with the rules of the game of the Cold War in the first case and of détente in the second, while an increase of political considerations in the second case as compared with the first was significant because it coincided with the decline of American strategic-nuclear as well as naval superiority and reflected the intervening diminution of the American-Soviet rivalry. If the role of the political factor could be seen as increasing relative to the hardware factor during a decade, nothing precluded the indefinite continuance and amplification of the trend as part of a systematically nurtured parity-evolving process related to detente over a still longer time span.

Parity is, in the last analysis, along with several other key normative and strategic political concepts (such as intervention and the balance of power itself) essentially and fruitfully a metaphysical notion. It is such in both the literal sense, of being above the physical aspect of hardware calculations (if not above the physics of power dynamics), and in the wider sense of being a concept with a debatable concrete meaning but also with meaningful and objectively self-evident connotations (differing thus favorably from, say, the notion of sufficiency in mere weaponry). Apart from the symbolic-educative functions of arms-control discussions, neither formal nor material parity can be, therefore, usefully negotiated as a succession of states or conditions, but it must be assimilated into foreign policy in the twin guise of a working process and an accepted terminus to modified competition.

The potentially positive relationship of detente and quest for parity will be manifest when the former contributes a psychopolitical mind-set to attenuating the disruptive impact of the dilemmas and quandaries unavoidably posed by the latter in the spheres of both arms and geopolitical assets. When so established, the relationship between détente and parity would qualify as the successor to one between cold war and containment. It would denote American success in the earlier process and strategy as to substance, insofar as the Soviet Union became eligible for the détente-parity combination as a conventionalized (regardless of whether also a mellowed) power. But the new process pair (encompassing the previously itemized issue pairs) would also denote the procedural impossibility (and undesirability, rather than the substantive failure) of indefinitely confining a so transmuted Soviet Union within the East-European and Eurasian continental heartland, either at all or at a universally acceptable cost in American material deployment, internal sociopolitical development (beyond or away from welfare to military "warfare" state), and evolution in external policy (beyond imperial role within a loose empire to imperialistic rigors within a tight empire).

Just as there was a possible positive relationship between détente and the quest for parity, however, there could be and largely was a negative relationship between the two. A workable, parity-evolving détente will be both punctuated and actuated (we have noted earlier[4]) by successive transitions between (stages in the movement toward) parity in military capabilities and (stages in the movement toward) parity in geopolitical positions corresponding to the capabilities. As part of resistance to that dynamic, the American political arena displayed instead, in fluctuating emphases, verbal critiques of (or denials of Soviet entitlement to) either the

4. See p. 182.

employment of tacitly conceded capabilities for geopolitically meaningful ends (mainly in the Nixon-Kissinger era) or the growth in Soviet military capabilities as such (more prominently in the ensuing period). The fluctuations in verbal and other interdicts were not likely to implement the desirable mix of inhibitions and incentives. Nor were they apt to mediate either the subsidiary short-term transitions (between specifically increased capability and its unopposed or legitimized employment) or the paramount long-term transition (from inconclusive contentions over the terms of parity to configurations both supporting and controlling the results of the process). It was no more productive, finally, to assail the dual process from the parity side than from the détente side. One such approach was to inhibit or derail the progression toward a quantitative-qualitative capability-mix constituting formal parity by scoring specific Soviet and American gains and losses from détente explicitly, while implicitly viewing détente as a mechanism for perpetuating Soviet military and geopolitical inferiority. Another such approach was to indirectly inhibit détente by frontally assailing the Soviet approach to the capability-mix (or formal parity) as denoting a Soviet drive for both military and geopolitical superiority.

Playing off détente against parity and vice versa in a critical mode constituted one (and narrowly "conservative") impediment to a progressive exit from the East-West conflict. A corresponding (loosely "liberal") derangement inhibited the advance to viable South-North adjustments. At issue was the relationship of the Southern claim to socioeconomic equity on a global plane to actual economic development on national planes and to politico-military equilibria or imperialisms regionally. In those respects, one defective approach was to represent the quest for global equity as conducive to the economic and political development of the least development-capable third-world countries in particular, while condoning demands for concessions and easements that were liable to obviate the need for, and nullify the incentives to, an economically disciplined and disciplining (as well as sociopolitically formative) development process. And a related fault was to disjoin the concession-mongering process from a coercion-capable American stance, and to treat the strategy for coopting the development-capable third-world middle (or middle-income) powers into the North-dominated global industrial system as one separable from a political strategy that would, one, meaningfully discriminate between economic subversives and strategic surrogates and, two, alternately condone and contain in a calculated manner the parallel politico-military self-assertion of either or both types of middle powers within the several regional theaters.

The intellectually predominating attitudes toward the South and the Soviet Union held positions diametrically opposed to one another in regard to short-term approaches, and risked being reciprocally frustrating in their long-term implications. The dominant approach to the South deemphasized the employment of American military capability (or force), and the relevance of the overall military-strategic framework for readjustments in the world economic order. It subordinated both force and framework to the assumed potential for negotiated convergence of economic interests, producing convergence of economic (and political) structures by virtue of more or less far-reaching economic redistribution. The converse attitude toward military redistribution and geopolitical reapportionment with respect to the Soviet Union was critically hostile to Soviet employment of military capabilities for geopolitical ends at the peripheries while laying heavy stress on the technical, both quantitative and qualitative, aspects of the military-strategic framework and its implications for action in the central theater. The same view of things also subordinated to the inherently incalculable factor of military capability, in itself and in relation to its employment, the hypothetical effects of growing inter-superpower symmetry in qualitative status. It discounted as a result the possibly beneficial consequence of status symmetry between the major powers for their progressing convergence in sociopolitical structures, leading to greater concordance in their interests and actions as the ongoing prerequisite to and a possible final result of effectively synchronizing constructive American strategies and global trends. Variously opposed by the two contrasting schools of thought were thus American and Soviet employment of military capabilities; and each school either deemphasized or overemphasized the strategic framework, either subordinated the framework to more organic convergence between the relevant parties or gave it marked precedence over such convergence, and either viewed the latter optimistically as progressing from interests to sociopolitical structures (in relations with the South) or minimized the probability that convergence both could and had to proceed inversely from structures to interests and action (in relations with the Soviet Union).

The one-sided, narrowly conservative and loosely liberal, doctrines and attitudes inhibited about equally an effective strategy for global equilibrium over time and across pitfalls. Ultraconservative elites opposed redistributive military equilibrium either directly by way of SALT or indirectly by way of détente. A formally if not materially, procedurally if not substantively, politicized conservative stance played down the technical military equations; but it failed to infer and implement the geopolitical implications. Both varieties of the conservative attitude reflected an extreme sensitivity to the presumption of irreversibility (or noncontrollability) of Soviet advance should it progress beyond a fairly proximate point in either military capabilities or geopolitical dispersion. When concentrating on the military-technological features, the attitude was a conservative-nationalistic replay in the Soviet case of the earlier, liberal-imperial, opposition to the French *force de frappe*. Each successive stance buried under technical arguments about either utility or usability of armaments a dogmatic opposition to a qualitative transformation of either ally or adversary in the direction of categorical status-equalization with the United States.

It was uncertain whether the conservative response was either a substitute or a revenge of erstwhile "hawks" for Vietnam, and thus essentially empire-related; or whether it was more narrowly nationalist (and anti-Soviet imperialist) in the imperial aftermath confining itself to the defense of territorial United States and its essential allies against maximum imaginable dangers, and oriented thus toward a strict conception of the balance of power focusing on quantitative "overbalance" and mechanical derivation of intentions from capabilities. An answer to that particular question might be progressively found in the evolving nationalist-conservative attitudes on the Southern issues. Meanwhile, the ultraconservative elites were more clearly differentiable from the humanist-or-humanitarian liberal ones in regard to fundamental attitudes than in respect to specific positions on détente and arms so long as the liberal elites were being as much or as little motivated by frustrations over domestic social programs (and the post-Vietnam "peace dividend") as the conservatives were actuated by fears for armaments-related industrial activity and domestic employment. It was uncertain whether and when liberal frustrations over economic interdependence in the world at large would follow disappointments with socioeconomic reform programs at home and weaken resistance to the utilization of "force" in one form or another, inducing a renewed support for circumscribing accommodation with the South no less authoritatively than conciliation with the Soviet Union. At such a future stage, the frustrations of liberals abroad would consummate the retribution for "dovish" posture on Vietnam, which helped weaken, by the fact of American defeat, the U.S.-managed strategic framework, and removed, by the fact of the defeat's domestic accompaniments, American capacity for strategic intervention in the peripheries. A different state of both framework and facility would have permitted economic interdependence (and redistribution) to proceed within the setting of U.S. authority as a given, without requiring recourse to specific acts of force as finally unavoidable.

Pending clarifications and possible corrections, apolitical militarism (or military technologism) complemented nonstrategic economism in a paralyzing effect on different aspects of American foreign policy. Both could be held to reflect an innate American preference for concrete and tangible features, amenable to organization and planning, over hypothetical speculation and diplomatic strategies when dealing with international contingencies and configurations. More serious would be the conclusion that both deformations disclosed also an incipient national decay and decline, reflected in elite diffidence. On the ultraconservative side, diffidence took the allied forms of suspicion and fear of national weakness in depth and doubt about elite skills, to be either compensated for or obscured by physical strength. On the liberal side, diffidence was focused on the innermost justice and worth of the national society and its politico-economic system, to be redeemed by identification with the materially weak at the moderate center and, at the extreme radical fringe, by identification also with the ideologically hostile and by deliberate material self-weakening.

A not inherently illiberal, but confidently conserving, corrective to such attitudes was, on the one hand, to reaffirm the primacy of the political (in the sense of long-term diplomatic strategy) over the military (in the form of concrete hardware and associated abstract rationality); and, on the other hand, to reassert the legitimacy of forceful uses of power in the last resort, as an instrument for equity usefully supplemental to diffuse compassion and propitiatory self-denial within a system of states. Implementing *politique d'abord* always, and applying force when necessary, would recreate a balance in dispositions which must underlie all other, more specific balances in promoting overall equilibrium. To emphasize the *political* side in politico-military relations will be apposite for both the central and the peripheral theaters in transactions with a Soviet Union that was doctrinally poised between accepting massive use of force as inevitable and rejecting it as impossible in relations with the United States and among the major powers generally. Similarly, to rehabilitate the *military* dimension in the politico-military setting of economic transactions with the South would correspond to the South's being itself in the evolutionary stage highly tolerant of, and in key respects dependent on, the use of force in both doctrine and practice. It will be propitious, furthermore, to stress employment over against capability in both classes of relationships, making more elastic the margin for unopposed employment of Soviet material capabilities for peripheral geo-political gain, and viewing again a comparably targeted employment of force by the United States as a legitimate last-resort regulator of interde-pendent economic relations with the South directly and of the interlocked détente and parity-evolving processes with the Soviet Union indirectly. An occasional employment of force and demonstration of resolve in the peripheries will help more than can any feasible central-systemic military build-up, compensating for systematic inaction, to reduce to a practically irrelevant minimum the likelihood of major conflict with the Soviet Union, either provoked by persistent denials of outlets to the Soviets or encouraged by prolonged absence of checks on all others. Manifest readiness for self-assertion will also reduce the chances for an economic collapse at the center of the American defense system, within a Western Europe or a Japan less provoked than prostrate, less denied political payoffs than deprived of economic wherewithals for ideal (or viable) polity, real (and vitalizing) power, or both.

It was a more likely danger for the United States and for its essential allies to be estranged from one another politico-economically by the agency of an unrestrained South than for the United States to be denied access to, and be thus isolated from, the major allies militarily or navally by the agency of a both unrestrainable and unsatisfiable Soviet Union. Moreover, not to be estranged in one way or another from Europe in particular was a more pressing concern for the United States than was the risk of being isolated from the poorest and most chaotic segments of the South. To avoid such estrangement was more than ever incumbent on an America that, having ascended to prominence by pathways staked out by all of Europe's agonies, has moved near, and might unwittingly move past, the capacity to break through the repetitive cycles in her own foreign policy and to balance, in the process, the lopsided Euro-American account books in the sight of history and in the interest of a progressively renewed and eventually also enlarged Occident.

POSTSCRIPT. *From the Middle Ages to the Middle East: Conflict Resolution in a Regional Microcosm*

To speak of either settlement of conflicts or termination of wars is to evoke the image of a contention finite in time and specific as well as stable in its stakes and parties, that is brought to a close by clearly discernible and conclusive military and diplomatic acts. However, unless a particular phase is artificially isolated from a prolonged conflict, such a conflict resolution is an exception for serious contentions among viable parties. The contemporary installment of the "Eastern Question" in the Middle East is no exception to the rule.

Territorially bounded and in part at least militarily enacted conflicts differ according to what are their stakes and structure; what is the identity of parties; and what is the conflict's rhythm and duration in time.

Stakes affect or reflect the rest. They are more or less divisible in fact or in the perception of parties. When stakes are extensive and involve the shape of the international system, without impinging upon the survival

This following essay is substantially the paper presented originally under the title "Wars in Rounds: Termination and Erosion" at the Symposium or Termination of Wars, held June 14-16, 1976, at the Hebrew University of Jerusalem, under the auspices of The Leonard Davis Institute for International Relations.

of either party, they are apt to be more readily adjustable and divisible than are stakes raising the issue of survival. But psychological complications will attend even systemic stakes when the conflict is over succession. The series of Anglo-French conflicts covered more than half-a-millenium, from the first or second Hundred Years War to 1870. The conflict series started out as a war for survival in dynastic terms, and it evolved into a systemic conflict in Europe and overseas. The enduringly intense emotional tone of the centuries-long contention was in part due to its raising repeatedly the question of succession. After the chain-of-wars had begun as a conflict over succession (to the Capetian royal line in France), it was reintensified over yet another succession (to the Spanish empire globally), and it culminated in the same broad framework of reference, if anachronistically (insofar as the Napoleonic wars reopened once again the succession to the Roman empire). Similarly, the millenial Franco-Germanic contention alternated between survival stakes (defined "nationally" in increasingly self-conscious terms) and systemic stakes (in the Mediterranean or in Europe at large). But it was, essentially, a drawn-out contention over who was rightfully to inherit the mantle of Charlemagne, as the *empire des rêves* shaded off into the nightmare of a *tausendjähriges Reich*.

Conflicts over succession will typically occur between parties that are physically close or even intertwined, while they are disparate in critical features of their respective make-ups; are at once conjoined and induced to confront one another by the shared pretension to an end-goal that is itself inherently indivisible and is sustained by both interests and values. When the realm to succeed to is identical for the contenders, and is invested with psychological if no other reality, the conflict will have the emotional or ideological overtones of civil strife. It will not be a strictly pragmatic, or routine, or conventional interstate war by the same token. A civil war will characteristically comprise actors different from "states" or "governments" in their identity; and it will often display, next to radical ideological differences, also significant asymmetries in matters other than values (e.g., structures as well as magnitudes of resources). The crisis will deepen when asymmetry has escalated beyond inequalities to felt incompatibility, and beyond disparity to a relationship that can only be described as schismatic. In a schism, the core-values and the identities or characteristics of parties will overlap substantially, even as the stakes are approached from diametrically opposed positions or perspectives and are viewed as being indivisible.

An ideological civil war, or a war over succession, will be commonly polar, unfolding between two main parties over one central issue defined as possession. But nothing prevents such a conflict from being encased in a setting that is structurally plural and combines a number of secondary parties and a range of interlocking issues. It would be tedious to identify the multiplicities of parties and issues in any one phase of, say, the Franco-Germanic (or Valois/Bourbon-Habsburg) conflict. Suffice it here to record the difference between material or territorial stakes and immaterial (mainly juridical or religio-ideological) issues. Another aspect of pluralism is to be found in the number and character of the levels on which a conflict unfolds. Well-crystallized conflicts in a formed and autonomous system, such as that of Renaissance Italy, can be progressively overshadowed and be relegated to subsystemic status by conflicts among larger extraneous powers, such as the European "northern monarchies." The situation is different when diffuse conflicts cutting across a fundamental cleavage (e.g., Christian vs. Moslem; Slav vs. Teuton) are being crystallized only *pari passu* with their being subsumed within a hierarchy of minor and major actors (e.g., in the first instance, among small Balkan states or communities and between these and the Ottoman empire under the supervisory auspices of the European great powers before World War I and, in the second instance, between Czech and Sudeten German in like systemic subordination if in less formal interstate crystallization prior to World War II). But, in either case, differentiation as to levels of conflict will substantially affect the settlement or termination of conflicts by mechanisms that range from imposition of terms by great powers to insurgence by the lesser parties against any such attempt. Analytically, it is possible to discount the habitual intensity of conflicts among smaller states within a microcosmic equilibrium-hegemonial system and their (seeming) autonomy relative to great powers that are temporarily aloof; or one may blow up a lower-level conflict as if it were intrinsically identical with larger-scale conflicts free of constraints by superior powers. But practically, when a conflict is a prolonged one, even fundamental transformations within and between the small parties are apt to have a less decisive impact on the conflict's termination than do reorientations among either the greater powers or in the relations between the minor and the major actors.

Prolonged conflicts will almost by necessity have several phases, each with a number of combat rounds. Thus, the half-millenial Anglo-French conflict had an interdynastic phase over feudal stakes (in the Hundred Years War or wars) and an interstate phase over the European and overseas balances of power (from the early reign of Louis XIV to 1870). The "rounds" in the first phase had the form of campaigns, major battles or raids; in the second phase, they assumed the shape of full-scale wars. The millenial Franco-German conflict, both before and after the Thirty Years War, could be similarly decomposed into phases of early French usurpations (interrupted by the Austro-Spanish dynastic union encompassing France's encirclement) and later German reciprocation, with several spells or rounds within each. In such a perspective, even a decisive campaign or conclusive termination of the war (e.g., in 1871) constitute but a round within a phase. The outcome is not materially different from a de facto suspension of belligerency without formal conclusion in a peace treaty, when it comes to the question of how and when a conflict such as the Franco-Germanic one has been terminated or settled.[1]

What about a contemporary conflict such as the Arab-Israeli one? The latest phase of the Eastern Question began as one over survival (of Israel and the Palestinians, as autonomous political entities). And it has veered increasingly toward being actually a contention over the shape of the Middle Eastern subsystem in function of its pluralism in parties, stakes, and levels. Stakes and conflicts other than the still dominant Arab-Israeli one have surfaced intraregionally on several political, economic, and confessional axes among the Arabs themselves, and between Arab and third actors such as Iran and, latently, Black Africa; and the great-power level has been increasingly significant because balanced and engaged, as the conflict evolved from one between Arab and Jew into one within a microcosmic equilibrium-hegemonial system of states alternately dwarfed and upgraded by the American-Soviet contest over preeminence and parity. Increasingly significant has been, moreover, the lowermost domestic level within at least some of the international parties. Such pluralism offers room for defusing the conflict and thus eventually terminating it. But features intensifying the conflict have continued to affect a contest that was, fundamentally, one over succession to Biblical or British Palestine and has had, as such, overtones of a historically conditioned civil or schismatic conflict aggravated by con-temporaneously-bred material and functional asymmetries.

Insofar as the subjectively significant characteristics have predominated, the conflict was susceptible of only a catastrophic termination for one or both parties. Only if and when the original biases were absorbed in the objectively growing conflict-pluralism would other terminal outcomes be-come possible. Barring extermination of one party that is achieved without a major cost to the other, the outcome was apt to be in the no-win category if victory has been properly defined as, one, the achievement of the conflict-originating goals; two, by the original party or parties unchanged in their

1. Readily accessible sources for the two major prolonged conflicts on which I draw for illustrations are, for the Hundred Years War, Edward R. Cheyney, *The Dawn of a New Era 1250-1453* (New York: Harper and Row, 1936), and Georges Pages, *La guerre de cent ans* (Paris: Gallimard, 1945); for the Thirty Years War, David Ogg, *Europe in the Seventeenth Century* (London: A. and C. Black, 1931), Sigfrid H. Steinberg, *The "Hundred Years War" and the Conflict for European Hegemony 1600-1660* (London: Edward Arnold, 1966), and C. V. Wedgwood, *The Thirty Years War* (New Haven: Yale University Press, 1939). For essays on conflict termination in general, see William T. R. Fox, ed., *How Wars End* (Philadelphia: American Academy of Political and Social Science, 1970).

essential internal or external features; and three, by virtue of a decisive application of forcible, and a determinative one of diplomatic, instruments, Consequently, in terms of a final distinction, the Arab-Israeli conflict's best prospect for noncatastrophic termination was tied up with its being or becoming an evolutionary one with regard to its outcome, to be distinguished from the revolutionary aspects of its enactment. Such a war is one that centers less on producing a previously unattainable decision or set of decisions between the parties (e.g., how to divide British Palestine) and more on promoting evolution within and between the parties. A decision will be typically achieved by military decimation or overall material attrition of one party; evolution entails the normative erosion of the original stakes and goals and (concurrently) the actual erosion of original actor identities in ways that shift attainable objectives toward the conditions of reciprocal toleration or even acceptance.

It might be argued that, despite brief apparent victories, prolonged conflicts produce only losers in the long run. Just as no empire is eternal any more than it is universal, so no victory is permanent any more than it can be unadulterated. There were few absolute victories even before the onset of the nuclear age.

A party can win militarily, to be sure, and either exterminate the adversary physically or eliminate him politically as an equivalent or significant actor. Even then, however, the victory is apt to be qualified by transformations of the victor, who may absorb key traits (including weaknesses) of the defeated; and of the system, as the defeated party is replaced by another and possibly more powerful or dangerous rival in an enlarged arena. Who is prepared to say that, even before she was partitioned, Prussia had actually won as a power and a culture in the contest with either Austria or France in any sense that would be meaningful to the proponents of any one of the several versions of the Prussian ideal?

The no-win outcome is altogether clear in wars that do not terminate in the suppression of one contestant, but end in tactical or strategic stalemate or in structural supersession. A stalemate makes the conflict subside indefinitely; supersession displaces or replaces it finally. In stalemated subsidence, the thing exhausted is apt to be the parties, and their material or moral resilience; in supersession, it is the issue or stake itself and its political relevance. The dissipation or disappearance of a conflict as it breeds another, its fading as part of a re-forming, supply the stuff and the data of the genealogy of conflicts. And the energy that actuates the termination of one conflict through the gestation of another will often come from "new" or "emergent" factors that revise stakes by way of the mind (including new creeds, concerns, or institutions) or matter (including material goods and technology). Such emergences or innovations provide the extra nurture for the indefinitely ramifying tree of related successor conflicts. Thus, telescoping and simplifying history, the several contests of the French monarchy or nation with the changing incumbents of the empire idea on the continent constituted the essential Europe. They were in their various phases successively superseded by colonial conflicts, engaging mainly but not only England with Spain and France, which expanded the European system. The inherently colonial conflicts, starting in Europe's own south, were at one point briefly overshadowed by ideologically (i.e., religiously) defined conflicts. And they were finally superseded by the Anglo-Russian contest, itself temporarily interrupted and ultimately expanded by the involvement of the successively dominant Anglo-Saxon wing powers with Germany. The latest supersession, in the form of the U.S.-Soviet rivalry, produced an (apparently) final termination of the Franco-Germanic struggle following upon the Anglo-French conflict, and along with them of the Europe-centered system, with the aid of both military-technological and institutional innovations.

The precise pattern of saliences in the tangled skein of the Euro-global historical process is not at issue. What matters is that the several multiphase series of conflicts ended only when stakes, parties, or both had been either transvalued or transformed. They were so changed characteristically with powerful assistance from a new conflict or concern, arising from the ashes and highlighting the anachronism of the preceding ones.

It is difficult to identify the indisputable victor in a protracted pluralistic conflict because it is nearly impossible to identify the unequivocally primary party to, and issue in, such a contention. The ambiguity is confirmed when the difficulty to determine "how" such a conflict ends is coupled with the uncertainty as to "when" it finally ended. The Hundred Years War displayed a tension between dynastic and primitively national, or else between feudal and territorial, issues, and between principal contenders and provincial and peripheral actors. And the last of the several truces did not terminate active Anglo-French hostilities more meaningfully or, for all that, authoritatively than did the waning of the (English) will, even more than capacity, to resume the fighting. That material erosion of energies coincided, moreover, with a normative one, of the war's original stakes, as the French succession crisis yielded to the crisis of the Burgundian succession and the territorial stakes shifted from continental France to peninsular Italy and to the consolidation of the "British" insular realm. And, in the even more complex Thirty Years War, which were the key parties? Was the determining conflict between Catholicism and Protestantism; between Bourbon and Habsburg; between Emperor and the territorial princes and Sweden; or between France and Spain? And was the critical "issue" (comprising in that term stake *and* outcome) dynastic, revolving around the disruption of the Habsburg Family Complex; "national," focused on independence for the Dutch (and its loss by the Bohemians); organic, in some powers rising meteorically or gradually (Sweden, United Provinces, Prussia) and others declining (Spain); or, lastly, economic, as the foreground conflict camouflaged the incipient one between Protestant Dutch and English (to involve later also Catholic France)?

Furthermore, did the "Thirty" Years War end in its essentials as early as 1635 (appeasing the "central" German issue), in 1648 (pacifying the "eastern" theater), in 1659 (extending pacification to the "western" sector), or only in 1756 (with the Habsburg-Bourbon reconciliation)? Was the war terminated mainly by virtue of the widespread physical or moral exhaustion; the recoil by the principals from extremes on both sides or from universal chaos; or the internal transformation and reciprocal assimilation of some belligerents, and the transvaluation and reciprocal confusion of territorial-material and immaterial-confessional stakes? And did the structural transformations within and among actors "cause" the war to terminate or did they matter most, instead, as the outward settings that allowed other, more elusive or more specific, determinants to finally assert themselves with effect?

Queries such as these cannot be reliably addressed. If so, however, it may not make much sense to fasten on final and determinate settlements, and be more profitable to explore how prolonged conficts gradually subside; not make much sense to view a conflict as settleed by negotiations, when the key question is whether and how the parties settle down to reciprocal toleration. In such cases formal peacemaking, including negotiations, is not the decisively creative element; and its role is mainly either to ratify what already came to pass or, at the most, break the inertial momentum of a conflict that already lost its original or revised structural or psychological foundations.

The conflict hardest to terminate permanently on a no-win basis is one that is confined to two parties and revolves around a finite, physically or perceptually indivisible, material stake. Such was, for instance, the conflict over Alsace-Lorraine between France and Germany. When parties and stakes are several, this will prolong a conflict but will also create openings for terminating it at least partially. The plurality of stakes will attentuate the indivisibility of material ones and the rigidity of immaterial ones by facilitating compensations among all issues and a more pragmatic approach to some. And if there are several parties with different priorities, a conflict among conflicts on either side will eventually erode the will to continue one or more of the controversies, including often the previously salient one, diminishing thus the incentives to escalation and expansion that are rooted in solidarity. Escalation of conflict is favored by polarity or, in plural structures, polarization. Conversely, its dispersion through introduction or differentiation of "third" parties will moderate a conflict. Yet, if it is true that structural (and psychological) transformations are more creative than are negotiations, the critical third-party activity is not skillful mediation; and if such a party can be most helpful when it is itself ensconced in the plural conflict, least promising mediation is one by an impartial outsider. Whereas the crucial activity is third-party involvement, the critical achievement is not to compose differences between parties by contriving a compromise; it is to induce the perceptions of alternatives by the contestants and their consequent dispositions to converge. Such a convergence will ideally put into effect whatever mutual assimilation or symmetrization resulted from waging the prolonged conflict in the first place.

A third party or an emergent new factor will help in terminating a conflict by virtue of one or several of the most common possible impingements. One, it can bring pressure to bear on *contracting* an otherwise unbridgeable disparity in goals and perceptions between two contending *parties*. Two, it can have a direct effect by *dispersing* a conflict between two *sides* into a tripartite or triangular situation. And three, it can supply impetus to *repolarizing* a conflict unfolding on two *levels*. In the first eventuality, the two parties will be helped to evolve coincident terms of pacification that permit both of them to *optimize* their respective balances or ratios of costs, from continuing the conflict, and net benefits, from terminating it, in the light of anticipated military odds and larger structural trends. As in other quests for parity, some kind of pressure or incentive from a third party or from a new factor will be most probably necessary for making such an effort and bringing it off. The second situation is that of a conflict between two sides of which at least one is a coalition, or a three-cornered contest. The requisite is then that one of the actors is anxious to *maximize* his advantage by initiating the termination of the contest (and to minimize thereby whatever loss he would incur from being left out of the first stage of war-termination). And the final situation requires that parties contending on one of the two levels of power magnitude have become prepared to *equalize* their postures in relations with the other level, acting as the third factor between them. To be equalized for lesser contenders is then either dependence on the auspices or guarantees by the greater powers as one result of pacification or, alternatively, resistance to the greater powers dictating the peace or exploiting the conflict (just as, for contending major powers, to be equalized are most generally their positions relative to smaller-power supporters or claimants).

Whichever direction the equalization takes, there will be elements of a separate peace, which is the very essence of tripartite dispersion. Either it is the greater-power sponsors or guarantors who make common cause relative to the guaranteed; or it is the smaller-power defectors who defuse their conflict to eschew either pressure, or need for support, from their erstwhile patrons. Beyond that, all three situations, including that of an unbridgeable disparity and its reduction, will rule out "total" victory for any direct party to the conflict. A shared "optimum" precludes anyone's maximum; a "separate peace" must be bought by concessions; and neither a concerted guarantee by two or more previously rival great powers nor a collusive smaller-party resistance to such powers will be compatible with the undiluted triumph of any individual direct or indirect participant. In all three cases, moreover, an eventual (and then decisive) supersession of the conflict will have been prepared by prior evolution. Such evolution may involve a measure of transcendence, in the two-party dichotomy; of depolarization, in tripartite dispersion; and of repolarization, in the dialectic between two levels.

An effort to transcend conflict between two parties in a new relationship is implicit in the quest for parity. Parity may signify no more than equivalence of costs and benefits from suspending acute conflict. Or, consolidating peace more substantially, parity may bear on qualitative status, material capabilities, and the productive utilization or employment of the latter for meaningful goals. Such accommodations do not spring, unaided, from either pure or prudential reason. Thus, even the much-vaunted termination of the War of American Independence by virtue of enlightened British calculations and concessions was not a stable accomplishment. It was consolidated only by the defeat of subsequent British efforts to reduce or reverse its implications, and by the gradual defusing of a continuing Anglo-American contention over the shape of first the North American, and then the west-hemispheric, balances of power. And it took, most importantly, the growing Anglo-German (alongside the Anglo-Russian) conflict to supply Britain in due course with the incentive to accept the American view of the regional implications of global parity and to reconcile the two English-speaking sister-nations at long last in depth.

Transcending a two-sided conflict is fully compatible with the conflict's temporary suspension or subsidence, and periodic renewals. Tripartite dispersion makes subsidence (en route to termination) more likely. It introduces ambiguities into the situation and ambivalence into attitudes, replacing clear-cut polarities and antagonisms. The role of the third party is thus to defuse a conflict. That achievement is different from deflecting the conflict to a new adversary, even though the prospect of deflection will help achieve the principal purpose in most cases. The third-party role will not substantially differ under the various possible configurations. The simplest is a three-cornered contest, including one in which an actor broke ranks with his coalition partners. The third actor, such as the duke of Burgundy in the

Anglo-French Hundred Years War, will on balance tend to moderate the contest while the tide of conflict runs strong, and to accelerate the movement toward termination when the tide has receded. His concern is to help any one of the other parties just enough to help himself most toward securing his objective, while avoiding being left out of a peace-making that would transpire over his head; nor do the other two, main contestants feel differently about the third party. The configuration is more complex, but the considerations of tactics and strategy remain the same, when two coalitions of two or more members face one another. Neither member of either coalition is then likely to desire a big enough success for another member that would disinterest the latter in the fate of the ally that was still embattled and unsatisfied. In the Seven Years War, the Anglo-Prussian alliance faced a Franco-Austrian (cum Russian) coalition; tripartisms interlocked, in that France was the critical third party for her ally Austria, and Britain for Prussia, in the second-named powers' conflict over the German balance of power, whereas Prussia and Austria occupied third-party positions in relation to the Anglo-French contention. Tripartite dispersion can, finally, encompass both of the power levels. In the Thirty Years War, a reciprocally checking tripartite relationship came into being between the Emperor, the allied Catholic princes (headed by Bavaria), and the rival Protestant party; alternatively, viewed from the Protestant side, the mixed, great- and smaller-power interplays involved Sweden, the allied Protestant princes (headed by Saxony), and the rival Catholic party (including France). Finally, crucial on the more uniformly greater-power level was the Franco-Habsburg-Swedish triangle. The resulting complex games of support and subversion or secession helped terminate the German phase (in the Peace of Prague) and, subsequently, the European phase (in the Peace of Westphalia). The introduction of Cromwellian England as the third party into the residual Franco-Spanish contest, even though misguidedly on the stronger French side, may have marginally aided in setting the course toward the "final" peace (of the Pyrennees).

Depolarization in tripartite dispersion defuses the conflict and sets the stage for its termination. By contrast, the dialectic between two levels will help terminate the conflict mainly by repolarizing the more or less directly involved parties. At the extremes, this can mean dictatorial imposition of the end of war by the "higher" on the "lower" level; it can also mean the rebellious insurgence of the lesser contenders against their patrons or protectors. Ideally, the higher-ranking actor or actors will be actively engaged, because of a stake in seeing the conflict terminated as part of larger interests; but they ought to display also a measure of detachment as to the specifics of settlement. The French popes at Avignon, who tried to appease the Hundred Years War, had the right posture and attitude, but they did not have the authority to impose peace and deflect the conflict to a crusade. When the schism had created a dual papacy, both ecclesiastical factions proceeded instead to stimulate the conflict between their respective secular supporters. Such competitive incitement will be reduced, and the chances to terminate a conflict enhanced, when an established major power allows a share in joint mediation or guarantee to a power that was so far involved only illegitimately and confers thus equal ad hoc status on that power. The beneficial result attended apparently the admission of Russia by France to joint mediation in the war of Bavarian succession, legitimizing Russia's concern in German affairs, at the end of the eighteenth century.

Rival great powers will augment pressures for terminating a conflict of lesser powers when they share the fear lest the conflict expand and engulf them. Or they may feel that the control of both over their respective dependents will decrease if the conflict is allowed to grow or one of the belligerents permitted to win too big. Conversely, the lesser parties will rebel against the great powers and seek mutual accommodation when they conclude that neither could win a preferable outcome by continuing combat in conditions of dependence. The major powers will be concerned about likely gains from continuing to assume risks and expend resources on behalf of an embattled protégé; and the smaller parties will assess alternative outcomes against the possibility of declining support and the likelihood of increasing control by an exasperated patron over time. A close examination of the two-level interplay in relation to, say, the Balkans would more likely than not produce examples of termination or suspension of conflict resulting from great-power injunctions (e.g., in 1912, in contrast with incitement to conflict on other occasions) as well as of smaller-state insurgence (e.g., through attempts to forge regional ensembles in the period between the two world wars, in contrast to entangling major powers in small-state conflicts).

The perspectives opened up by history for the Middle Eastern conflict engender a philosophic bias rather than a blueprint for policy. The distilled guidelines are only very general; and the situation in the Middle East was too fluid to permit confidently applying even the generalities. At the same time, a gradual evolution in structures and attitudes has been underway for three decades; and it has been both punctuated and propelled, next to a series of military engagements and diplomatic initiatives, by wholly new or emergent factors. Prominent among such factors were a heightened resource based on oil for one side, and a potential for deterrent-retaliatory capacity based on nuclear weaponry mainly for the other side. More even than the military events and factors (including nuclear), the new economic (oil) factor has commanded attention as it affected the setting within which the conflict could be defused preparatory to its being deflected to successor concerns by one or another of the three aforementioned mechanisms.

In a conflict of two parties, we have noted in regard to the first mechanism, the appearance of a third party or a previously absent factor will be commonly necessary, and always helpful, to accentuate any existing dispositions to wind down conflict on a basis "optimizing" costs and benefits for both parties (always subject to estimates of military odds and evolutionary trends). In the Middle East, it was possible to discount provisionally the common threat from nuclearization as one too abstract or diffuse to promote the "right" parity calculations and *convergence* in the immediate future. One might, conversely, focus on the newly salient oil factor, without expecting conclusive or early effects from any economic factor working in isolation. Even so, the new vistas of economic development could not but affect the critical cost-benefit calculations. Both the costs of continuing the war, and the benefits from terminating it, have been rising, both absolutely and relative to one another, for the development-capable Arab states, notably if they were also actually or potentially situated in the front-line zone. They have risen sufficiently to approach the point of common optimum with the cost-benefit pattern of Israel which, in contra-distinction from the Arab side, was more one of actually rising costs of conflict that of increasing potential benefits jeopardized by conflict.

In conditions such as these, permanent military mobilization can easily become a threat to important actors on both sides of the conflict. In the class of forces making for diversion of resources were the Arabs in the so-called rejection front and the Israeli committed to security-through-expansion. They held out for maximum satisfaction on the strength of either basic interests or ideological commitments (e.g., radical Palestinian and Libyan leaderships and advocates of Greater Israel) or of tactical calculations, involving security or status in the relevant regional or domestic political system (a spectrum comprising Iraq and Saudi Arabia in the Arab camp and comparably opportunist political factions in Israel). As a rule, cross-cutting intransigence of some is a standing invitation to conciliation for others. But, so long as the conflict-perpetuating group on the Arab side included development-capable countries and politically conservative governments, while genuine extremists retained vetoes of sorts on both sides, there was apt to be only lagging or latent convergence between the moderate centers on the basis of parallel recoils from extremes.

Other factors were necessary in these conditions to make the potential for convergence, implicit in oil-based Arab economic development, operational. One possible impetus could come from third-party pressures originating outside the region, and either deriving from economics or rooted in geography. An economically conditioned pressure might emanate from industrial West and preindustrial Black Africa as the former reacted to the price-and-supply, and the latter to the price-and-aid, policies of the oil-rich Arab states. A geopolitically conditioned pressure might emanate from an outsider, such as Iran. Any tactical interest to see the Arab-Israeli conflict continue was likely to last in Iran only so long as the advantage of deflecting Arab energies from the Persian Gulf was not outweighed by the influx of ever more Soviet energies into the area in function of the conflict. By the same token, Iran's regional ambitions could gradually inflect at least some of the Arab states to look with favor on terminating the dispute with Israel. While a shared desire to exploit the oil boom dampened the politico-territorial Iran-Iraq conflict for the time being, the oil factor itself could reintensify the chronic rivalry any time by adding economic to geopolitical stakes. Conversely, so long as Israel held on to her territorial bargaining chips, and the Arabs did not provoke the West into forcible reactions to their oil policies, Western (i.e., American) pressures were apt to weigh more heavily on the more West-dependent Israel, even if far from decisively. As regards the Black Africans, finally, the oil crisis estranged them from Israel in expectation of Arab-wrought relief from its consequences; but discriminatory policies of Arab aid from oil revenues were susceptible of gradually recasting the diplomatic if no other equations.

Such considerations suggested that the several specific impacts of the newly emergent oil factor on the politics of the Middle Eastern conflict, if left to themselves, were likely to fluctuate and to cancel out one another. The one equation that the oil factor did unequivocally change so far was very basic, however. It concerned the geo-economic complexion of the Arab-Israeli conflict. With some license, it may be said that the conflict had started out as one between an overseas-oriented state with a considerable industrial-mercantile component and a set of economically more primitive and inward-turned polities. If Israel was not literally insular, she was largely insulated from the Arab states. As is characteristic for powers so situated, Israel depended for continuing insulation and immunity on either an indirectly exerted hegemony over the Arab states and groups or a conflictually enacted balance of power among them. Only in part figuratively, therefore, Israel's relation to the Arab world was initially the alternately glorious and precarious one of a Venice relative to the states on the Italian terra firma and of England relative to the European continent. In those cases, an inherently irreconcileable conflict of outlooks and objectives between the differently situated and constituted parties proved eventually disastrous for the state-system in question, and was ultimately fatal to the exposed insular or quasi-insular power. The oil factor may have made it possible to transmute the foundation of Israel's security, by shifting it from precarious balancing of inter-Arab rivalries to a prolonged quest for more stable parity with the developing Arab state or states emerging as concilia-tion-prone because cooperation-capable. Israel had previously sought, and could only seek, appeasement by virtue of regulating and rationing Arab economic and technical development from a position of economic and technological supremacy. It has become possible henceforth for the two sides to develop complementary strengths, in resources and skills, amounting to elements in reciprocal parity as a condition and mutual assimilation as a process.

So far, the effect of the activated oil factor was the initial one of stalemating the conflict and the contestants. Arab oil offset the material advantage of Israel, by enabling the Arabs to purchase arms with abandon; the diplomatic one, by inflecting powers dependent on oil to the Arab viewpoint; and the psychological one, by intensifying the confident wave-of-the-future psychosis in Arab ranks set off by improved performance in the coincident round of warfare (in 1973). Only in the longer run could economic development based on oil revenues divert Arab energies materially from confrontation with Israeli ingenuity. Any such transcendence or supersession of the conflict was apt to be slow and hesitant, however, if left to the economics of oil and isolated from the dynamic of politico-military inducements to appeasement. And the conflict would not be superseded at all, or not in a way consonant with stable regional equilibrium, if the material trends appeared to favor indefinitely one (Arab) side or if their political repercussions fluctuated ever more widely and wildly. It was crucial, therefore, whether a materially rooted structural transformation could be accelerated and its bearing channeled. Deliberately designed military and related politico-diplomatic activities were most likely to have that possible effect.[2] The oil factor itself might be helpful, however, insofar as it helped disperse the Arab-Israeli conflict by engendering disparities and tensions between oil-rich and oil-poor Arab countries and regimes.

A key factor in any *tripartite dispersion* in the Middle East, constituting the second of the three critical mechanisms, was the position of Egypt. The Egyptian position on the Arab side has been as ambiguous as the Egyptian policy attitudes have become ambivalent. Egypt has been a leader in military-political coalition while being a financial client of the oil-rich Arab states; and she has been such a client while being an agro-industrial giant when compared with her financial patrons. Egyptian cost-benefit calculations have been, consequently, complicated by the uncertainty whether the benefits of terminating the war (i.e., diverting resources from military to developmental tasks) would not be offset by the cost of seeing the subsidies dry out. Conjointly, the strictly national Egyptian objective of greater power by means of a stronger economy has been potentially at variance with the goal of regional preeminence. In this respect alone, the situation of Egypt was comparable to that of Burgundy in the Hundred Years War. The

2. See pp. 236–44.

Burgundian dukes, too, wavered between securing a dominant position in the larger theater (France) and segregating their hereditary domain from the feudal network as an aggrandized territorial, if not yet national, entity. Since several actors shared competitively the vaster, hegemonial objective in both the remote and the contemporary settings, ambivalence could not but seep into attitudes toward both technically allied and ostensibly adversary parties. Appropriately nuanced, the attitudes of the Burgundian dukes vis-à-vis the kings of France and England were of a piece with those of post-Nasser Egyptian leadership vis-à-vis Arab sister states and Israel.

The practical consequence of ambiguity and ambivalence will be separate peace as a process or, at least, tendency. Whether an actual transaction or only a latent tendency, separate peace will take time to unfold even in favorable psychological and structural conditions. Both will have to mature thoughout a protracted conflict interspersed with differently frustrating rounds of active warfare. The dispersion of conflict that is initiated by the partial disengagement or complete defection of one (henceforth the "third") party will be most effective if that party controls assets that are critical for the capacity of its (prior) partners to continue the conflict. It will help, moreover, if the third party has been member of a coalition rather than being a separate if parallel actor. A previously allied defector cannot just drop out of a contest without engendering adverse psychopolitical as well as military consequences for the other contestants; nor is he likely to have an interest in seeing the conflict continue without him, for fear of maximizing, along with advantages from the separate peace, also exposure to reprisals by the still embattled ex-allies for his betrayal. The factor of betrayal will be weakened in both diplomatic and moral terms if the contestants (temporarily) left out of pacification had previously rejected "reasonable" conditions of peace; and the risk of exposure is less severe if the defector extracts from the initially separate peace initiatives the capacity to replace leadership in a military coalition with a prominent role in a rearranged peacetime alignment or concert. Both considerations will prolong the peace-making process for seemingly irrational reasons.

If tripartite dispersion unfolds on both sides to a conflict, the resulting interlock will have more than usually hard-to-predict consequences for the rate at which the conflict subsides and the terms on which it is terminated. But even if it affects only one side directly, triangularization can operate in more than one way. Egyptian policy-makers might give national goals priority over regional ones, and reduce or reshape their active, military engagement with a view to terminating it gradually. Embarking on the road to separate peace would be calculated to either reduce clientage (by virtue of a compensating aid from outside the oil-rich countries) or enhance Egypt's leverage as coalition leader (by endowing Egypt with a genuine alternative to carrying on with her role in the war). Conversely, the oil-rich and population-poor Arab countries might be the ones to move to disengage from pan-Arab solidarity vis-à-vis Israel, as they ceased to view the conflict as a desirable source of influence and immunity. They might do so, for instance, if they came to fear a classic expansionist thrust by an Egypt determined to exploit her military superiority while it lasted. Were Egypt to veer toward freeing herself from precarious clientship by the conquest of fellow-Arabs, rather than by conciliation with Israel (and the West), Israel would become valuable to the endangered oil-rich Arab countries as either a counterpoise (for Libya) or a physical barrier and political buffer (for the Arabian peninsula). Israel's being located between the western and the eastern Arabs would then cease being a symbolic challenge and a physical block to Arab unity, and might become a safeguard against either Egyptian hegemony or against Egyptian interference with internal conflicts in different parts of the Arab world. Notably a deflection of the eastern Arabs to conflicts within the Fertile Crescent and with Iran would complete the defusing of the Arab-Israeli conflict attendant on its tripartite dispersion, converting Israel into an actual or potential, tactical and tacit, ally for one or another Arab party. If, in addition, Egyptian control over Libyan oil were to supplement Western aid (and replace Saudi subsidies), the balance of power in the Meshrik would be recast somewhat as the conquest of Spanish Saharan phosphates by Morocco recast the equilibrium in the Maghreb, with consequent dangers for inter-Arab solidary and possibilities for the erosion of the Arab-Israeli conflict.

Tripartite dispersion could originate on the non-Arab side as well. It would take place if U.S. policy set out to maximize regional goals, in the form of consolidating ascendancy in the Middle East, or national goals, in the form of retrenching worldwide or consolidating Atlantic ties in the short run. It might then move in the direction of a "separate peace" with the Arab side, to be found on terms favorable to the Arabs and imposed on Israel. Highly unlikely as such an approach was because of domestic constraints, it was no more inconceivable in principle or as a subtheme than was a Soviet-Arab alienation in function of a Soviet-Israeli separate accommodation. Parallel and interacting tripartisms might either mutually stimulate and reinforce one another, and then promote the trend to depolarization (and conflict erosion); or else they might be mutually paralyzing if each possible third party should hold back in the expectation of improving its bargaining position with every further step in the disintegration of the adversary coalition.

Including extraregional great powers as possible third parties introduces the final of the three mechanisms, the *two-level interplay*, into the triangular dynamic. If an active third party connotes dispersion and (transient) depolarization, interactions across two levels of power magnitudes can differently crystallize actors and repolarize relationships. The conflict among the lesser parties is superseded when the bigger powers preempt the contest or the lesser ones resist an attempt at preemption.

Insofar as involvement by great powers helped crystallize inferior contestants into forms of organization that are contemporaneously legitimate, the involvement helps preclude the surgical resolution of a conflict by the elimination of one of the contending parties. The Moslems in Spain, the Teutonic knights in Poland, and the Germans in Bohemia failed ultimately to impose a hegemonic solution on their immediate environment, and were exterminated in one form or another. The intrusive, imperialist elements failed also because they had not achieved a consolidated statelike form and no systemic interplay came into being on the two critical levels. A statelike existence for the Sudeten Germans, within a multiethnic federation or confederation in Central Europe, under the guarantee or mutually balanced and equally involved European great powers, might have been the only way to terminate the secular ethnic conflict in Bohemia without the extermination of one side, considering the failure of the hegemonic German solution before World War I and during World War II and of the more moderate and reequilibrating, but still basically hegemonic, Czech solution in the interlude. Accordingly, the fact that the Arabo-Jewish (or Pan Arab-Zionist) conflict had progressively crystallized into one involving states on both sides and levels of power was a necessary prerequisite to a nonsurgical resolution, as the original parties' prophetic exaltation collided with the pragmatic expediencies of their own statecrafts and of the great powers when dealing with subordinate contentions.

The option between exterminating one party and otherwise terminating a conflict will be thus tied up with the option between escalating a conflict indefinitely and finitely expanding the relevant system. Expanding the system only among the smaller states might deflect attention and energies. Adding Iran as a contender in the larger Middle East might, we have noted, relieve the previously more critical conflict while having little or nothing in common with introducing Iran (or Turkey) into the contention as a diplomatic moderator or mediator. Only great powers, preferably from outside the region, might help terminate the conflict by exerting diplomatic moderation or offering guarantee. In some situations, expanding the directly relevant system by means of contractual guarantees may be the only alternative to a conflict's indefinite escalation in intensity or extension in time, due to the smaller powers' pursuing competitively physical, or territorial, safeguards. A guarantee by treaty will equalize the status not only of the great powers if they act as coguarantors, but also of the smaller powers as jointly guaranteed parties. Such equalization may usefully supplement, in prefacing or promoting conflict termination, the pragmatization of interests and the relativization of stakes which great-power involvement injects into schismatic and successional, or otherwise passional, small-power contentions. On the other hand, the issue of great-power guarantee will arouse sensitivities and activate special interests within the smaller states more intensely than can any other action by a great power outside all-out coercion or desertion. It will expand the interplay to a third, domestic, level and depend on a multifaceted stalemate for a propitious outcome.

In its modern phase, the Franco-German contention was one that was focused on the option between competing territorial safeguards against current and hypothetical future threats engineered by the parties themselves and a higher-level agency decompressing and preempting the conflict in some way. Neither the envisaged Anglo-American guarantee at the end of World War I nor the substitutive Anglo-Italian Locarno guarantee managed, however, to unite the requisite conditions in the last phase preceding the supersession of the European system as a whole. Such conditions include a simultaneously perceived and relatively symmetrical stalemate between the contending parties (in terms of actual-or-mobilized and potential-or-organic capabilities); effective and involved, if relatively "disinterested" and reciprocally balanced, guarantors; and domestic publics equally and simultaneously acquiescent in the coordinate declension in status attendant on an outside guarantee. In the Middle East it has continued to be questionable when and how an American-Soviet guarantee could do better, perhaps because the two potential coguarantors would be more steadily involved than had been the United States, and Britain as well, after the First World War; because they would be more evenly balanced in capabilities and biases when compared with Britain and Italy; or because their joint superiority over the guaranteed parties (and potential leverage relative to them) would be greater than it had been in the abortive instance. It was also true, however, that the Franco-German and the Arab-Israeli conflicts were alike in displaying an asymmetric stalemate as to capabilities (whenever in being) and volatile domestic responses to the implications of a hard-to-equalize and synchronize dependence on outside guarantees.

In such circumstances, the odds in favor of conflict terminating as a result of great-power imposition of sorts will be about even with the conflict ending by virtue of smaller-state insurgence. It is possible, moreover, that the insufficient potential of the first approach had to be exhausted before contestants would be able to progress toward, let alone consummate, the second. For example, the greater powers might promote a succession of stalemates in the local military engagements, depriving both lesser sides of a decisive success, lest hostilities escalate to the higher level. And the recurrent stalemate might eventually predispose the smaller states in favor of a direct deal. The sequence would then surface the split between an inclination of the smaller states, to blow up their conflict as one autonomous and all-important because intensely felt, and the contrasting inclination of the great powers, to shrink the conflict to its proper place in the larger system. And the resulting process would implement a desire by the lesser powers to thwart the tendency of the greater ones to preempt the stakes of a conflict after having dwarfed the conflict itself, and to impose the will for peace after having condoned or incited militancy in a different earlier setting of great-power interests. When they are apparent or suspected, such tendencies will shift small-state allegiance and alignments in degrees and stages. And if disaffections of the lesser states grow along parallel lines, they may eventually converge into the capacity for a common front and a separate (that is, direct) peace, repolarizing the military conflict into a politico-diplomatic cleavage between the smaller and the greater powers.

Egypt's vacillations between the superpowers conferred most recently a provisional diplomatic monopoly of overt action, as distinct from effective potency, as the peace-broker on the United States. In due course, Egypt's shift might be usefully complemented by Israel's compensating movement in the direction of the Soviet Union. This would, in turn, further loosen Soviet ties with clients other than Egypt, the diminution of which ties could no longer seriously jeopardize Soviet Union's pretension to participate in Middle Eastern war- and peace-making by virtue of its status as a regionally adjoining and an incipiently global power. In such a setting, partial Israeli dealignment from her long-standing, and parallel Egyptian disillusionment with her latest, patron might equalize interplays spanning both power levels and repolarize relationships sufficiently to erode the conflict by one more degree.

Military activities help terminate prolonged conflicts not least by catalyzing transformations in structures and attitudes. But the course of military processes is as important as are specific military outcomes. It may be more so. Consequently, military engagements have to be deliberately managed when the object is to stalemate, suspend, or supplant the contest at least as much as to subdue the adversary.

In the Middle East, Israel won over time a string of technical military victories. In political effect the victories were nullified, however, by activating potentials on the defeated side (the Arabs, similar in this respect to the French in the Hundred Years War) and reserves on the great-power side (the Soviet Union, analogous to France's midterm intervention in the Thirty Years War). Importance accrued in consequence to transformations originating in the military outcomes only partially. One major and, if sustained from the outside, potentially stable change was the shift from Nasser's transcendent pan-Arab propensities to Sadat's prosaic Egyptian priorities. The implied "nationalization" was reminiscent of the shift to narrowly Austrian from pan-Habsburg and pan-Catholic biases late in the Thirty Years War by the successor of Emperor Ferdinand II; and the shift to economic concerns from politico-military adventures recalled the evolution of the English at the end of the Hundred Years War. Internal consolidation and improved organization favored on balance the Arabs, just as they had worked to the advantage of the French in the medieval contest. Intervening shifts in attitudes outside the Middle East were likewise unfavorable to the previously ascendant Israelis, whereas the compensating reactions to too great a success have barely begun to focus resentments on the Arabs along the lines of, say, the Dutch and the papal defections from France in the final stages of the Thirty Years War.

Internal and international transformations will often convert the technical defeat for a party into an effective draw before a prolonged conflict has run its course. Conversely, a military stalemate does not necessarily suffice to terminate a conflict by means of a negotiated compromise. For instance, in the mid-eighteenth century War of Austrian Succession, an inconclusive military result failed to produce a lasting peace even though the separate-peace approach did lead to a general peace. Discordance between overt compromise and unresolved contentiousness underneath soon had the powers clash in renewed conflict (changing only their alignment, in the Seven Years War). Accordingly, in the Middle East, even if the elements of a separate peace brought into existence by the tactical military stalemate of 1973 were to set off a momentum, the resulting general peace would not automatically constitute an enduring appeasement. Tactical stalemate as a provisional outcome denotes equality in battlefield performance. Strategic stalemate, as an evolving condition, is different in that it signals dovetailing asymmetries in both military and nonmilitary structures and capabilities. It will most readily obtain in relations between a relatively "developed" or consolidated actor and a basically viable or resilient, but disorganized and only "developing," party. So long as the asymmetry lasts, the latter party will be inadequate in offense but impossible to defeat conclusively. A consequently prolonged conflict will crystallize such a party's latent identity while tending to enervate or corrode the maturer party, possessed of an appropriately smaller margin of extra potential to actualize by conflict. France's wars with the members and successors of the Holy Roman Empire had this kind of disparate effect, as have had more recently the wars of decolonization. In such conflicts, technical military victories that do not promptly enough eliminate the developmentally lagging adversary as a serious rival, or promote a future rapport on the basis of reciprocal utilities, will be tantamount to eventual political defeat for the initially more advanced belligerent.

An essentially imperial Israeli strategy before 1973 could look to using partial technical victories so as to satellitize some lesser Arab countries (e.g., Jordan) and in effect delegate operative control over peace observance within the Arab world to one or two major Arab countries (e.g., Egypt) as part of a two-tier hegemonial system. After 1973, it became wholly implausible for Israel to reach for either direct, or indirect but substantial, control over structural developments in the Arab sector by applying combined economic and military superiority. In the military domain, the choice has become one between three options: one, Israel could seek to influence psychological and material developments in the Arab world by way of politically controlled and shaped military tactics and strategies; two, she could seek to suspend fundamentally uncontrollable transformations by military means; and three, she could try to precipitate a direct preemption or supersession of the local subsystemic conflict by the major powers.

Following the military stalemate in the October War, it has become both possible and more than ever necessary to subordinate military enactment of conflict to political criteria and concepts. The stalemate of 1973 had engendered a psychological Arab-Israeli "parity" with respect to the conventional dimension of warfare. It also rendered the terroristic component less psychologically vital or rewarding for Arabs other than the Palestinians, because no longer required to compensate for humiliating defeats in the open terrain; and it rendered terrorism more onerous and embarassing politically for prominent Arab actors, specifically including Egypt. Israeli strategists might have usefully simulated a military stalemate in 1967 as a method to promote eventual appeasement. But matters have moved since beyond the need to restore Arab military honor. Politically controlled military tactics and strategy had to foster henceforth other kinds of positive evolution by other means.

One possible desideratum was to augment the material cost of continuing warfare for the newly oil-rich Arab countries outside the front line, so as to move them closer to "parity" with both Israeli and Egyptian (and Syrian) cost-benefit calculations. To achieve that essentially political objective, Israel might confine any future military operations on the land front with Egypt and Syria to a defensive holding action, and direct airborne engines of destruction to the growing industrial plan and other development-related installations (other than oil) in countries such as Saudi Arabia and Iraq. The air-centered strategy would diffuse the military impact of the conflict. A different strategy would be required to promote the conflict's politico-diplomatic dispersion, including further detachment of Egypt from bellicose Arab states without fatally compromising her leadership in the Arab camp.

If it was to promote the diplomatic objective, a military strategy would have to assign priority to demonstrating the military dependence of the eastern Arabs on Egypt; it would also have to revitalize Israel's military reputation as no less invincible in battle rounds than the Arabs were in the overall conflict; and it would have to foster the two demonstrative purposes while preserving or enhancing the political gains that the Egyptians had garnered from their military performance in 1973. One possible scenario was a "phony war" on the western front at the inception of the next round while Israel was acquiring a clear-cut military advantage in the East, to be followed by an Egyptian military offensive just sufficient to save the eastern Arabs from total disaster and create the setting for one more ceasefire, round of diplomacy, and turn of the evolutionary wheel. Egyptian and Israeli military deployments would perforce combine elements of simulation and collusion, and be in any event such as to discourage an early, and contain the effects of the last-stage, Egyptian offensive. The course of military events would be of a kind to strengthen the diplomatic hand of Egypt with fellow-Arabs. But it would not substantiate any presumption of present or likely future Egyptian capacity to achieve more than a limited military success even against an Israel fighting on two (or, if the overland be combined with the aerial strategy, three) fronts. Nor would such a course of the military engagement jeopardize Egypt's national option by exposing the Egyptian heartland to the full weight and impact of the military superiority that Israel has presumably reacquired since 1973.

At some point, it may cease being possible to manage military rounds with a view to eroding the political foundations of conflict, and become necessary to redirect the military instrument from shaping diplomatic evolutions to suspending material transformations that were likely to do damage to the more vulnerable party to an asymmetrical strategic stalemate.

Active belligerency can be suspended by the nature's seasons, by the exhaustion or the calculations of combatants, or by higher-power (e.g., papal or, acting for superpower, U.N.) authority. Interruptions in prolonged conflicts permit deliberate diplomatic explorations and allow for unplanned developments conducive to appeasement. Were oil-related, demographic, and other material factors to evolve continuously against Israel and against the chances for an eventual no-win outcome, Israel's strategic imperative might well shift to suspending instead the political and possible physical manifestations of Arab material ascendancy by some form of military escalation, in the hopes of an eventual reequilibration on a more inclusive basis. In the conventional military domain, escalation would mean unrestrained use of momentary Israeli military superiority for producing a technical victory sufficiently striking to break for a decade or two the wave-of-future buoyancy of the Arabs. A militarily enacted psychological warfare would replace under the second option the politically managed warfare of the first; and a near-term diplomatic purpose would be subordinated to the objectives of gaining time rather than to govern events and of interrupting adverse trends rather than to inspire propitious transformations.

A similar primary purpose would attach to escalating the military confrontation to the nuclear level. The risks from a nuclear environment are differently calculable for the two sides and are not necessarily evenly distributed in the Middle East. If Israel alone went nuclear, this would freeze the military situation without promoting conflict resolution. It would set off an Arab drive for countervailing capability and, as importantly or more, increase Israeli subjection to American control over acts even remotely susceptible of sparking overt belligerency, unless nuclearization entailed all-out Israeli-American separation. Going nuclear unilaterally was thus a second-best remedy for Israel's problems. On the other hand, were nuclear deterrence to be mutual and mutually nonprovocative, because exposing both sides and strengthening neither offensively, it might come to differ favorably from, and be more enduringly effective than, partial mutual disengagements of conventional military forces, the functionally similar device for gaining time. Two-sided nuclearization might even engender pressures for composition in depth where separation of conventional forces removes such pressures, and fosters instead an indefinitely festering precarious coexistence. In a nuclear environment, neither side has a rational interest to stimulate and exploit, and even to favor, a continuous and cumulative decline of the other party to a conflict over survival, since irreversible decline is the one context for "rational" employment of the ultimate weapon by the despairing contestant. And finally, extension of nuclear deterrence to a subsystemic conflict was likely to encourage the conflict's preemption by the greater powers, anxious to minimize the risks to themselves and to the international system in its entirety, or just determined to affirm their prerogative to be the first to use the weapon of mass destruction even if no longer the only ones to possess it. Comparable preemption might be set off by Israel's bidding for a suspensive conventional military victory and, of course, the Arabs' moving close to a suppressive victory, insofar as neither would be tolerable for one of the superpowers, worth a superpower confrontation for the other, and outweigh larger common interests for both.

A preemption superseding the local contention and contestants by means of direct great-power intervention, imposition of terms, and guarantee was the third option, not necessarily for all time equally undesirable for both sides to the Middle Eastern conflict.[3] Preferences of local parties between

---

3. The author has dealt more extensively with the issue of guarantee in *Beyond Kissinger* (Baltimore: The Johns Hopkins University Press, 1975) pp. 143–59.

different possible forms of military impact on trends were liable to be influenced by political considerations sooner or later. These included the question of which military recourse was: one, most conducive to long-term appeasement on a basis acceptable to mainstream elements on both sides; and two, reserved greater autonomy for local actors relative to the larger powers. In the Middle East, barring profound upheavals in the Arab camp in particular, politically controlled conventional warfare might prove to be most promising in the next phase, without holding out the promise of an abrupt breakthrough or immediate surcease. It was more difficult to opt between a smashing conventional-military outcome favorable to Israel, psychologically maiming for the Arabs, and a stalemate on a nuclear basis, psychologically upsetting for the Israeli if unstable and diplomatically enslaving (or isolating) for them if engineered unilaterally. As between the two inferior recourses, however, it was possible that, from the Israeli viewpoint, the "smash" might have to precede the "stalemate" for maximum impact and stalemate only follow the smash for maximum possible insurance.

When fighting rounds occur over a long period of time, be they major battles or campaigns of yesteryear or individual wars in more recent times, they will be identifiable with larger phases. Just as the Plantagenet phase differed in key active combatants and both issues and techniques from the Lancasterian, or the strictly English from the Anglo-Burgundian, phases in the Hundred Years War, and the Bohemian-Palatine spell from the Danish, Swedish, or French phases in the Thirty Years War, so in the Middle Eastern conflict the British phase differed from the succeeding Egyptian and the latter may be replaced in due course by yet another, Saudi or Syrian, phase. As important as changes in principal actors and preferred techniques is the basic, linear or fluctuating, pattern of the fighting rounds. The pattern is linear when each successive round is more violent than the preceding engagement, and has either the same winner or the same outcome (i.e., stalemate). The two-to-three rounds of the Indo-Pakistani conflict were marked by rising, or increasingly organized, violence and had the same winner (except possibly in the first round at the time of independence). The Anglo-French conflict was on balance increasingly violent in the culminating phase from early Louis XIV to late Napoleonic wars, but fluctuated rather narrowly around the no-win norm as to outcomes. The modern phase of the Franco-German conflict between 1870 and 1945 grew in the scale of environmental violence while fluctuating widely as to the identity of the winner and the scope of the victory from one war to another and, in the course of World War II, also within one war. The Franco-German contest may also suggest, and do so more clearly than does the long Anglo-French duel, that most likely to help terminate a conflict is a costly victory in a round following upon preceding defeat or defeats and susceptible to being promptly devalued and rendered nonrepeatable by changes including the military resurgence of the "defeated" adversary or the emergence of a militarily superior third party. When this happens, repetitive rounds of active fighting might help terminate a prolonged conflict by way of a mechanism grossly comparable to that of fluctuating performances in competitive arming, which is supposed to be coresponsible for the origination of armed conflict. The appeasing effect will be greatest and last longest when both sides share the experience if at different junctures. If the mechanism worked manifestly to make the French side prone to appeasement following World War I, the dynamic was also in evidence within narrowly Franco-German relations on the German side following World War II.

Different patterns of intensities and outcomes will correlate differently with different frequencies in occurrence. Frequent rounds will terminate a conflict by virtue of sheer physical factors if the outcomes are linear (e.g., in the Indo-Pakistani conflict), and by virtue of primarily psychological ones if they are not (e.g., in the modern Franco-German series). If the interludes between rounds are lengthy relative to impact (e.g., in the Anglo-French contest), structural changes will be more likely to intervene but the psychological impetus that greater round frequency may impart to conflict termination will be correspondingly diminished. In the Arab-Israeli conflict, the already transpired rounds have been moving into the zone of sufficiency when assessed by intuitive common sense and projected against historical precedents, whereas their considerable frequency mirrored the overall tendency in modern times to foreshorten and telescope evolutions. But, if material changes occur rapidly and correspondingly alter the objectively pertinent configuration of stakes and issues, changes of attitudes in survival conflicts will lag even farther behind than they do in systemic conflicts. This is true despite the rapid-fire psychological impact of a compressed war-series, and notwithstanding self-conscious attempts to mold attitudes by controlling actions and events (including military processes and outcomes) in the desired direction.

On balance, the Middle Eastern conflict may prove to wither away sooner than did the centuries-long European contentions of comparable kinds. Even if it terminates this side of, say, the hundred-year mark, however, the conflict can no longer be ended this side of the thirty-year limit. The most propitious pattern of its unfolding might be a modification of the Franco-German contention. Both sides might become ready for compromises as each of them in succession saw once or more than once the costly gains made in one round be reduced or nullified in the next. If both sides retained the basic capacity for trying to reverse military fortunes yet once again, the inclination to do so might fade conjointly and at a faster rate than did the capacity. Israel had an inkling of that experience in 1973. Extending the experience to the Arab side in a controlled measure in the "next" round might be required to round off the bases for appeasement if (as is likely) a mere suspicion that the wheel of military fortunes might turn again, and adversely, did not suffice.

If psychological and structural transformations are indeed decisive for terminating a conflict, techniques and blueprints for negotiations will be no more sufficient in themselves to accommodate the full spectrum of material and immaterial stakes than is a mere will-to-peace. Even a fully negotiated compromise will be meaningless if it is not rooted in supporting conditions. This was as true for the agreements ending the American involvement in the second Indochina war as it had been for the treaties pacifying the "first" Hundred Years War (in 1258) and the second eighteenth-century succession war (in 1748); and the rule was liable to apply to ceasefires (solemnized by U.N. auspices or not) in the Middle East and elsewhere that left issues unresolved, configurations unchanged, and spirits unappeased. Such transactions mark only a pause in most cases while the very ambiguities that made them possible will reignite and may escalate the conflict at a later date. Nor will even the emergence of a peace party be sufficient to tame the dogs of war, if the readiness for concessions remains isolated and unsupported. Propeace Richard II had made the experience in the Hundred Years War as did the last Habsburg emperor in the First World War, and only provisionally superior results were achieved on behalf of Queen Anne and King George III in the "global" wars of the eighteenth century. Where peacefully inclined principals can be thwarted, peace-making by third-party outsiders can be hardly more determining independently of a context that is more than transient or contrived.

Is there an area in which negotiations can do substantially more than translate into formulae of peace the balances of forces and of inclinations, and significantly aid in breaking through a deadlock on issues or inertial militancy? Such an opportunity would seem to be provided by the tension between material or territorial, and immaterial or formal, stakes and issues. Negotiations that aim to trade one set of issues against another ought to make both kinds somewhat more adjustable if the allocation of tangibles can be made strictly enforceable and contain thus the volatile effect of ambiguities designed to obfuscate the intangibles. In principle, any expansion in the range of issues facilitates tradeoffs in negotiations. But the record of interstate tractations suggests, even if that of labor-management negotiations does not, that certain immaterial issues are intrinsically nonnegotiable. Their formal omission from a settlement is, therefore, the only way to fit them into a war-ending whose conditions speak for themselves. A disposition of territorial issues reflecting military outcomes and future prospects was more or less explicitly formalized or ratified at the end of both the hundred and the thirty years-long wars, and the allocation of actual control over French territory was at all times negotiable in the course of the longer conflict. But the same was not true for key and live immaterial issues. They had to be ignored in the war-terminating formal instruments to permit the war to terminate in fact. Nonnegotiable and altogether nonmentionable, but actually "settled," was the question of ultimate authority or sovereignty within France and Germany respectively, involved in the issue of recognition, of the indigenous dynasty by the English as the legitimate kings of France and of the German territorial potentates by the Holy Roman Emperor as effectively independent. Another, and ostensibly central, immaterial issue in the "German" war was the religious one. It could be formally disposed of only when one side (the emperor) was conspiciously winning for a time (in the Peace of Prague) or (in the Peace of Westphalia) when the issue was universally if tacitly perceived as obsolete.

A renewable truce, one of several, terminated the Hundred Years War in both fact and, it was to appear retrospectively, form. It confirmed the reconquests by the Valois Kings in France, while a dynastic marriage merely implied the otherwise impossible recognition of their title and renunciation by the English claimant. In the Middle Eastern setting, functional interpenetration was a possible, and the only available, substitute in the long term for the forever lost convenience (and irritant) of a dynastic marriage. Before any such consummation would transpire, the historical record suggests, a formal recognition of a right (i.e., Israel's to existence) was the last, rather than the first, concession to obtain, even and perhaps especially from a party that had lost out militarily on technical points. Insistence upon such recognition as the key preliminary will, therefore, be most useful for delaying serious negotiations that are deemed premature. And a formal recognition of a critical right was apt to be both forthcoming and dependable only when actual conditions had made the object to which the right referred so stable and reliably acquired as to make its formal recognition materially redundant.

Analyzing conflicts that unfold in several rounds means moving in circles for much of the time, just as a certain determinism will surface when tracing the pathway out of the last round into lasting peace. In the ensuing vision, the factor of evolution will be supreme over the capacity of military engagements to decide issues by themselves, not least in the revolutionary wars over survival; and the existential or also normative erosion of the conflict-initiating actors, conditions, and stakes will overshadow both military decimation and material attrition in terminating conflicts, notably the prolonged ones over succession.

The Arab-Israeli conflict in the Middle East has been only one, if the latest, installment of the Eastern Question. That "question" has been historically the object of many sterile partition schemes, futile negotiations, and militarily influenced transformations. The contemporary conflict, too, will depend for its conclusion on so conditioned transformations more than on either tricks or triumphs of the diplomatic trade. It will have to go on changing from a conflict over survival and succession, bearing on absolute and exclusive rights to existence or possession, into a systemic conflict over balances of power on two (small- and greater-power) tiers and within an alternately contracting and expanding compass; from an ideologically colored quasi-civil war into a pragmatically managed interstate conflict; from a contention that is both salient and polarized to one covering only one segment of relationships within a plural structure of conflicts; and from a conflict that both sides perceived as inherently winnable in regard to stakes that could be no more divided than they could be compromised, into one that the front-line and front-rank contestants on both sides had come to see as one that can be won only by outsiders. Furthermore, the existing asymmetries between the key parties will have to be attenuated by mutual assimilation in both endowments and outlooks, as the politics of catastrophe yields to a process of convergence, the former having unwittingly crystallized actors and issues rather than eliminating either and the latter promoting toleration even if not immediately integration among actors that were proven viable.

A prolonged strife fosters a measure of convergence between adversaries as unavoidably as some narrowing of differences is necessary for terminating the conflict. If convergence in the Middle East meant for the Arabs to develop both middle classes and middle powers, it meant for the Israeli an authentic Middle Eastern identity and a middling solution, insuring survival but discarding the role of a controller over the Arabs, as either hegemon or active balancer, for that of a convenience for the Arabs, as a background factor or actual barrier in the inter-Arab balance of power. If it was Israel's right to exist but not to predominate, it was the Arab's right to expect Israel to cease being a Middle Eastern Brandenburg or Hanoi but not in order to become one more Lebanon; to relinquish any semblance of pretension to disguised imperium, but not to become an emporium naked before its enemies. Increased Arab material strength and psychological self-confidence, if contained by Arab sagacity and regulated by Israeli strategies, should gradually permit the toleration of an Israel that was viable in terms of civic spirit as well as civilian economy, and to do so first on the basis of a many-faceted stalemate.

A key transformation bears upon the configuration of conflict, toward its dispersion and its supersession by other conflicts and other, including cooperative, concerns. The Arab-Israeli conflict has long resisted being superseded by an equivalent contention or preoccupation. The resistance has only begun to be relieved by incipient dispersion of concerns and by realignments in intra-Arab conflicts, such as those focused on the continuing crisis in Lebanon. A substantial measure of rigidity between the parties was kept alive by matching weaknesses within them. Spells of compulsive diplomatic solidarity among the Arabs were alike in their retarding effect with the unrelieved siege mentality among the Israelis, just as the converse tendency to subject diplomatic solidarity to either competitive or compensatory exaggerations in verbal and symbolic militancy on one side had its counterpart in aggressively enacted internecine political divisions alternately straining and hardening the defensive unity of the other. They all have militated against converting into appeasement the new self-image and widened vistas of key Arab actors, without wholly preventing a decline in interstate bellicosity. It fell to the Palestinians to take up the slack and to focus dramatically both the territorial and the immaterial stakes during the period of their prominence and, to a point, ascendancy. The issue of a Palestinian state lent itself least to devices for decomposing "indivisible" territorial stakes functionally (e.g., by demilitarization or neutralization) and for tacitly spiriting away or artfully camouflaging "uncompromisable" immaterial stakes (such as recognition and sovereignty). Only further evolution could make it possible to reassess or transvalue specific odds, particular stakes, and wider perspectives in cost-benefit calculations that would reassure in depth even while being precise only superficially. And only when that had come to pass would the still-outstanding divisive issues, including the Palestinian one, be either composed by negotiation or consigned to the consequences of neglect; be parleyed into agreements or permitted to atrophy.

The ending of conflicts depends on evolution, as changes within and among participants overshadow one-time priorities that clamored for a clear-cut decision. Being partially controllable, however, the course and conduct of such conflicts can also inflect evolution in a direction favorable to their termination. When this happens, the conduct of a conflict contains within it the seeds of peaceful composition. Evolution, even more than wars, is the mother of all things. But war can be, and often is, evolution's midwife. That which is often most needed is to use time so as to gain more time. The only quick cure for political as for physical ills is the surgical one, at risk; the promptest termination is extermination. It has begun to be said that time ceased to work for Israel and started to work for the Arabs. This is probably true in regard to any Israeli objective of security rooted in supremacy. It will take more time to give Israel the requisite minimum of long-term security, and the Arabs the tolerable maximum of inner strength and self-respect, on the objective basis of something like Israel-Arab parity. To all appearances, the requisites were in the making; for a certainty, they and the goal remained to be achieved in full.

INDEX

Alliances: and deterrence, 129; functions of, 5, 119, 131–32, 201; and land-sea power schism, 11–13, 16–17, 39, 129, 135, 197–98; and liberalization, 196, 198–201; moderating function of, 10–11, 69; and parity, 180; and power aggregation, 6, 8; and quasi-constitutional unions, 10, 18; regulatory function of, 5–8, 129, 130, 201; and "rise and fall," 8–10, 129, 131–32; among sea powers, 61–62, 130; and separate peace, 232; and U.S.-Soviet relations, 184, 196–201. *See also* North Atlantic Alliance; Triple Alliance; Triple Entente; Warsaw Pact

Arab states. *See* Middle East

Balance of power: and alliances, 5–8, 13, 17, 19; and American foreign policy, xi–xii, xv, 116–18; and collective security, 116; and complementary imbalances, 29, 33, 157–58; and diplomatic options, 117; and equivalence, 21–22; and foremost actor, 53, 109; and hegemony, 5–8; and international system, 3–4; kinds of "balancer" in, 123–24; kinds of "power" in, 79, 98–99, 100; and land-sea power schism, 11, 13–16, 17, 18, 127, 141; in Middle-Eastern microcosm, 220–21, 236, 245–46; and normative constraints, 10; and "organic" dimension, 4–5, 8–9, 10, 19, 81, 176–77; and reserve powers, xiii; and resource-risk ratios, 126. *See also* Equilibrium; International System (European and Eurocentric); Power

Balfour, Arthur James, 78
Bethmann-Hollweg, Theobald von, 45, 78
Bismarck, Otto von, 35, 47, 51, 66, 128, 176
Brandt, Willy, 134
Brezhnev, Leonid, 169

Capabilities (military): airborne, 140; and changing international environment, 121; employment of, 145-46, 148, 152, 156, 158, 159; naval, 133, 135–36, 138–46, 152–53, 161–62, 178; nuclear, 117, 140, 144, 145, 162, 163; and parity, 149, 151, 170, 178, 210–16; and primacy of politics, 216; and use of force, 213–16. *See also* Seapower

China: and Anglo-German accommodation efforts, 69; "open door" to, 66, 72, 175; partition of, 154; and Russia, 119. *See also* People's Republic of China

Choiseul, duc (Etienne François) de, 13, 35, 45, 55

Churchill, Sir Winston, 68

Civil War (American): British attitudes toward, 85–87; compared with German "civil war," 65, 85–86; possible revival of, xviii; and U.S. foreign-policy phases, xii

Cleveland, Grover, 66, 79, 90

Cold War: and alliance rigidities, 129; character and dynamic of, 100–112, 134, 181–82; deceleration of, 105; and difference from other wars, 100–101, 106; effect of, on international system, 106; origins of, 94, 99–104; possible revival of, 207, 208; rela-

THE JOHNS HOPKINS UNIVERSITY PRESS

This book was composed in Compugraphic Bem text and Garmond display
type by Brushwood Graphics, from a design by Susan Bishop. It was
printed and bound by The Murray Printing Company.

LIBRARY OF CONGRESS CATALOGING IN PUBLICATION DATA

Liska, George.
  Quest for equilibrium.

  (Studies in international affairs)
  Includes index.
  1. Balance of power. 2. United States—Foreign relations. I. Title. II. Series: Washington Center of Foreign Policy Research. Studies in International affairs.

JX1318.L47 327'.112 77—4780
ISBN 0—8018—1968—7